Praise for

A Pocketful of Happiness

"Richard E. Grant is a wonderful actor and, it seems, a rather wonderful (goofy, talented, loving) man. His new memoir, written in diary form, is about his terrific thirty-five-year marriage-of-opposites to Joan Washington (he the eternal adolescent, star-struck optimist, and gifted actor, she a sharp-tongued, no-nonsense, and equally gifted dialect coach) . . . Genuine and compelling."

—*The New York Times*

"His decision to form the book's narrative jointly out of the most enchanting highs (the Oscars, karaoke with Olivia Colman in a house formerly owned by Bette Davis) and the bleakest lows (Joan's diagnosis, her fury when Grant inadvertently used the word 'terminal' one day to describe her illness) came, he said, out of his desire to accurately capture what most people's lives are like . . . [Richard and Joan's] relationship is the fascinating central pillar of the book."

—*The Atlantic*

"The term 'soulmate' gets thrown around with abandon, often in the throes of young lust, long before love is tested by time, financial hardship, or even illness. But when Richard E. Grant calls his late wife, Joan Washington, his 'soulmate' in his new memoir, *A Pocketful of Happiness*, it almost seems an understatement . . . The Oscar-nominated British actor writes tenderly, heart on his sleeve."

—*USA Today*

"One of the bravest, strongest, funniest memoirs I've ever read."

—Bonnie Garmus, *New York Times* bestselling author of *Lessons in Chemistry*

"Actor Grant delivers an excellent memoir that's part journal, part love letter to his late wife, Joan Washington. Grant's tender recollections effectively conjure on the page the couple's enduring connection. The result is a moving and entertaining celebration of life and love."

—*Publishers Weekly* (starred review)

"Grant's prose is charming and witty . . . An engaging story of life, love, and grief that will resonate with anyone who has ever loved and lost."

—Booklist

"A diary-keeper since childhood, the author draws on his candid entries to weave together an absorbing, moving chronicle . . . Ebullience and grief mark a touching memoir."

—*Kirkus Reviews*

"A gorgeously candid account of acting and show business. And an intimate and heartfelt story of love, loss, and a life spent together. It is an honor to be invited in on these diaries. I cannot remember being so moved by a book."

—Dolly Alderton, internationally bestselling author of *Everything I Know About Love*

"An emotional roller coaster—profoundly moving and wonderfully entertaining. A brilliant memoir about living, loving, and losing."

—Bernardine Evaristo, winner of the Booker Prize and author of *Girl, Woman, Other*

"What a book! To put it one way, you could describe the lovely Richard E. Grant's *A Pocketful of Happiness* as love, death, and showbiz stories—and while accurate, that would be to miss both its fierceness and tenderness."

—Nigella Lawson, bestselling cookbook author and television host

"*A Pocketful of Happiness* documents the head- and heart-exploding overwhelm of grief . . . Brutal but necessary."

—The Sunday Times

"Grant's profoundly moving book, part love letter to his beloved wife, part gossipy memoir about his life and times, will resonate with anyone who ever lost a loved one."

—Daily Express

"Richard E. Grant's heartbreaking memoir recalls a long, happy marriage—and leaves us shattered for his loss."

—*The Spectator*

"A touching account."

—*The Observer* (UK)

"An elegant exploration of the profundity of loss. While the memoir will appeal to Grant's many fans, it may also comfort those struggling with an impending or recent loss."

—*Library Journal*

"The title of Richard E. Grant's memoir, *A Pocketful of Happiness*, is both misleading and utterly truthful. On the one hand, the book is full of charming anecdotes which are indicative of the Swaziland-born, British actor's sunny disposition, but, on the other, it charts the grim journey of losing his wife . . . An endearing read."

—Associated Press

"Incredibly moving."

—*The Daily Telegraph*

RICHARD E. GRANT

A Pocketful of Happiness

A Memoir

Simon & Schuster Paperbacks
New York London Toronto Sydney New Delhi

An Imprint of Simon & Schuster, LLC
1230 Avenue of the Americas
New York, NY 10020

First Simon & Schuster trade paperback edition August 2024

SIMON & SCHUSTER PAPERBACKS and colophon are registered trademarks of Simon & Schuster, LLC

Simon & Schuster: Celebrating 100 Years of Publishing in 2024

For information about special discounts for bulk purchases, please contact Simon & Schuster Special Sales at 1-866-506-1949 or business@simonandschuster.com.

The Simon & Schuster Speakers Bureau can bring authors to your live event. For more information or to book an event, contact the Simon & Schuster Speakers Bureau at 1-866-248-3049 or visit our website at www.simonspeakers.com.

Manufactured in the United States of America

10 9 8 7 6 5 4 3 2 1

Library of Congress Cataloging-in-Publication Data is available.

ISBN 978-1-6680-3069-1
ISBN 978-1-6680-3084-4 (pbk)
ISBN 978-1-6680-3085-1 (ebook)

For Oilly—our supreme and perfect being

CONTENTS

PROLOGUE

On December 31, 2021, I posted the following message on Instagram:

> Lockdown last year turned out to be a blessing in disguise, because my wife and I spent 9 months, after our 38 years together, with each other every single minute of the day and night, and then . . . had 8 months together for the last months of her Life, this year. And she said to me, just before she died, "You're going to be all right—try to find a pocketful of happiness in every single day," and I'm just so grateful for almost 4 decades that we had together, and the gift that is our daughter. So, on that note, Happy New Year to you.

When last I looked, it had been viewed over a quarter of a million times and 1,748 comments were posted by friends, acquaintances, and complete strangers. Confirmation that almost without exception, especially during this wretched pandemic, someone has suffered a loss or losses in tandem with mine. Being widowed and embarking on the year ahead on my own felt daunting. These social media messages have been hugely welcome, uplifting and inspiring by turns.

Whatever cynicism I'd accrued like an old crab-shell in my sixty-four years was cracked and dissolved by the compassion, kindness, and love I've been engulfed by this past year. The consequence of which is that I feel completely vulnerable and exposed, *yet* protected.

Honouring my wife's edict became my New Year's resolution, and my mantra. Having never followed any religion, brought up to regard all of it as superstition, Joan's simple challenge has proved to be profoundly powerful. Whenever I waver towards the canyon of grief, her instruction pings across my cranium and I endeavour to try to find a pocketful of happiness wherever I can.

It already feels like a welcome habit, my daily bread and buffer.

Our daughter, Oilly, and her partner, Florian, generously invited me to go with them to Venice for four days before Christmas, so I wouldn't be home alone on Joan's posthumous birthday on December 21, then on to Austria to spend Christmas with his family. Generous, diverting, and a complete contrast to our home traditions. *Sound of Music* mountains, covered in snow, and a Christmas Eve feast with presents and everyone valiantly speaking English as neither Oilly nor I know more than a *schnell*'s worth of German.

Anticipated Teutonic reserve and humourectomy—only to be enveloped by boundless warmth, both fireside and human, and much hilarity.

Horse-drawn sleigh ride on a frozen lake on Christmas Day and, just when it didn't seem possible to eat any more, managed to stuff down two frankfurters, bunned-up and mustard-slathered, to the manor born!

"Don't eat so quickly!" Joan's voice in my head reiterates silently. She must have said this to me at least a thousand times over: "I've gone to the trouble to cook something delicious, and you've gobbled it down in seconds!"

"That's because it is so delicious, and you know I love food when it's hot. Take it as a compliment."

Her large monkey eyes fixed me with admonishment. "Always got an answer, smartarse!"

Trying to do anything slowly has been a lifelong challenge, as I was born with the impatience button firmly pressed down. When I was nine years old, my father identified me as an overwound clock!

Joan died in September 2021 and, two months later, I flew to South Africa to visit my 90-year-old mother, whom I'd not seen for four years, other than on Skype.

A twelve-hour flight later, I was thrilled to see her on such feisty form. Still driving, playing bridge regularly, reading five novels per week and writing summaries for a book company. She announces that all the electricity has been accidentally cut off by a plumber who severed the wrong pipe and it's been off for two days already. As her backup generator has now run out too, I diplomatically suggest that we book into a hotel nearby until the power is reconnected.

"Out of the question," is her unequivocal response.

"But I've been travelling for fourteen hours and would like to have a shower."

"Boil a kettle!"

"There's no electricity!"

She won't relent. "I'm not going to sleep in any bed other than my own."

A pocketful of patience is what's required.

Even though I am sixty-four years old, it is with the greatest trepidation that I go ahead and book myself a hotel room. Her barely concealed contempt reminds me of the nine months when she refused to speak to my father in 1967, prior to their divorce. Her capacity to silently sulk is epic and I remember my father trying every subterfuge to get a word out of her, to no avail. I was used as piggy-in-the-middle: "Ask your father to pass me the salt/car keys/mail"—you name it.

Shortly after Joan and I coupled up, we disagreed about something and I shut off.

"You're not sulking by any chance, are you?" she said incredulously. "Because if you are, you'd better snap right out of it, *pronto presto*, as I won't stand for it!"

I was so taken aback that this well-learnt ploy, which had always stood me in such good stead, was being detonated that I burst out laughing and never dared sulk with Joan ever again.

I made the mistake of chuckling in response to my mother's intransigence, remembering Joan's rebuke. Eyebrow raised, Roger Moore–style, she snapped: "It's *not* funny."

The thing about death is that after the past eight months of bearing witness to the love of my life deteriorating daily, negotiating with my mother about a hotel bed versus her own bed *is* funny. I silently register that this would have made Joan cackle, which instantly reminds me that I can never share these trivials with her ever again.

Not face to face, nor on the phone or by text, or whisper to pillow.

Yet, just the act of writing this down conjures her present again. It feels like an act of resurrection.

I began writing a diary when I was ten years old, after waking up on the back seat of a car to witness my mother bonking my father's best friend on the front seat in 1967. A sentence that can hurtle trippingly off my tongue several decades later.

But back in the last century, I couldn't tell anyone, least of all my father, or any of my friends. Tried God, but got no reply, so I began writing in secret. Somehow it rendered the unreality real.

I've kept a diary ever since. During Joan's illness, writing was the only vestige of control I could cling on to, as each day, as her health declined, underlined how helpless we were. I wanted a record of *everything* we shared, "for better or for worse, in sickness and in health," honouring our marriage vows made on November 1, 1986.

Her fierce privacy was the antithesis of both my public life and my iron-clad belief that secrets are toxic. But she accepted that this counterbalance was the yin and yang of our relationship.

Reading Martin Amis's *Inside Story*, and on life-writing, he surmises that "somehow, the very act of composition, is an act of love."

Bullseye! That's been my intention in writing this diary.

I truly hope that my scribblings will give you an idea why I loved her so utterly and completely for thirty-eight years. A journalist once asked me what the secret was for managing to stay together for almost four decades, especially in show business (which would make us golden wedding anniversary veterans by that standard), and my reply was immediate and simple. We began a conversation in 1983 and we never stopped talking, or sleeping together in the same bed.

Our marriage is *the* story of my adult life. Which concluded with her last earthly breath on Thursday, September 2, 2021, at 7:30 p.m. Holding each other's hand.

Chapter One

DECEMBER

1982

Newly arrived in London, I was waitering at Tuttons brasserie in Covent Garden, and had just secured an acting agent, who suggested getting accent coaching to help me play Northern Irish, as there were so many dramas being made about the Troubles and "you're dark-haired and blue-eyed, so you could go up for Irish roles."

A pal told me about the Actors Centre, where you could take classes at an affordable price, so I signed up for Joan Washington's accent course. Boiler-suited, Kicker-booted, and sporting a Laurie Anderson spiked haircut, she was a charismatic and formidable presence, with a rich, deep voice that contrasted with her petite figure. At the end of the first session, I asked if she would consider teaching me privately.

"What for?"

"To iron out my colonial accent."

"I don't really have the time, as I'm coaching at various theatres and at RADA."

"Please. I'm begging you!" That made her laugh. "*Please?*"

She gave me the once-over, sighed, and replied: "Okay."

"*Thank you!* What do you charge?"

"£20 per hour."

"But I can only afford £12 . . ."

She fixed me with her big monkey eyes and said, "All right—but you'll have to repay me, if you ever make it."

"Done deal!"

I was renting a bedsit in Blenheim Crescent, a few blocks down from where it intersects with Portobello Road, in Notting Hill Gate, for £30 per week, which puts the price of her lesson into (my) financial perspective. Plus the cost of taking the tube all the way to Richmond, then a twenty-minute walk to her house, situated behind the ice rink in East Twickenham. Trying to work out how many sessions I'd need and what to budget accordingly. Anticipating *months* of classes to sound acceptable to the natives.

"So how long do you reckon it'll take to sort me out?"

"No more than a couple of sessions."

I was astonished. Her innate gift, as has been reiterated by everyone lucky enough to have been taught by her, is the confidence she instilled with *her* belief that you can crack it. Which inspired *this* pupil to believe he *could* do it. And all for the princely sum of £24!

"You just have one sound that you need to be aware of—when you say 'basin' or 'council' or 'pencil,' you overcompensate and say 'bay-SIN,' 'coun-CIL,' and 'pen-CIL.' Instead, say 'pen-SULL' rhyming with 'pull' and throw it away."

Even after almost four decades together, the teacher in her never missed the opportunity to correct this defect in my speech. Occasionally, when we were mid-argument, she'd go Henry Higgins on me, with an accent correction, simultaneously *increasing* my fury and trip-switching us into hilarity.

While I was grateful that she didn't think I needed endless coaching, I was also frustrated that after only two sessions I no longer had a legitimate reason to see her again. She was also a few years older than me, married-but-separated, with a young son, and with a string of prestigious productions and a movie to her credit.

I was an out-of-work actor from the southern hemisphere, from *nowhere*, earning a subsistence wage as a waiter, schlepping home after midnight, listening to "Sweet Dreams (Are Made of This)" on my prized Walkman. Not exactly a "catch" of *any* kind—*and* pipe-cleaner thin. Joan on the other hand was already a legend in her field. Such was the success of Richard Eyre's landmark National Theatre production of *Guys and Dolls* in 1982, and Joan's accent coaching, that Barbra Streisand enquired, "Who are these American actors I've never heard of?" Which resulted in Joan being interviewed to coach Mitteleuropean accents for Streisand's directorial debut movie, *Yentl*. As I've been a Streisand fanatic for half a century, the details she recalled of their first meeting have been imprinted, like a talisman, on my memory ever since.

She'd never coached on a film before and had been summoned to Lee International Studios in Wembley, where she met producer Larry "DeWaay We Were" as he was nicknamed (the double "a" in his surname isn't a spelling mistake) and casting director Cis Corman, who'd known Streisand since she was a teenager. Told that she was wearing a colour that Barbra liked, before going in to meet her—"That's a good sign."

Joan found Streisand surprisingly petite compared to her screen persona, softly spoken, and fast.

"Can you do some accents for me?"

"I'm a trained phonetician and don't really work that way. Any more than I'd ask you to sing me a medley of your greatest hits."

"I understand. This is my Princess Margaret. What d'you think?"

"Not very good—it's an impression rather than the real thing and you couldn't sustain a whole performance doing that. Needs to be as accurate and authentic as possible."

"You're very direct. I like that. So am I. How many movies have you done?"

"None."

"Then this will be *your* first, and it's *my* first time directing."

It's only when she left the room that her knees buckled with the impact of securing this prestigious job. Joan has never been starstruck in the way that I continue to be, but reluctantly admitted that she was *really* chuffed, as a Scottish girl from Aberdeen, to be coaching Yiddish accents on *Yentl*. An endorsement from on high that defied all those naysayers and male theatre directors who once dismissed accent coaching as "irrelevant" at the start of her career.

Probably a very good thing that I didn't know any of this when we first got together, otherwise she might have run for the Highlands at the prospect of having to accommodate three people in this relationship. Herself, Barbra, and me!

She never tired of teasing me about my adolescent-adult obsession with "Babs," and it's a true measure of how secure our love is for each other that she wasn't threatened by my fantasy idolatry, even after I'd commissioned a two-foot-tall sculpture of Streisand's face for the garden.

"I get it. She's unique and beautiful and extraordinary, but you're mine! And besides, she's married to James Brolin." For someone as territorial and jealous of any "comers" as Joan was, I count myself lucky that she never banished Barbra from our life together.

In January 1983, Joan unexpectedly contacted me, leaving a message on my answering machine, asking if I'd record a script that she was coaching for the RSC, which required a Siswati speaker—"and as you're the only person I've ever met who can speak the language, come over and I'll cook you dinner."

Didn't wait tables on a Monday night, so I suggested

coming over then. Very excited, and it was snowing, which for a boy from Swaziland, *is*, *was*, and *always will be* a magical phenomenon. Bought a bunch of tulips, wondering if this might be inappropriate/patronising/non-her and held them behind my back when I rang the doorbell, keeping them hidden until I was inside.

"Your hand all right?"

"Yes, why d'you ask?"

"You've held it behind your back for the past five minutes."

Blushed and offered up the tulips, which thankfully turned out to be more than acceptable. Fired off lots of questions which she answered unreservedly and, in turn, asked me as many, mirroring my curiosity, which culminated in her casually asking, "Are you in a relationship?" while taking a casserole out of the oven.

"Not at the moment."

She smiled again.

"Let's eat first, then do the recording."

Delicious home-made boeuf bourguignon that I put my nose to instantly.

"What's wrong with it?"

"Sorry, should have said, I like to smell *everything* in sight. Always have done. Ever since I can remember. Can't understand why everyone *doesn't*. You're a brilliant cook."

"Thank you. You have very brown, hairy arms, considering it's the middle of winter. Have you been skiing?" I was wearing a cream cable-knit sweater, and had pulled the sleeves up while eating.

"Never skied in my life, but was born olive-skinned. Do you always ask so many questions?"

"You can talk! You're very unusual for an Englishman, but then I suppose you're a colonial."

The transition from pupil and teacher into flirter and flirtee happened seamlessly. After dinner, we went into the living room, recorded the script, continued talking, and when I checked my watch it was gone midnight, so no chance of getting to the station in time.

"Would you mind if I stayed the night in your guest bedroom, as I've missed the last tube? *My* fault."

"Sure."

Went upstairs and she opened the door into an icebox. "I'm sorry, but the radiator's been turned off in here. I'll get you an extra duvet." This pantomime lasted all of ten minutes, before I gingerly knocked on her door and said, "I'm really sorry, but it's arctic in there. May I join you?"

Got into bed and, just when I thought things were hunky-dory, she de-hunked me by declaring, "You're as skinny as a stick-insect!" A passion-killing phrase if ever there was one, which every thin man will sympathise with.

Monday, December 21, 2020

Joan's birthday. We are unabashed Christmas-aholics, and the house is baubled-up, tree kissing the ceiling, and enough fairy lights to host a Tinker Bell convention. For the past week she's mentioned feeling breathless and has to pause halfway up the stairs. Nothing more than that. Uncharacteristically, for a doctor's daughter who has resolutely resisted *any* and *every* encouragement to see a medic about anything, she suggests calling the doctor, a first in our decades together.

"Have you lost your sense of smell or taste?"

"Don't be daft."

Manage to get through to our local health centre immediately and given an appointment at 5 p.m. for a chest X-ray and blood test at Kingston Hospital.

Wish that I could go in with her, but restrictions in place, so wait outside. Very few people. No queue. No waiting around. Doesn't take long and she returns feeling calm and reassured.

Oilly and Florian come over and help me cook birthday dinner. Candles lit, "Happy Birthday" sung, and presents opened. Everything as familiar and familial as can be. I once made the mistake of asking Joan whether she wanted a *main* combined birthday-Christmas present, to which she said, "Makes sense as they're only three days apart." Perhaps she thought I couldn't afford both, back then?

Idiot, idiot, *idiot*!

My father's advice to me as a teenager was: "What a woman *says* she wants, and what she *actually* wants, are two entirely different things." Summarily dismissed by me as advice from an unevolved olde-school brontosaurus.

Until I saw how disappointed Joan was! I can still *feel* the gigantic Jurassic imprint of putting my foot in it and never tried that ploy ever again.

Tuesday, December 22, 2020

Alex Dunkerley, the lung coordinator at Kingston Hospital, calls to say that the X-ray has revealed a "small abnormal knot in the right lung, which is likely to be residual scar tissue from when Joan had pneumonia a couple of years ago. I'd like to book her in for a CT scan this evening."

Distract ourselves playing Scrabble most of the afternoon, trying not to fixate on anything other than the here and now. But we know one another too well not to wonder and finally worry out loud—

"What do you think?"

"No idea. Best not to speculate and wait to see what the scan shows up."

Instead of easing the tension, it feels that giving it air has ramped it up and made it feel real.

We walk, arm in arm, in silence to the car, through the cold evening air.

Only thing she says en route is: "Sounds like it's something serious." Reach across and squeeze her arm.

Again the frustration of not being able to be by her side when she's having the scan. She reappears twenty minutes later.

"That was quick! What did it feel like?"

"Amazingly straightforward. Just had to lie very still and breathe slowly."

Palpable relief that it's done, radio on and we yakety-yak all the way home. As per.

Wednesday, December 23, 2020

Counting down. Wondering how long it will take for the results of the CT scan to come through.

At 11 a.m. lung coordinator Alex calls and asks to speak to Joan. I know instantly from the tone of her voice that the news isn't good. Too calm. Too conciliatory. Joan is still in bed when I hand her my phone.

"The CT scan has revealed a dark mass on your left lung, Joan, so we need you to go to the Marsden Hospital in Sutton for a PET scan at eight fifteen tomorrow morning."

Joan looks at me and unequivocally says: "It's lung cancer, isn't it?"

Tongue-tied, I can only slowly nod in agreement. It's the first time that either of us has dared utter that toxic "C" word.

Grandfather clock chimes on the landing outside our bedroom door. It's been ticking in her family's lives for more than two centuries. Yet at this moment, it feels like time has stopped for both of us.

She takes a deep breath and declares, "Promise me that you won't share *any* of this with Oilly, *until* we've had confirmation from the medics. Do you promise me?"

"I promise."

Her assertion unites and fortifies us.

"Darling, please bring me a cup of tea and some toast with Marmite."

Walk, lurch downstairs, utterly overwhelmed and discombobulated. Tears blurring everything. Grateful to have something to do.

Despite being cursed with misophonia (hypersensitivity to sounds like crunching, swallowing, lip smacking, slurping, and chewing, all of which provoke intense irrational anger) I'm grateful, at this moment, to hear her chomping on toast and taking gulps of tea.

Click on the TV and watch a blur of cooking/travel/interviews/pets, all the while holding hands, until she drifts into sleep.

Lying shoulder to shoulder, I look across to where this "dark mass" is hiding inside her. Waiting. Just like we are, on the outside, waiting to identify what it's doing and how far it's spread.

Waiting.

Thursday, December 24, 2020

Wake at 6 a.m. and feel like I've spent the entire night sprinting around my own brain.

Must stay calm for Joan. Must stay calm for her, no matter what.

Drive for half an hour through deserted streets to the hospital.

Large-lettered CANCER RESEARCH CENTRE sign panics Joan. Reach for her hand. Park up, hug her, and whisper love and assurance as best I can. Walk arm in arm into the deserted reception. Eerie. As though everyone has been vacuumed away. The staff are incredibly kind, soft-spoken and gentle, which underlines the gravity of our situation. Form filling then ushered into a small room where a nurse asks her to lie down and injects a saline solution into her arm, followed by a radiation drug that will circulate through her bloodstream, taking an hour to fully absorb, during which she has to lie still and not talk.

That's a challenge for us, as yakety-yakking is the modus operandi of our marriage. Look at one another with incredible intensity and naked tenderness. Once the initial unease of being here subsides, she asks me to hand her the book she's brought along. Titled *Just My Luck*.

Irony of ironies and we both silently laugh. Walk together into a room straight out of *2001: A Space Odyssey*. Joan lies down on the elevated narrow platform. Nurse presses buttons and Joan slides backwards into the giant white Polo mint–shaped contraption. Like a Kubrickian sleep-pod.

During the ten-minute scanning process, I'm catapulted back to 1973, when my chemistry master instructed me to comment out loud on the scientific process whereby one component changed from one colour to another, declaring, "It's an incredible shade of indigo, sir." Prompting him to bellow, "*Sit down!*"

My mock O-level result was a truly mockable 16 percent.

Home. Oilly is upbeat and excited about Christmas, totally unaware of the seriousness of our situation. *Yet.* Which is how Joan is determined to maintain things. So much so that when we leave for our 2 p.m. appointment, she says, "I'm sure it's going to be all right, Mum."

Mask up and both allowed to go in to meet with lung coordinator Alex and Dr. Chinegwundoh.

"The right lung is ninety-five percent intact and it's clear to see that the left lung has a growth all over it, which is why you're experiencing such shortness of breath. You're breathing with only one lung."

Looks to me like a disintegrated cauliflower.

"It's also spread into your clavicle lymph nodes. It could be some kind of severe infection, but is most likely to be a form of lung cancer, so I'd like to do a biopsy under local anaesthetic next week."

We look at one another, as our whole world spins, stumbles and judders before us.

Brutal to witness Joan telling Oilly that "more tests are required, chemotherapy is likely, as I have an as yet undiagnosed form of lung cancer."

Mother and daughter hug each other and our brave child says, "Let's have a great Christmas together."

It's as if we've made an unspoken pact not to family-fall-apart and go about prepping food for tomorrow. Those old clichés "business as usual" and "the show must go on" apply.

Friday, December 25, 2020, Christmas Day

Woken up twelve hours later at 10 a.m. by Oilly and Florian, who pile on to our bed with the Christmas stockings, both giving Oscar-worthy performances—bright-eyed and full of bonhomie.

Every gift given and opened, every memory shared, every carol sung and listened to, is supercharged with a poignancy so painful that it's a titanic struggle not to go under.

The "kids" go downstairs to make breakfast. Joan takes my hands, and asks: "You will stay with me through all of this, won't you?"

"*Of course, I will!! Every* step of the way. Don't doubt me for so much as a nanosecond."

Attempting to be "normal" in this uniquely abnormal situation exhausts us all, and we're in bed by 9 p.m.

Saturday, December 26, 2020, Boxing Day

Post-Christmas lull and slump. Played Scrabble and the first word Joan puts down is "memorial" and, without missing a beat, quips, "I'm still here, Swaz!"

Joan's distinctive "gravy" voice—full of rich, delicious brown notes—has begun to alter, as her breath support has halved, and sounds more like her Scottish mother, sometimes leaping into a higher octave. Her Central School of Speech and Drama–trained standard English accent is sounding more Aberdonian than I've ever noticed before.

Sunday, December 27, 2020

Joan goes to the loo mid-morning and hear her yelp and thump down. Weirdly, she has collapsed on to the step into the shower, thinking that she was sitting on the lav. Says she feels confused, but is luckily unhurt.

Oilly brings us breakfast in bed and questions Joan about how long she's felt breathless and had a cough. It's a completely honest and open exchange, which enables us to share everything that the doctors and scans have revealed. The parental push-me-pull-you of wanting to protect our grown-up child, by withholding detailed medical information, is subverted by her open-hearted need to know and share everything.

"We were just worried that telling you *everything* would be too much of a burden."

"*Not* knowing everything is worse."

When Joan asks how she has been coping, Oilly replies that she wobbles between tears and denial.

"It's the same for us."

Being able to talk about *everything* so openly is a genuine relief.

Thursday, December 31, 2020, New Year's Eve

Drove to Sandys Fishmongers in Twickenham and bought lobsters and champagne for New Year's Eve dinner. A fragile, brutal day and emotionally charged evening, where the ghosts of all our previous thirty-six celebrations haunted our conversation. Joan is exhausted and goes to bed by 11 p.m.

Stay up with Oilly and Florian watching TV as the rest of the world whoop and firework their way into 2021, around the globe.

Where have the past four decades gone? I feel the same age as when we were first together.

1983

In the summer of 1983 I was playing the juvenile subplot love interest opposite Judi Bowker in a production of *Tartuffe*, with Leonard Rossiter in the titular role, at the Churchill Theatre, in Bromley. His demeanour was permanently dialled up to splenetic, especially during my scenes with Judi, banging his prop walking stick in the wings in the misguided belief that this would provoke Ms. Bowker to increase her volume above a stage whisper. Had zero effect on *her* and drove *him* into a Rumpelstiltskin-stick-banging apoplexy, audible at the back of the stalls.

During a matinee interval, the stage manager went

around the dressing rooms, asking if anyone knew "the very tanned woman wearing Bermuda shorts and a Hawaiian shirt, who was fast asleep in a house seat and snoring *very* loudly."

"Haven't a clue, I'm sorry."

"Well, *someone* must know her, as those seats are reserved exclusively for friends of the cast."

You guessed correctly. After the curtain came down, said tanned woman came backstage "looking for Richard Grant" and was shown to my dressing room by the stage manager, who eyeballed and vigorously nodded that this was the snoring culprit.

"What are *you* doing here?"

"My flight from Tahiti landed earlier than expected, so I thought I'd surprise you!"

"You *surely* have!"

"You're very good in the show."

"Oh, did you enjoy it then? *Liar*—you were fast asleep and snoring *loudly* all the way through it!"

"Must be jet lag. But let's face it, Swaz, it's *really* boring, and I couldn't hear a word that young woman was whispering."

I had to sneak her out of the emergency exit and begged the stage manager not to grass me up.

Joan had been in Tahiti coaching Mel Gibson on *The Bounty*. We hadn't even moved in together yet, and my career prospects were provincial to put it politely, compared to the stellar company she was keeping. But she never allowed that to come between us, even though I felt it keenly.

"I love you, Swaziboy, and that's all that matters."

Six months prior to this, I was still a waiter, so getting this job in Bromley felt like a *major* advance. The twilight year cast included Dulcie Gray, Michael Denison, Judy Geeson, Dilys Watling, and Denys Hawthorne. Whereas she'd been coaching on a big-budget movie starring Mel Gibson and Anthony Hopkins, with a supporting cast featuring Liam Neeson, Daniel Day-Lewis, Dexter Fletcher, Edward Fox, Bernard Hill, and Sir Laurence Olivier.

Around this time, I received a letter from Equity, the actors' union, and was informed that a retired actor called Richard Grant had complained, after seeing his name outside the Churchill Theatre, requiring me to change mine. Called Equity in a panic and explained that I had no money, and that my name was printed on all my ten-by-eight photos already.

"Please may I speak to Mr. Grant on the phone?"

Begrudgingly given his number and he was charm itself.

"I'm a retired character actor, and my real name is Peter Grant, but I had to change it in 1929, as there was an actor with that name already."

"Is there any possibility that you would allow me to add a middle name?"

"I don't see why not."

"Any chance you might consider my inserting a *single*

capital letter in between, as I don't have the funds to get all my printed photos redone?"

He generously agreed, and I called the stentorian-voiced Equity Bunty, who barked, "*What* letter, then?"

Stammered, and started with Richard A. Grant/Richard B. Grant/Richard C. Grant/Richard D. Grant—

"I haven't got all *day*!"

"Richard E. Grant."

"Right, that's it. I'll get it changed on the membership list."

Some years later, I was promoting a film on Channel 4's *The Big Breakfast* and there was a live phone-in segment where a member of the public called in to speak to the TV guest. It was Mrs. Grant from Bromley who advised that I could drop the "E." as her husband Peter had died six months previously.

In early 1983, when Joan was coaching on three different productions at the RSC and National Theatre and I was doing a lunch-hour play in a pub theatre on a profit share basis, which meant zero pay, she wrote me a letter, declaring that:

> The world feels beautiful to me at the moment. I've never felt quite like this before about anyone. I can't find the right words to tell you how I feel, because the sensations are new to me. I so love everything about it—just being in the same room with you is wonderful. You're a very special person—I've always

thought so, even before I fell in love with you—so open, so generous, so . . . EVERYTHING. I want you to be happy, to be successful, to feel complete, whatever happens between us. At the moment I want US to happen together. Read "The Good-Morrow" by John Donne—that's how I feel about you—

My face in thine eye, thine in mine appears
And true plain hearts do in the faces rest;
Where can we find two better hemispheres,
Without sharp north, without declining west?
Whatever dies, was not mixed equally;
If our two loves be one, or, thou and I
Love so alike, that none do slacken, none can die.

Something metaphysical is certainly happening to *me*!!! I've never written a letter like this before. How wonderful life is. I love you, my darling. Joan X

Chapter Two

January

Saturday, January 2, 2021

Joan helps me put away all the Christmas decorations, while Oilly and Florian pack up to return to their flat. She seems completely *herself* today. House suddenly feels very quiet after they've gone.

In the afternoon, Joan says that she feels very dizzy whenever she stands up, and I suggest that it's probably 'cos she doesn't have enough oxygen.

We tele-surf and settle on *The Bridge on the River Kwai*, mainly because she told me in the last century that she fancied William Holden. The plot is very straightforward and we've both seen it before, so alarm bells start clanging when she questions what's going on.

When she goes to bed at 8 p.m., she mumbles, "I feel very disorientated" and takes a left turn into the living room.

"I don't know where I am."

Monday, January 4, 2021

Oilly's thirty-second birthday. Phone and tell her that Joan has rallied for the breathing test at the hospital.

Alex has confirmed that the headaches and dizziness are *not* due to lack of oxygen. The consultant has suggested a brain scan as soon as possible.

My stomach plunge is akin to one of those mid-air pressure drops.

Wednesday, January 6, 2021

Undergoes the forty-minute MRI brain scan, which proves noisy and uncomfortable, but am mightily relieved that this will be the final test before all her results are collated and diagnosed by the oncologist. She is her perky, provocative and funnily restored self on the drive home.

"Will my brain ever get back to normal?"

"Well, as you've told me enough times that you think I'm crazy, I don't really feel qualified to reply."

She slaps my shoulder and laughs. Which makes me laugh. Which makes *us* both laugh.

Thursday, January 7, 2021

Noon call from Wanda Cui, the Australian oncologist from the Royal Marsden cancer hospital, who speaks delicately and with immense vocal calm. "The MRI scan has revealed lesions on the brain and there is swelling around them, which accounts for Joan's current symptoms, so I've prescribed steroids which will alleviate the pressure. They can take a few days to start working, so don't expect an immediate result."

The room turns upside down and I hear myself agreeing to everything that Wanda is saying and advising, though, in actuality, not taking in a single thing. Like that moment when you're driving and suddenly catch your breath, realising that you've travelled for ten minutes or longer without *any* sense of how you've done so.

Yet, confirmation that it's brain lesions causing her confusion is its own odd relief. Better to know than live in unblissful ignorance.

Relay the news to Oilly who is relieved that it's not dementia or Alzheimer's.

Friday, January 8, 2021

Unbelievably, Joan wakes up at 6:30 a.m. able to see properly, walk normally, talk coherently, and eat a proper breakfast. *Fully* restored in less than twenty-four hours with the steroid pills.

If this illness has begun to teach us anything, it's that living in the moment, for the moment, is the most positive way forward.

It's the ultimate taunting cruelty of this disease that we are so hope-filled, but for how long?

"No matter what happens, *please* don't let me be alone in a hospital, Swaziboy. I want to be at home with you. I know you can't promise, but *promise* me."

"I *promise,* Monkee"—even though I know that this might not be in my power to keep.

Oilly confides that Joan has voiced her fears about chemo, losing all her hair and "my identity." This demon bass chord resounds beneath everything we say and do.

Dread.

Dread.

Dread.

Echoing Brando's "The horror, the horror" incantation in *Apocalypse Now*.

The diagnosis/prognosis with the oncologist has been brought forward to Monday afternoon, rendering the hours of the weekend ahead aeons-long. Recall that our Belgian friend, Felix de Loose, who survived leukaemia, convinced himself to have zero expectations in order not to have his hopes dashed. So that *any* progress was a bonus. The problem for me is that I've always travelled "in hope," the price for which is that inevitable canyon-deep plunge when hope doesn't hold up.

Sunday, January 10, 2021

How do we *not* project about tomorrow's prognosis? Is it better to be in this no-man's-land, *not* knowing, or to find out precisely where you stand and what to prepare for?

Like Hamlet philosophised: "There's a special providence in the fall of a sparrow. If it be now, 'tis not to come; if it be not to come, it will be now; if it be not now, yet it will come—the readiness is all."

Monday, January 11, 2021

Joan is her complete self. Positive, sharp, and funny. Takes steroid pills, drinks coffee, eats a full breakfast, in contrast to Oilly and I, who look and feel utterly steamrollered. Delivery of cashmere leggings, top and loose-fitting sweater to make Joan feel comfy and cosseted, courtesy of our thoughtful and generous daughter.

The hours until our appointment stretch ahead in an infinity of excruciation. Cannot imagine what Joan must be feeling like. My shoulders have invisible anvils pressing down on them. No matter how I try to focus and stay calm, every nightmare scenario competes for the centre of my shaky attention.

The readiness is all. Readiness is all. Readiness is all.

How can you *ever* be ready for this?

Drive as sedately as possible to the hospital for 3:15 p.m. Covid restrictions preclude Oilly being present, but she's able to listen via speakerphone. Once inside, we wait for a further hour. *The longest* of our lives. Covertly look at the other two patients in the reception area, awaiting their fate. None of us make direct eye contact.

Wanda Cui, the Australian oncologist, finally arrives and

ushers us into a room. She is petite, looks preternaturally young, apologises profusely for the delay, then calmly delivers the atom bomb diagnosis:

Stage 4 lung cancer.

Never have I dreaded or loathed a number so instantaneously as this one. Closely followed by the word "spread" . . .

To the lymph nodes. To the adrenal glands. To the brain.

A Catherine wheel of information. Flaring and firing in every direction.

What has taken eight short sentences to write took almost twenty carefully cushioned and considered minutes to reveal.

With Joan's permission, I dare ask, "How long?"

Wanda answers with, "That's a very good question. If you're sure you want to know, understanding that this isn't an exact science . . ."

"Yes, please, tell us?"

"At best, twelve to eighteen months. Or less."

The room tips in on itself as our world spins off its axis.

Hurtling.

Free-falling.

Words compete for attention—radiation/statistics/scans/terminal/blood tests/immunotherapy/combined/with chemotherapy/steroids/terminal—zoning in and out.

Bizarre as this may sound, among all the other hurtling

emotions there's a weird relief in finally knowing. Wanda manages to combine the unenviable task of delivering the most brutal news possible with compassion, kindness, and medical expertise.

Joan is devastated.

All three of us, utterly devastated.

Poleaxed.

Except it's Joan, not us, who's been sentenced.

Drive home blurry-eyed and blinking. Sucker-punched by a tidal wave of grief.

Tuesday, January 12, 2021

Chaotic day of disbelief and discord. Joan is very chipper—in contrast to Oilly and me, lurching in and out of tears, not quite knowing what to do with ourselves. Even though we hesitantly anticipated what the diagnosis might be, *nothing* has properly prepared us for the head-and-heart-exploding overwhelm of it all.

We resolve to share the news with all our friends, as it just feels too much to bear on our own. Joan is fiercely against doing so.

"We need our friends to know and to have their love and support," is Oilly's reasoning.

"Remember how grateful I was when Victoria Wood told me when she had cancer the first time, then how hurt I felt when it returned and she chose *not* to include me?" I add. "Hearing about her death made me feel that

I'd failed her, and wasn't a worthy or close enough friend to tell. I'm sure that's not what she meant, but that's how it felt, so *please* allow us to tell our friends."

Oilly added, "You're so loved, Mum. Everyone will want to help us. *Please.*"

"But it won't cure me!"

"But it'll help *us*!"

Feels brutal to be arguing with each other, but Oilly holds her ground, holds her mother and insists that it's the only way we can begin to navigate what's ahead.

While Joan naps, we both email and message all our friends. No sooner sent, than our news is reciprocated by a cyber-avalanche of love, shock, disbelief, and compassion. All-engulfing.

The relief of not having to hide this any longer feels profound.

Wednesday, January 13, 2021

Steroids working their magic, enabling Joan to walk unaided. Eating heartily. Tasting normally.

More and more messages of love pour in. Joan acknowledges that sharing our situation *is* beneficial and a real support. It's as if we've been exiled in outer space for the past three weeks, locked into that *Alien* movie tagline: "In space, no one can hear you scream."

It's poignant how normal our day feels. Knowing that this is one of the precious few we have left before the chemo/radiation onslaught begins. Can it truly be only forty-eight hours since receiving her diagnosis?

Don't project. Live in the moment.

1985

In December 1985, Joan's father died and she offered to take her mother to Paris.

When Joan had told her Aberdonian mother that she had fallen in love with a Swazi, she delighted in her mum's, "Oooh no, Joan, what have you gone and done now?"

But I adored Maggie, who was outwardly nonplussed when I took her to a hardware shop in Twickenham to buy a replacement wooden loo seat, attempting to part-exchange it for the cracked and stained plastic one I'd brought with me. It seemed perfectly logical to me, and it was only when I reported back to Joan and she said, "What the hell did you think you were doing?!" that I realised it might have been slightly inappropriate.

I took the opportunity while they were away to go back to Africa for the first time since emigrating to England in April 1982. It was the longest we'd been apart, and we wrote two aerogrammes to each other every day, as phoning was prohibitively expensive. The first of which, read:

> My darling Richard—here's my favourite D. H. Lawrence poem, since falling deeply and totally in love with you. He wrote it to Frieda—

You are the call and I am the answer
You are the wish and I the fulfilment
You are the night and I the day
What else?
It is perfect enough
It is perfectly complete
You and I
Strange how we suffer in spite of this!

Let's be very happy together all our lives, because I believe we have a very special and great love. Come home to me safely, my sweet darling. I also found your message on the answering machine, which I've played at least ten times! I love you so much, my sweet darling. Have a really good and interesting time in Africa and come back to me. All my love, forever, Joan XXX

PS. You're all around me all the time. I can feel you and smell you and I quite often have talks with you out loud—as well as my constant conversation with you inside my head. I adore you, Rich. Yours now and always, Joan xxxxxxxxxxx

PPS. Sight-seeing with my mum and we passed a cinema in Pigalle, advertising "LES PETITS TROUS FARCIS." She asked me what it meant, which I reluctantly told her was the title of a porn film called "Little Stuffed Holes." Made both of us really laugh.

The issue of the age gap between us (ten years) periodically surfaced as a worry for her in our early years, but never bothered this toyboy one iota. Six weeks apart convinced me that we should get married, so I bought the most expensive diamond I couldn't afford and, at 6 a.m. at Heathrow airport in January 1986, I got down on one knee, beside the luggage trolley, and proposed.

Saturday, January 16, 2021

Pouring rain, rendering the lawn sponge-squelchy wet. While Joan naps, Oilly and I take the opportunity to clear all her evening clothes out of the wardrobe in Oilly's childhood bedroom, so that her and Florian's clothes don't end up scattered all over the floor, student-style, while they stay here.

Very emotional bagging up our past together, in clothing form. Knowing that she will never wear any of them again.

Oilly compares notes about her friendship group's response, and her renewed faith in the kindness of people. I feel exactly the same. Both of us buoyed up by this outpouring of generosity and compassion. When Joan wakes up, Oilly quietly says, "We love you *so, so* much, Mama."

Nigella Lawson WhatsApps that she's booked a cab to deliver a home-made rice dish, a cake, and her latest cookbook, which arrives accompanied by an incredibly loving dedication and generous note. Wholly unexpected and mightily welcome. It's the perfect moment to share with Joan all the messages we've received. She is genuinely moved.

"Sounds like my memorial!"

"All hail and hallelujah to that. I think it's a real gift to hear what your friends have to say and feel about you. Not morbid in any way. Something to celebrate."

She concurs. It's a juggle to keep the word "death" out of our conversation, even though it's constantly hovering.

"I'd like to record a thank-you video message for Nigella."

Joan has never done anything like this before, as she hates all technology, so it's a real measure of how grateful she feels.

Sunday, January 17, 2021

Sun's out and spirits lifted. Complete three circuits of the garden. No breathlessness. No dizziness. Good appetite. Ticks and gold stars on the invisible progress chart I keep in my head.

We've now established a daily bath ritual—she undresses herself, gets in and out of the bath, unaided, and sits like a little girl on the loo seat, while I towel her down, then apply body cream.

"Feels like a spa, Swaz"—which makes her happy.

Blow-dries and brushes her own hair. These little things that we take for granted. Grateful that she can complete these tasks for herself. She's as witty, feisty, and forthright as ever she was when we first met in late 1982, at the Actors Centre in Covent Garden, where she was doing a six-week course teaching regional British accents.

"I still fancy you, you know?"

"Don't sound so bloody surprised!"

"But I do. Even though we've been together for a hundred years, you're the only person I've ever truly loved, in the romantic sense. I'm genuinely amazed that you've managed to change gears from being so frenetic, to being calm and controlled."

"It's exhausting!"—which makes her laugh.

Monday, January 18, 2021

I read the oncology report that's just landed on the doormat. Addressed to Joan, but am resolved that she will never read it. The atomic bombshell diagnosis/prognosis verbally delivered a week ago, here in black and white. With all the medical terminology I never want to read, ever again. The words "incurable" and "terminal" hang, like unlit neon, in the air.

The committee has opted to do radiation surgery. To blast the brain tumours in three days, rather than do whole-brain radiation over ten days. Joan's hair will all fall out a week after radiation treatment, and there will be brain swelling and possible incoherence, which we will counteract by doubling her steroid dosage. This will be followed by chemo or immunotherapy.

How can this be?

Joan is on such good form today, and here's the thing—even though those deadly words are fixed to the page, we are going to *live* each day, for the here-and-now of it. The alternative would be to duvet-dive and will ourselves dead already.

Binge-watched all ten episodes of *The Morning Show* on Apple TV+. Script, direction, and performances all stellar. Especially Jennifer Aniston. Whom I met, three years ago, backstage with Melissa McCarthy at the *Good Morning America* studios in New York. Melissa and I on the publicity trail for the film *Can You Ever Forgive Me?* and I asked what Jennifer was promoting.

"I'm not. Here researching behind-the-scenes for a series I'm doing about breakfast TV."

She is as friendly and accessible as I'd hoped she might be, looks unfeasibly unaged since *Friends*, with the silhouette of a teenager, at *fifty*! As on screen, she possesses that particular kinetic quality that makes you want to imitate her—by which I mean, when she gestures, picks up props, angles her head, flicks her hair, or expressively uses her hands, it's hypnotic. To this viewer anyway. The other actor who has this by the bucket-load is Diane Keaton. Sometimes turn the sound off and just watch how both of them move and physically react to everything. Like a second language. Jennifer's voice sounds deeper than expected and am thrilled when she blows some flattery smoke signals up our tepees. Shamelessly ask for a selfie, which she readily agrees to, with the steely proviso, "*No* social media, okay?"

Her question is unequivocally rhetorical. Iron-clad. No-shit-Sherlock clear. A pinprick recognition that she is as tough as her "Rachel" hair is silky-soft. A *very* beguiling combination.

"You look like a hypnotised puppy, watching her," quips Joan midway through our binge. "Small but tough, just like me."

My soulmate may be seriously ill, but *nothing* wrong with her antennae. Cheering and reassuring. I've observed her from a distance, flirting up a can-can skirt's worth, but always assured that we are swan/seahorse/beaver/bald eagle monogamous. It's literally been the bedrock of our marriage.

Wednesday, January 20, 2021

Reading lights off at midnight, then Joan woke up at 2 a.m. Ate breakfast and took steroids. Read together, then back to sleep at 3 a.m. She's up again at 4 a.m. and goes downstairs. Woke at 7 a.m. and found her reading and texting, insistent that I go back to bed to catch up.

"This feels like precious, peaceful time. Don't worry about me. I've been emailing and telling people that I've got cancer, but that I'm feeling feisty and accepting. Their immediate, shocked response and the love expressed has buoyed up my spirits. Made me feel euphoric."

Most surprising of all, she added:

"Thank you and Oilly, for showing me the way and how beneficial it is to share my situation. Made me feel a lot better that I've taken ownership. Feel calm. Feel like I'm a grown-up, for the first time in my life."

Huge psychic relief for me and her. Our morning smooths calmly along, but by 2:40 p.m., anticipating the radiation doctor's phone call, scheduled for 3:20 p.m., agitation manifests in shortness of breath and suppressed panic.

Hollow gut and twisted nerve ends. Panic. Reality encroaching upon us, too fast.

Phone rings at precisely 3:20 on speaker mode and a very calm, controlled, and compassionate Dr. Liam Welsh fills the next fifty minutes, detailing everything about Joan's forthcoming radiation treatment. Side effects. Statistics. Percentages. Positives.

Joan has calmed down completely and asks a few questions, all of which he answers, honestly and compassionately. So cogent is his prognosis that you'd almost believe we were heading towards a curable conclusion. Any vestige of hope is grasped at and held tight. Such is our combined willpower to alter the inevitable. Within the parameters of her terminal condition, this is heartening and even cheering news to receive. Sounds contradictory, but it's action, rather than passivity.

Skye Gyngell, the Australian chef supreme, whose cookbooks we've road-tasted from cover to cover, sends three large boxes of the most delicious food, with a note thanking

Joan for being so generous and kind to her at a particular moment in her life. Joan is genuinely taken aback by her generosity.

"I feel I haven't done anything worthy enough to deserve all of this."

Watched Donald Trump finally exiting the White House to a soundtrack of "YMCA" by the Village People. I interviewed him in 2013 for docu-series *Hotel Secrets* on the gazillionth floor of Trump Tower in Manhattan. Strictly prescribed—ten questions in ten minutes—which he insisted on vetting in advance.

Entered, flanked by two wardrobe-sized bodyguards, smelling of hairspray. (Him, not them.)

"Fire away, kid."

I asked about how his German-Scottish parents influenced the way he brought up *his* children.

"This wasn't on the list."

"Yes, but I'm not David Letterman. I'm curious to understand your Calvinist work ethic. My wife is from Aberdeen."

"I own a golf course there, do you play?"

"No, because when I was ten years old, I inadvertently woke up on the back seat of a car and witnessed my mother schtupping someone who wasn't my father, on the front seat, and *he* was a golfer, so I don't play."

"You're saying this on TV?"

"Yes. How have you brought up your children to avoid the Paris Hilton school of hotel-parenting?"

"Rules! No room service. No alcohol and no drugs."

Ten minutes expanded to fifty. Once he'd started, he was unstoppable. On his way out, he turned and said, "You did good, kid. You'll go far."

Felt like being in the company of a Teflon-coated Barnum & Bailey ringmaster, polished from the top of his golden Ford Fairlane hair to the tips of his shiny shoes.

Friday, January 22, 2021

New sleeping pills have countered the steroids and, for the first time in a fortnight, she's managed to sleep through the night! Today feels like I've got her totally back. Profound relief and gratitude. Quips me with: "I've never done what I'm supposed to have done. You should etch that on my tombstone."

Am dumbfounded. These shards of deadly humour come obliquely and without warning. How can she not think about her own mortality?

Oilly's friends send more flowers, adding to the florist's worth we've already received, scenting every room. As Joan doesn't seem "critically ill" at this moment, we're in a slightly heightened state of euphoria. Is this denial? Of sorts. Yet every five minutes, we're reminded that this is all too real.

Sit in her room, where she usually coaches actors privately or in prep for film roles. Looking around at all our loot, she identifies when and where we bought, or were given, or inherited, all of the furniture, ornaments, objects, books, masks, portraits, and paintings that cover every surface, from floor to ceiling. Taking inventory of our maximalist life together.

"Play something for me on the piano."

In all our years together, we have *never* taken time quite like this, to take stock. Improvise a tune on the upright that Allan Corduner (best man at our register office wedding) has permanently loaned us, as he no longer has room for it. Age and central heating have rendered it slightly out of tune, giving it a honky-tonk tone. Melancholic music emits from my fingertips, which makes her tear up.

"Don't stop!"

Thursday, January 28, 2021

That time of year when, if you're not deducting from your paycheque, the tax behemoth haemorrhages through your bank account.

Make onion soup for lunch and encourage Joan to circuit the garden a few times. Manages three. Oilly offers to cook this evening, relieving me of my daily chef duties.

"Wonder if she'll do mushroom stroganoff?"

"Hope not. Can't stand it. Seem to have eaten it every four days."

Joan catches herself going Larry David on me, and apologises, while laughing!

"I love your cooking, darling, but we do seem to have eaten strog ad nauseam."

Her diplomacy button clearly fell off at birth. For the record, I certainly haven't offered up stroganoff every four days. Her propensity to drop a clanger is well known. We were once singing carols at Sting and Trudie's annual Christmas sleepover party, when she confided to a total stranger, seated beside her, "Oh, don't worry, I'm tone deaf too. Can't sing a note."

This came to light a couple of years later, when the self-same woman came up to me at some event and told me that she was mortified by Joan's comment, as she'd always believed that she *could* sing!

I apologised and said, "That's just Joan. Doesn't pussyfoot about her opinions." The lady had the grace to laugh. I know all too well that Joan would have said it without any malice, which is what renders it all the more lethal as she genuinely believes that she's being honest and direct! It's this feistiness that continues to keep me on my toes and fully engaged. And laughing. Apart from her audible intake of breath, she looks great and in apparently good health today.

Cancer is concealed, cruel, and confounding.

Could we love each other more? I don't think that's possible. We complete one another, like a pair of well-worn bookends, our lives in large volumes, bound together, in between.

Friday, January 29, 2021

Wanda calls with astonishing news. "The FDA-approved tepotinib wonder drug has been granted on compassionate grounds, completely free. You're only required to take two pills per day."

It's a new drug that only works for a very specific type of lung cancer. To be given this end-of-week hope-filled news is extraordinary. Christen it the "Wanda drug."

HOPE.

The all-time magic ingredient.

She won't have to undergo chemotherapy. Won't lose her hair. Feels like a lottery win.

Wanda is so happy to be sharing this positive news that she "encores" by reading out the email from the US drug company. No sooner has she said goodbye, than all three of us burst into tears and dance around the kitchen to Queen and Bowie's "Under Pressure," which happens to be playing on the radio.

Saturday, January 30, 2021

Joan gently wakes me up at 6 a.m. and asks me to get her a cup of tea.

"Do you honestly think this new medication will enable me to live a little longer? Wanda originally said I had a year to eighteen months. Do you think I'll still be here next Christmas?"

"Yes! I should damn well hope so, Monkee. We've got our thirty-fifth wedding anniversary in November, so you better be here! Can't do it without you." Jocular as I try to be, she maintains her serenity.

"Thank you, Swaz. I feel completely loved and supported, and accepting that I've made my mark and had a good life."

Hearing her articulate out loud what Oilly and I have been thinking makes my jaw invisibly drop.

"Sometimes, I fantasise about us jumping into your Z4 and doing a *Thelma & Louise*, driving at 200 miles an hour over a cliff together." She laughs and don't-be-dafts me, adding, "One thing that's clear to me, since getting my diagnosis, is that you and Oilly are going to be all right. Strong. Bonded. She's a real grown-up now. So evolved, mature, and wise."

Oilly and Florian sensibly return to their flat for the night. Mightily generous of them to stay with us, but also an incredible strain for a young couple to have to cope with all of this.

Joan's asleep on the sofa and the house suddenly feels empty, vast, and lonely. Presaging what's to come.

Multiple texts from friends, checking in on us, and every single message and act of kindness is profoundly welcome. Keeps us connected in our enforced isolation.

Struck by this passage from Saul Bellow's novel *More Die of Heartbreak*: "Towards the end of your life, you have something like a pain schedule to fill out . . . First, physical causes . . . Next category, injured vanity, betrayal, swindle, injustice. But the hardest items of all have to do with love."

Read it out to Joan, who replies, "Our love renders that second category obsolete."

Chapter Three

February

Monday, February 1, 2021

First day of another month, in this new decade, feels in itself like a mini victory. Spent the morning strimming ivy off the arches in the garden, stuffing it into the car, and taking it to the municipal dump. Aware that anything I do that's distracting is undertowed by unease. The countdown until radiation treatment begins. Just tidying up the garden is its own satisfaction, as there is a visible result.

Joan suggests face-timing with Bruce and Sophie Robinson. He is on fine Grumpelstiltskin form and hilariously describes reinventing the potato chip, which goes something like this:

"Grab a huge fucker, *shove* it in the Aga, like you were doing a baked potato. When it's thoroughly cooked through, slice it up, like a loaf of white, then deep-fry the fuckers, and you won't *believe* how good they are."

A "gourmet" recipe, delivered with trademark Withnailian

conviction. He was at the Central School of Speech and Drama in the mid-sixties, when Joan was training on the teachers' course. She remembers his gang, which included Vivian MacKerrell (on whom Withnail was based), as being very glamorous, despite Bruce's assurances that they were always skint. These lifelong connections thread through our lives and friendship, in a way that feels unbreakable. Capable of withstanding whatever strength or strain we test it with.

1986

Joan's faith in me never wavered, despite being unemployed for nine months in 1985. The year had begun promisingly when I was cast in an improvised film for the BBC called *Honest, Decent and True*, set in an advertising agency, alongside Adrian Edmondson, Arabella Weir, and Gary Oldman, so I knew I had *something* to show for it. But the toll of being out of work for that long was debilitating. The worst moment being my misguided decision to paint the loo in Joan's house pillar-box red. It was tiled halfway up the wall, and I slathered it with gloss paint, which wouldn't adhere. Looked like that scene in *Carrie* where Sissy Spacek is drenched in pig's blood at her school prom. *Only* moment when Joan truly lost it and spluttered, "*Nitromors!*"

Required five tins of the paint stripper and took three gruesome days to get it all off. The pay-off for that long resting period was that casting director Mary Selway saw the BBC film when it transmitted on February 9, 1986, and called me in to audition for *Withnail and I*, to play an actor riddled with frustration at being out of work for months on end. That breakthrough role single-handedly transformed my career prospects and bank account. They had been trying to cast the part for two months and Bruce Robinson had rejected every actor on the grounds that no one had yet made him laugh speaking his dialogue. I read for him and bellowed "FORK IT!," referring to matter growing in the mouldy kitchen sink. He laughed and on the basis of saying these two words "as he'd heard them in his head," I was called back every day for the next fortnight to audition with other actors, after which I was finally offered the role.

As he was a first-time writer-director, and Paul McGann and I were likewise movie first-timers, we were given two weeks of rehearsal. Which is not how films usually get made. At the end of the first week, Joan went into premature labour.

Hurtled through the morning traffic to the hospital and our daughter Tiffany was born, but tragically only lived for half an hour. Her lungs were too underdeveloped to survive. It felt as though this euphoric life- and career-defining role came at the most heartbreaking price imaginable.

Dread my way to Hammersmith municipal offices and handed a form on which I am legally required to write down our daughter's name, date of birth, date of death. One little half hour. Same day. Same hour. This confuses the clerk who whinges that I will have to do the form again "'cos it's not possible to have the same date of birth and death on the same line." I lower my voice and say, "Excuse me, I don't want to argue with you, but my baby daughter was born and died within half an hour of birth on the same day, within the same hour, and is therefore registered on this form on the same line in the same section." A couple of sullen eyes meet mine with the distant blink of a light bulb going on and I wonder if she's ever going to stamp the fucking paper. "Get a move on, love," bleats someone behind me, which galvanises her into action, grips the stamp, inks up and blots down on the words that I never thought would relate to me.

Joan was asked to coach Christopher Lambert on *The Sicilian*, and escaped to Italy. She is not keen to go but it seems better to be abroad while I am filming on location in Cumbria than to be alone at home with a baby's room that has no infant.

I felt incredibly insecure playing this lead role, especially as I'm allergic to alcohol, and Withnail is in a near-perpetual state of drunkenness. Bruce insisted that I get drunk the night before the final day of rehearsal "in order to have a chemical memory" to draw upon, which I somehow managed to do. Throwing up throughout the night, and topping up on more drink at the studio the next morning, until I finally passed out midway through the rehearsal, to the delight of Bruce and Paul!

Joan and I wrote to one another every day and she gave me this sage advice:

My darling, dearest love

Thank you for your phone call to me tonight. It was *so* comforting to talk to you after all that we have suffered together. It has made us all the stronger and more committed to one another. I love your voice on the phone—what joy, what peace I feel to hear you—like an erotic hot-water bottle. Comfort and thrills at the same time. Rich, I'm thrilled for your success. Brilliant, isn't it. I feel flooding, overpowering love for you. I miss you. I hope that all is going as well as it possibly can, on your first movie! Whatever is happening with you at the moment, whether good, bad or indifferent in terms of the work, keep channelling your energy into positives. Don't play the dialogue, play *actions*. Play the moments—you *know* the *whole*! This part *is* you, and that's why they chose you. Don't worry about whether you're being "good" or not—concern yourself only with whether the moments feel true! This is not written as a lesson, because you're probably in the middle of a very good shoot—only because I want to say I love you and I believe in you and I want to be sure that you believe and trust in yourself as much as I do in you. Oh I do love you, bandage! Thank you again for my lovely pearls and *beautiful* diamond rings.

> They make me feel so close to you and such a part of you when we're apart. I know these things shouldn't matter, but they are concrete symbols of our love, which I wear with me every day. Darling, hope all's well with you. I love you and for the first time ever in my life, I swear to love you till I die. I have *no* doubts. Joan XXXXXX

My £20,000 paycheque for *Withnail* was more money than I'd earned in my entire professional career up to that point and, the moment the film wrapped, we set a wedding date for November 1, 1986. When Joan's divorce was finalised in 1984, she had told me that "we should wait a while before moving in together." That "while" lasted all of a week and she said, "What's the worst that can happen? Let's give it a go and see if it works, and, by the way, I *never* want to get married ever again."

My parents' incredibly acrimonious divorce had likewise sworn me off ever getting married or having a child, and here I was married with a stepson, whom I adored, and Joan determined that we should keep trying to have a baby of our own.

Bought a second-hand red MG, booked the Richmond registry for the official bit, then lunch with Joan's family at the Waterside Inn, Bray. My brother-in-law, David, filmed everything on my suitcase-sized home video camera, and for years afterwards we greatly enjoyed replaying the wedding lunch, as it's dominated by Joan's hypochondriacal sister Anne telling everyone about her health issues. Which Joan delighted in riffing on with "*and then I had my kidneys removed . . . and THEN I had a heart transplant . . . and THEN . . .*"

Joan decided that we should cater our own wedding party at home—for eighty people! Everyone thought we were nuts, but Joan persuasively argued that as she was a good cook, it was her act of friendship to do so for our guests. My culinary experience was limited to tin-opening and spaghetti bolognese, so she gave me Delia Smith's *How to Cook* manual, which begins with how to boil an egg and I learnt *fast*. At the time I assumed that she was doing this for budgetary reasons, but, without exception, we cooked for *all* of our subsequent Christmas parties, brunches, and dinners, when it would have been quite easy to pay someone to do so.

"Wouldn't feel personal doing that, and I think people appreciate it more, knowing that we've done it ourselves." *Every* party I suggested we get help and she remained adamant. Never panicked no matter how many people poured through our door.

When *Withnail and I* premiered in London in January 1988, I was already filming *Warlock* in Boston and had to miss it. Joan attended and wrote me an aerogramme:

> Dear Swaz—just back from the *Withnail* premiere with an immediate letter about my feelings and impressions of the evening. Got picked up by the

> driver, along with Susie Wooldridge, and arrived at Piccadilly too early, so we asked to be taken to the Ritz for a drink. Haymarket cinema was abuzz with cameras, squash of penguin suits and every woman bedecked in black silk, taffeta and jewels. Including me! Watched your movie very nervously to begin with and then in total confidence about the production and your performance. The film got lots of laughs and applause at the end. Then went to the party and the response was *incredible*. Oh, I wish you'd been there, especially as you're such a fan of Annie Lennox and could have met her. Spoke a lot to Ralph Brown. Kept a low profile, but everyone who clocked that you were my husband said, "He's a star" and I could only reply, "Yes he is!" Bruce announced that, "It's rare to meet an actor who is so cerebral. Grant had never done a movie before, so he was a big risk and when the casting director showed me his photo, I said, 'I don't like the look of him,' but I was wrong. He is in fact mad, but in a socially acceptable way and he reacts to the material in the way I want."

Some irony that almost every job I've had since was the result of playing an out-of-work actor in my first film. Which is why I'm eternally indebted to Bruce for taking the risk and for writing the funniest script I've ever read. Every journalist asks if I'm wary of talking about it, but I've never baulked at doing so. It has afforded me lifelong friendships with the cast and continues to accumulate cult followers.

Tuesday, February 2, 2021

Everything is preternaturally quiet today, in anticipation of the radiation treatment beginning tomorrow. Joan spends much of the day on her own, dozing and intermittently thumbing through Skye's inspirational cookery books.

Mine taken up with answering emails, household maintenance, replacing light bulbs, fixing things, and writing down everything that the nurse, calling from the Marsden Hospital in Sutton, outlines about what to expect tomorrow. Where to park. Who to call. Instructions about the rota of steroid pills to be taken at breakfast and at lunchtime. Reassured that the radiation will be pain-free.

Receive confirmation that the tepotinib drugs will be ready to pick up on February 9th.

Respected Joan's determination to be entirely independent today. Leaving her to do everything for herself. By herself.

This is the first time, since our world turned upside down on December 23, 2020, that we've felt able, strong, and trusting enough to allow each other to be alone. We meet up for supper and she confesses that "as well as feeling breathless, it feels like there's a weight pressing down on my chest."

Roast chicken and all goes swimmingly, until Joan snaps

at me about something I've either done or not done, can't even remember which, but everything escalates out of all proportion, very rapidly. Retreat early to bed, knowing full well that this is all to do with her anxiety about the brain radiation surgery.

Wednesday, February 3, 2021

Finally here—the first day of Joan's treatment plan. When I get downstairs, Joan and Oilly are already awake and the atmosphere is antsy and irritable. At the very moment that we need to be united and supporting one another, everything feels scratchy and out of sorts. Escape back upstairs with a bowl of muesli, and Oilly goes for a walk along the Thames. Deep, deep breaths, then we're in the car and negotiating rain and heavy traffic to the Marsden. Met by a very calm nurse who takes us down into the basement where the CyberKnife unit is located. Past a waiting room filled with patients in wheelchairs and visibly poor health. Very sobering. Covert eye contact as we walk by.

The nurse asks if I'd like to see where the treatment will take place and am led in to see the *Space Odyssey*-style machine.

Almost four decades ago, my 53-year-old father underwent actual rather than radiation surgery, to remove his subsidiary brain tumours. Requiring a complete head-shave, anaesthetic, sawing into his skull, stitches, bandages, and the trauma of major surgery. Seems barbaric compared to the ease and precision of this CyberKnife machine. Whereas he was so fear-filled, Joan is mercifully calm, awake, and relatively in control.

Feel profound relief that her treatment programme has finally begun.

Thursday, February 4, 2021

Joan is on markedly independent form this morning. Our drive to the hospital in acute contrast to the nerve-rack of yesterday. Perky, positive, and went straight into her second radiation "surgery" as if she'd done it a hundred times before. Shorter session today and, despite the prognosis, we're both weirdly hope-filled.

Overwhelmed with longing for everything to be healthy and safe again. Against the ghastly recognition that this will never be. Joan asks, "Do you feel that this is all happening to someone else?"

"I'm afraid so. You?"

She nods. Looks exhausted and ill. For the first time. Or is that just me daring to acknowledge this to myself?

Cook supper. And the mood swings round again. Feels like everything has returned to normal. Familial. Warm. Convivial. Relieved.

Friday, February 5, 2021

Bright-blue-sky walk along the Thames with Oilly, for an hour, sharing how our friends have reacted or failed to. This disease is so egocentric—vacuuming all conversation into its vortex. Walking back into the real world is bracing and life-enhancingly welcome.

Back to the Marsden for Joan's third and final brain session. How soon will we know if it's worked? Will the miracle drug tepotinib have any effect on stage 4 cancer? Will chemotherapy even be an option? The questions squall up on the horizon.

Joan is completely calm and Zen-like today, and falls fast asleep during the radiation. Hannah, Adriana, and Jennifer give her five-star care and tell us that it will take two weeks for the radiation results to emerge, once the brain swelling has subsided. Warned that Joan will feel exhausted in the weeks ahead. Right now, she is calm and completely compos mentis.

Friday night takeaway fish and chips to celebrate!

Monday, February 8, 2021

Steroid pills reduced to three per day, which has the positive effect of enabling her to sleep through the night. Combined with the impact of the radiation, which has wiped her out.

Melissa McCarthy messages, noting how much "your

ladies keep you on your toes. The first time I met Joan, we were at a party with terrible acoustics, and I finally screamed, 'I feel like I'm screaming at you,' and she never flinched and said, 'It's because you *are*. You've been screaming at me for some time.' I knew at that moment I'd never be that funny. The 'Colonel' wins."

The Colonel, my nickname for Joan. Early on in our relationship, she and I had smoked a spliff of Swazi Gold, and at 2 a.m. she woke up demanding: "Why doesn't everyone just listen to what I say and do what I tell them to? I *am* the Colonel!"

My childhood friend Richard Clarke posts a book from Perth, *Being Mortal* by Atul Gawande, speed-read in a single sitting. Examines how Western cultures shy away from dealing with death. Hospice care at the end is the most civilised and loving decision to take, rather than endlessly pursuing chemo and medical options that won't alter the inevitable. The common denominator is that people *all* want to die at home, in their own beds.

Good appetite and stayed up till 11 p.m. watching TV and chatting, but she struggled to walk upstairs. Oilly assists, taking pit stops on the way, to give her time to muster her breath. Once in bed, she complains that her legs are cold, despite refusing to use a heavy cashmere rug, folded at the bottom of the bed.

"Would you like to wear the cashmere leggings that Oilly gave you?"

"*No.*"

"What if I pulled up the rug, at the end of the bed?"

Triggers her to go from zero to maniac, in seconds. Refusing the rug *and* the leggings. Awful to be snapped at when you're doing everything you possibly can to make things warmer, smoother, better. But that's the very thing I can't do. Make it better.

Any and every irritant or misunderstanding has to be absorbed, forgiven, and forgotten. No matter what. Feels like Joan will fade. From us. From me. From her former self. Felt for the first time that she is resentful that I am well, while she's not. Emerged in a casual aside. No answer to that. Resolved with Oilly to encourage her to go to bed earlier, so that she doesn't get so frazzled. Like the 1939 poster encouraged—"KEEP CALM AND CARRY ON."

Tuesday, February 9, 2021

"T" Day—tepotinib.

Our great Oz friend, Christine Mitchell, generously picks us up and takes us to the Royal Marsden, "as it's a nightmare to park in Chelsea, and I'll just wait till you're done." That's Christine. Incredibly impatient by nature, but willing to wait indefinitely in our hours of need. Unbelievable.

The hospital is packed, and it's a while before Joan can get a blood test, then an ECG. Except the machine's not working properly and, after three nurses each have a go, they give up. Blood pressure taken. Joan is shivering.

Irritable. Stubborn. Despite snow on the ground today, she insisted on wearing a summer, rather than winter, coat.

Height measured—5ft 3in; weight—55 kilos.

Finally get to see oncologist Wanda Cui, who reluctantly reveals that the tepotinib drugs haven't arrived and that they're currently held in customs due to Brexit regulations. This is a real blow. Joan is wiped out. While she's taken to the loo, manage to speak to Wanda on my own.

"If the tepotinib works, the tumours will shrink within the first eight weeks, and Joan's life will return to normal for the next twelve months. Thereafter, we might resort to chemo. This drug means that she won't lose her hair, but the radiation fatigue will continue for the next three weeks. She'll have to come in to the Marsden every fortnight for scans and blood tests."

The good news I'm holding on to is that we will make it to our thirty-fifth wedding anniversary in November and have one more Christmas, together. Double bonus!

Christine chariots us home and Joan requests that I set up a duvet and pillows on the sofa in the drawing room, so that she doesn't have to negotiate the stairs to our bedroom. Falls asleep instantly. After which Christine moots her plan to propose Joan for the New Year Honours List, which recognizes extraordinary people across the UK, for her career achievements.

"What d'you reckon?"

"That's a brilliant idea!"

She agrees to go ahead and find out the application

requirements. Typically proactive and generous of her to think of this. First night alone in our bed, with Joan asleep downstairs.

Saturday, February 13, 2021

Oilly and Florian have returned to their flat for his birthday weekend and take a much-needed break from caring duties.

Reading Martin Amis's book *Inside Story* again, which poignantly details the final months of his great friend Christopher Hitchens, observing that "sickness is itself a waiting room . . . Many, many people have written with great penetration on sickness, on the estrangement from the world of will and action, the indignity, the onerousness, but not many have evoked the boredom, as Christopher has."

Prompting me to ask if Joan has felt bored. Not so far, as she's always reading or sewing her tapestry cushions, snoozing, Scrabbling, or chatting. But I think he means the sheer, unalterable *boredom* of never getting better.

Scrabbling this morning, and the accumulated sleep has revived her spirits to full feistiness. Laughs a lot and she's drawing cartoons of us in the score book, as she did all through lockdown last year. She always manages to draw my face like an elongated peanut shell with sprouts of hair on top and a bulbous nose, accompanied by a cartoon balloon with my comment on winning or losing.

While she takes a nap after lunch, Christine messages that the honours application requires ten letters from the great and the good, to submit along with the forms. As Sir Richard Eyre was head of the National Theatre and gave Joan many job opportunities, including her big break *Guys and Dolls*, he is the first person I've emailed.

Astonishingly, he replies with his testimonial an hour later. Many more follow in quick succession.

Completely undone by this incredible response. Firstly, because they read like obituaries and, secondly, wondering if she will live long enough to be able to accept it, if awarded; and, lastly, because I would so like her to read these accolades *now*, rather than having to wait until September to find out if she's qualified for an honour.

Shared this news with our great friend Lady Ruth Kennedy-Dundas, who thought it a brilliant idea and offers to do all the applications, submissions, CV, and legalese, as she knows many of the people on the Arts and Media Committee, in the hope that she can get this expedited *within* twelve months.

Contacted Christine Mitchell immediately, and she generously said, "I'm absolutely delighted that your 'Lady' friend can do all the heavy-lifting work on this one. Glad to have been a fillip for it. I can honestly think of no one better than Joan as a recipient. Just hope it comes through in time."

Joan woken up by the doorbell and delivery of scented red roses, from Joely Richardson and Vanessa Redgrave. A family who have suffered unbearable tragedy. Joan has coached them all. I'd done the 1984 Shakespeare season in Regent's Park, which was Tasha's professional debut, and she was my premiere "date" for *L.A. Story*. Their dad, Tony Richardson, had called me weeks before he died, about being in his West End production of a Chekhov. Spaghetti junction of family connections, making our chat very open, easy, and loving.

"I can't get over how thoughtful and kind our friends are."

"*All* you. Do you have any idea how admired and respected you truly are, Monkee?"

"Don't be daft. I'd love a cup of tea, please, Swaz"—is her typical response, but I know that she's chuffed, as she's keeping *every* card and note that friends and colleagues have sent her.

Siberian cold front is keeping temperatures below freezing tonight.

Sunday, February 14, 2021

Valentine's Day—could it be our *final* one after thirty-eight years together? Hard to compute. Impossible to imagine. *Not* being a unit, pair, partnership, union, marriage . . . None of which we share or discuss out loud and, on the evidence of her ebullience today, clearly not something she is dwelling on or even thinking about. Scrabble, eat, cuddle, and cocoon ourselves against the arctic temperature outdoors. Her *only* irritant is an especially top-note-heavy violin concerto playing on Classic FM. The sound of violins and saxophones, both of which I love, are her bugbears and I've become adept at pressing ye olde mute button whenever they threaten to saw the air waves!

Monday, February 15, 2021

Bruce Robinson's default setting is Curmudgeon.com—always hilarious to listen to, as he launches his droll and witty missile attacks on *all* politicians, the weather, horses, Covid isolation, producers, the parlous state of this, and perilous state of that. All in the most fabulously Withnailian invective imaginable. His view of the world is as jaundiced as mine is sunny, which makes for a good yin 'n' yang balance to our long friendship. Found a letter he'd written to me in 1987, when I was doing a miniseries in Israel. Read it out loud to Joan, which made her *really* laugh:

> My Dear Grant
>
> Thank you for your scratching which I read this morning propped in bed with a pot of tea and an asthma inhaler. And why not. What's wrong with a bit of asthma to go with the herniated disc. The asthma struck at two forty-five a.m. September the first. Half an hour in the bathroom, staring at the mirror waiting for the pill to work, face like an abandoned cauliflower and tongue out the colour of a snuff-user's hanky. The pill didn't work, of course it didn't work. Into the hospital and they shove you on a

thing to measure your breath. The average breather hits about 350. I was coming up 48. (Apparently a prospective corpse can produce about 25 with a fucking death-rattle.) Anyway, they masked me and the needle went in featuring pure pharmaceutical adrenalin. Suddenly your heart is converted into a small diesel engine that could get a Honda up the street at about fifty. In comes the Quack with an ulcer and a divorce and his eyes asking the question (Is this the little cunt?) and his mouth saying, "I'm told you smoke?" "Like a fucking joss-stick, Doctor." (Get this attack over with so I can have another.) Am I insane? I'm getting too old for illness. I am clearly too old for cigarettes. Cigarettes should be reserved for children and it should be illegal to sell them to anyone over sixteen. It was as a child that I became addicted. How sweet was that first thrust of a Wills' Whiff on the garage roof? Smoking Wills' with a small boy called Roy Hurry who used to stick pieces of newspaper into his ears until they operated and stopped him. (Lord God, I'm going barmy up here staring at the fucking rain.) At some time in October I'm going into a clinic, called the Devonshire Clinic, for my sciatica and they're going to try and do something about the wanking. My specialist is convinced that 30 years of almost uninterrupted wanking has damaged my spine. I'm prepared to go along with this because something must be done. I'm getting genuinely panicked about my work. I fear this will be a short scratch because even 15 minutes in front of a typewriter feels like having a horse-shoe made on your leg. What am I going to do? If I can't write a fucking letter, how am I going to write a screenplay? I have "Germinal" and "The Boil" to complete before Christmas—Ah Christmas—you can smell it coming like warm drains. The failed wish-bones and decaying marzipan and huge underpants already being purchased by my mother. My mother has always considered vast underwear as appropriate excitement for me to wake up to on Christmas morning. (As a matter of fact my 41st birthday was celebrated with three pairs.) Anyway, it's your own fault for going there and I hope they circumcise you. I've had it now. I'm full of curry and have to go to bed. I'm completely and utterly drained. And so is my bottle. And so, goodbye.

Much love & great luck on picture
Bruce

Decades ago, I was invited to become an ambassador for The Prince's Trust and seated beside Camilla Parker Bowles at a dinner in St. James's Palace. She was so forthright, open, curious, and funny that we got along instantly and were subsequently invited to spend the weekend with her and Prince Charles at Sandringham, then Highgrove, and to attend their wedding at Windsor Castle. Camilla sends flowers with a note—"Thinking of you at this horrid time," which made both of us chuckle. No attempt at euphemisms. Much appreciated by my no-nonsense Aberdonian wife, who is equally direct. Joan's father was an NHS doctor and we are indebted to the health service for their amazing treatment. Never been asked to pay for a single appointment, pill, diagnosis, scan, or CyberKnife surgery.

Tuesday, February 16, 2021

Playing Scrabble and I picked up an apple, musing, "Imagine being an apple. Waiting for someone to just pick you and take a bite?"

"I'd be frightened. Especially as you eat so fast. I'd be chomped in a couple of mouthfuls!"

Prince Charles sends Joan a two-page, handwritten letter, full of love, compassion, empathy, and encouragement.

She wonders, "How has he managed to do this in between endless commitments and calls on his time?"—clearly very touched by his letter.

Drove to the Marsden Hospital in Chelsea to pick up the tepotinib drugs which have finally landed. Stare at the month's supply of large pink pills which will hopefully shrink and control the cancer tumours. Having waited so impatiently for them to arrive, it's anticlimactic to actually have them at last. That sense of "this is it." The last medical outpost of hope. Will they work? With what side effects?

Joan's still asleep when I return, then rings her alarm buzzer and reveals that she feels like she can't mentally connect to get her legs to function. Help her up and hand her a glass of water to swallow the two tepotinib pills for the first time.

"My cheeks look like a chipmunk. Must be the side effects of the steroids"—which are being reduced each week. What lies ahead of us is a bizarre combination of knowing and not knowing. In contrast to that eternity of days that we're genetically programmed to believe we each have to live.

2001

Twenty years ago, when we were invited by Prince Charles to spend the weekend with him and Camilla at Sandringham, it felt like the real-life royal version of *Gosford Park*. Car was unpacked by a valet, then driven away and returned on Monday, with a full tank and as immaculately clean as the day it left the factory. Every lunch and dinner was planned so that each guest was seated beside our royal hosts at some point, so that no one felt favoured or usurped.

I'd just returned from horse-riding training in Paris for a film called *Monsieur N*, detailing the last years of Napoleon's life in exile, playing the English governor Sir Hudson Lowe. My horse was so feisty that, without realising it, I'd been clinging on for dear life and ridden for so many days and hours that, when I changed for dinner,

Joan announced, "Your bum's *on fire.*" It was indeed. Bloody whiplashes across each cheek!

All our clothes had been unpacked, hung up, suitcases removed, and outfits laid out for the evening, so had nowhere to dispose of my bloodied boxers.

"You can't hide them under the bed *or* under the wardrobe, Swaz."

Assuming that no one would be checking on *top* of the high wardrobe, I flung the bloodstained shorts up there, convinced they would *never* be found. Then wrapped voluminous amounts of loo roll around my bahookie, to avoid the risk of staining any Sandringham sofas or cushions.

Completely forgot about them, until it came time to change for dinner the following evening. Went upstairs to our bedroom, and *there* they were. Freshly laundered, de-stained and immaculately pressed, on the bed alongside my black-tie suit. I was as *mortified* as Joan was mirth-filled. She instantly re-enacted how she'd imagined the guilty pants were discovered, hoisted with a pole from atop the cupboard and removed with great ceremony to the laundry, where the household staff would have been regaled with tales of the actor who clearly favoured heavy-duty S&M conjugals under a royal roof!

I was convinced there must be closed-circuit cameras *everywhere* and took to trying to locate where they were hidden. Our valet knocked and asked if there was anything we needed, giving away nothing about his discovery, retrieval, and return of said bloodied pants.

Joan then took great delight in telling *all* the other house guests what had happened and, whenever our paths have crossed in the intervening years, that's *all* they've talked to me about.

Wednesday, February 17, 2021

Joan managed to sleep for seven hours, took tepotinib, then dozed her way through the rest of the day, fatigued and "feeling like a zombie." Oilly pointed out that if Joan had just undergone chemotherapy, she'd be poleaxed for days. I naively assumed there would be few to no side effects. Seeing her so felled with fatigue, it's not hard to imagine a time when she is too exhausted to struggle on.

These thoughts come crowding in when she's gone to sleep, and I struggle to—eyes tight shut, but wide awake with worry. Hoping that her nomination can be processed in time and that she gets the recognition we all feel she deserves, before she's no longer here.

Much as I try to live in the moment, I find it impossible not to project. Find that I waver between the here-and-now and the dread of not-there-and-gone.

Only respite is going for a long riverside walk with Oilly, able to share all these burdens and joys, both of us gobsmacked by the written endorsements from her peers. The cruelty of this disease is that when she's fully herself, all our troubles melt away in an instant. Moment she goes zombie, it's brutal and abrupt.

Saturday, February 20, 2021

A friend has put me in touch with a cancer guru in San Francisco, whose speciality is to do phone consultations, after examining all available medical records, to find any gaps or missed opportunities, new therapies or alternatives. Made the mistake of broaching this with my family, all of whom shouted me down: "We're in the best possible hands with the Marsden oncology team, so don't muddy the waters." Clear as!

Against their better judgement, I decide to discreetly go ahead, as any and every option is worth pursuing. I need a sliver of hope. It's exhausting trying to keep peppy and positive all the time. Filled in the online form and paid $400 to book a phoner with this medical adjudicator, who, according to my friend, has had great success. "No harm in getting a second opinion," is his take. "Monitor every change and variation, keep listening, keep looking, keep ultra-vigilant. Follow your instinct."

This will doubtless sound bonkers, but it's made me feel like I've taken control by taking some action.

Sunday, February 21, 2021

All calm on the family front. Home alone with Joan.

"I know you meant well, Swaz, but I totally trust Wanda and her team."

Nigella habitually cabs over her Sunday afternoon

savoury and sweet treats. Called to thank her and she advises to "live for the moment. Ignore all the prognosis and life expectancy estimates. That way madness lies." Easier said than done, when you're a natural-born worrier!

Monday, February 22, 2021

Oilly's return after the weekend break has reset the barometer to family-neutral. *Relieved.*

Go for a 4-mile walk, during which she lovingly identifies that she's been brought up without any paternal boundaries, "and I think it's time to put some in place, Pops. You're very extreme in your reactions to people and things. Hot or cold. Love or loathe. Damn or deify. No moderation. *Not with me.* It's just that you don't censor anything and tend to tell me everything. Maybe you should tell me less. If that makes sense."

It does! Guilty as charged. On all counts.

How do you change the DNA of your personality? I've had this levelled at me since the get-go, in every school report from kindergarten to my A-levels and beyond. Top marks for arts subjects that interested me, and flatlining through all the sciences and maths. Understand from psychoanalysis, twenty years ago, that the pattern of always trying to make things right sprang specifically from having to parent my father, when his life fell apart after my mother divorced him, when I was ten. The curse of people pleasing. Having my own puppet theatre was the perfect distraction and escape. Likewise, taking part in school plays and joining the Swaziland Theatre Club as a junior member offered me an outlet to distract from the secret curse of my father's alcoholism. Gave me a much-needed sense of identity and single-minded purpose. Literally pretending to be someone else became the template for dealing with real-life problems. And here I am in my early sixties being given parental advice by my daughter. Resolve to get some more counselling.

To the supermarket and bumped into actor Sean Chapman, whom I'd not seen in fifteen years.

"How's Joan?"

Deep breath to tell him and he welled up instantly.

"She was always the best fun and most encouraging person in a rehearsal room."

Bizarre to be standing in a shopping aisle, sharing this information, while customers are pushing trolleys and reaching past for tins of tomatoes. Hearing about her at work, when she was well, is enormously heartening. Feel like a cuckoo, returning to the nest and plopping his complimentary worm into her grateful beak. Made her smile and divert down memory lane with her own anecdotes about working with Sean. Feel so lucky, considering how much she loved working with actors, that she chose this one to fall in love with and marry.

Watched home videos of when Oilly was a toddler, which is heartwarming on one hand, but also sobering seeing people alive and well who are no longer with us. Life. Cycles. Endings.

1989

After *multiple* miscarriages and the premature birth of our first daughter Tiffany, we'd been strongly advised not to try for another baby. But they hadn't reckoned on the willpower of Joan. A friend of mine in Swaziland who had also suffered miscarriages told me that she'd finally gone full term after having a cervical stitch in the neck of her womb to ensure that the foetus remained on board. So I took a chance and asked the gynaecologist if this stitch was a possible solution.

I will never forget the way he looked at me, pausing as if to demur, then conceded with a drawn-out: "Yeeeeees, it's a possibility."

The procedure was duly carried out, but six months into her pregnancy, Joan began bleeding, and we assumed the worst. She was hospitalised and diagnosed with placenta previa. Meaning that her placenta was covering the opening of her cervix. Meaning that infant *and* mother were at risk from haemorrhaging *at any time*. Meaning that she would require bed rest in the hospital for the remaining three months.

"This is our last chance, Swaz. *Whatever* it takes."

In order to alleviate the tedium, I decided to buy the smallest portable TV that Dixons had to offer, which I'd seen in Richmond high street. I parked on a double yellow line, ran in, and said, "I'd like to buy that small TV in the window. Please."

"I'm sorry, sir, but that's on display and we don't have any others in stock."

"No problem. If you don't stock them, then I'll buy *that* one."

"I'm sorry, sir, but that's not possible, it's not for sale."

"But, this is a shop, and I'm a customer and I *want* that TV in your window. You can't advertise something and then tell me I can't buy it, it doesn't make sense!"

I may as well have been speaking in hieroglyphics. While he went to find the manager, I climbed into the window display, retrieved the TV, counted out the £70 in cash, proffered the notes to the manager when he appeared, assured him I didn't need the box or instructions, as my wife was in hospital, that this was an emergency *and* I was double parked *and* I had to run.

We ended up addicted to watching *Neighbours*, which aired at 1:30 p.m. and was then repeated at 5:30 p.m., every weekday, delighting in bits we'd savoured the first time around. It was the lead-up to Kylie Minogue's on-screen marriage to Jason Donovan, which was broadcast in the UK on November 8, 1988. In the first year of our daughter's life, when she struggled to fall asleep, I'd play the *Neighbours* theme tune, and she instantly calmed down and nodded off.

Before she was born, we endlessly speculated what she

would look like, having been told we were having a daughter.

"With your oblong face and length of limb, she'll likely look like Olive Oyl."

"Synchronicity—because my father used to call me Popeye, as I always bemoaned my lack of muscles!"

Which is how we settled upon calling her Oilly, months before she was born. Telling her to "stay inside, until you're fully baked."

"We'll have to give her a *proper* name for her birth certificate *and* to appease our mothers *and* just in case she doesn't like it"—hence Olivia. (Neither of our mothers *ever* called her Oilly!)

She was born by Caesarean section at 12:56 p.m. on Wednesday, January 4, 1989, weighing 4½ pounds—2 kilos—and required to spend her first three days in an incubator.

When the nurse brought her, all swaddled up, to the glass-panelled door outside the operating theatre to show her to me, tears projectiled on to the glass, signalling the single most miraculous moment of my life. If there's a nanosecond's worth of choice when you fall in love, there was *no* measure of time between seeing Oilly and feeling the most profound, life-changing love *imaginable*. Beyond *all* counting! Our longed for, *miracle*, baby.

1997

When Oilly was eight years old, after I picked her up from school she always delighted in clicking on the answer machine messages when we got home. She hurtled into the kitchen and said, "Dadda, you *have* to do this job. You just *have to*," fervently pulling my arm to follow her back into my study, so that she could replay the message from my agent, offering me the role of the Spice Girls' manager in their forthcoming movie.

The moment I accepted, she leapt up and wrapped her legs around me like a spider monkey. "If you're their manager, does this mean I can come and meet all of them?" It most certainly did and I brought her to the set as often as I possibly could. The Spice Girls were incredibly friendly and accommodating and I realised that they were much closer to my daughter's age than they were to mine.

The first day of shooting at a country pile south of Guildford, and they were *each* assigned the most enormous Winnebago motorhome. They were having none of this isolationism, and insisted that they all share one, saving the producers an enormous amount of money from the get-go.

The script was there more as a guide, rather than something to be slavishly adhered to, and they were encouraged to improvise and just be themselves as much as possible. Geri *Ginger Spice* Halliwell predominated and had zero filter between what popped into her head and came out of her mouth. Disarming and hilarious by turns. *They* expressed genuine disbelief that global fame had engulfed them so completely. Emma *Baby Spice* Bunton was who Oilly gravitated to when set-visiting, as she was so maternal and inclusive and suggested that her hairdresser do Oilly's hair in exactly the same fountain ponytail style that she had. My eight-year-old daughter's fantasy, *come true*!

Mel *Scary Spice* Brown thwacked me on the bum and declared, "You're in pretty good shape, for an *old* guy!" I was instantly nicknamed *Old Spice*. Verbal Viagra! Victoria *Posh Spice* Beckham was unswervingly obsessed with fashion and flicked through *Vogue* at every opportunity, quick-witted and not anything like the serious-faced persona she has adopted since becoming a fashion designer. Mel *Sporty Spice* Chisholm was a fitness fanatic and the least forthcoming and most shy of the five of them.

I was chastised by the more serious members of the acting fraternity for taking the role, but had the last laugh two decades later when Lena Dunham wrote me into four episodes of *Girls*, as a result of knowing me from *Spice World—The Movie*. Likewise, Adele, with whom I share a birthday, sent me tickets to her sold-out O2 Arena concert as she is an obsessive Spice Girls fan. So win-win!

But, most importantly, it's the job that Oilly has been most thrilled about in my entire career. It gave me the highest school playground status of my life. Spice Girl mania was at its most hysterical, and I was besieged by mothers begging for tickets to the concert scene, filmed in the Albert Hall, requiring two minibuses to get them all there. Despite the reviews, the movie took a shedload of money at the global box office and, like Liberace quipped, "*I cried all the way to the bank*"!

Thursday, February 25, 2021

Steroids have made Joan incredibly tetchy and irritable due to interrupted and too little sleep. Know it's not meant, but all the same, very wearing.

Morning walk with Oilly and acutely mindful (there I go, being extreme again!) of her "No" boundary request. As in, when she says no to anything, not to try offering alternative options. She and Florian are moving back to theirs for a week to house-sit our friends David and Nikki's cats while they're in Liverpool for his father's funeral. A timely break that will hopefully give her some breathing space and distance.

Joan says that her hair is thinning. Came off in her brush. I haven't noticed, but know that this is a big worry for her. After she went to bed, am *hit* by a wave of loneliness.

Friday, February 26, 2021

Seventy-minute online session with psychotherapist who identified that I'm undergoing withdrawal symptoms from Joan, as she gets more ill, while Oilly needs me to be calm, controlled, and low-key.

Made the connection that my father's drinking meant that I had no boundaries with him. That *everything* was shared. When his alcoholic pendulum swung into Johnnie Walker mode after 9 p.m., I became his verbal, and sometimes physical, victim, in tandem with all his friends, whom he annihilated behind their backs, then was charm itself to their faces when sober. As he was with me. None of my friends had this father-son dynamic. Chimes with Oilly's observation that our father-daughter relationship is unique among *her* friendship group.

Never made this connection before. Like a giant bell clanging. Feel guilty. *Yet*, enormously grateful for the bond that we share. The difference being that my father's personality change was a constant betrayal, whereas my loyalty to Oilly is unbreakably steadfast. *Just* need to implement *her* boundary requests.

Coloured the rest of the day. Felt underwater.

1999

When I was forty-two, I was so angry and unhappy with my life and career that I had some kind of nervous collapse and became convinced that I was paralysed. Joan, my lodestar and no-nonsense Scot, pinched my thigh and asked, "Can you feel that?"

Nodded. "But I can't move my legs."

Unbidden tears running down my face convinced her that there was something seriously wrong and she picked up the phone and called Steve Martin, apologising for the late hour in LA.

"Swaziboy's in real meltdown. Can you give me the name and number of the brilliant analyst you told him about?"

Two hours later, I trudged from the station up the steep hill to Hampstead High Street as though wearing lead-filled ski boots, and slumped down in Christopher Bollas's all-white office. This extraordinary soul saved my psyche. Single-mindedly.

Having no idea how to begin analysis, I instinctively unspooled my life story in an uninterrupted outpouring, during which he made five connections, illuminating my past like fireworks.

"You're forty-two, the same age that your father was when he was cuckolded by your mother; he was in career crisis due to Swaziland gaining independence and had a 10-year-old son. His whole life imploded and he became a violent alcoholic.

"*You* have a 10-year-old daughter and you're acutely aware how young and vulnerable an age that is, as you were when your mother left home. Likewise, you feel that your film career is in free fall. You've hit your own 'wall' and feel paralysed."

Sounds so simple, put like this, but made perfect sense. The toxicity of keeping family secrets, suddenly liberated by exposing them. No one in here to judge, deride, or dismiss. Always struck by the Pandora's box myth that you're supposed to keep the lid tight shut in order not to release all of life's miseries into the world. But, of course, the last gift in Pandora's box was hope.

Which is the gift the analyst gave me after our first session. Hope-filled, I literally *skipped* back down the hill to the station, feeling like an Astaire-on-air. Eighteen months of weekly sessions resulted in a rapprochement with my estranged mother, career turnaround, and loving my life with Joan again, at full force 10!

Chapter Four

March

Tuesday, March 2, 2021

Nothing Joan reads or watches manages to hold her attention for more than a few minutes. Asleep most of the time. Wheezing breath with a disturbing crinkly sound. Like paper rustling in her chest. Saintly Christine Mitchell picks us up to go to the Marsden for her blood test and check-up. Is visibly shocked to see Joan like this. Too weak to walk into the hospital and requires a wheelchair.

Wanda Cui instantly detects that something is seriously wrong, observing that Joan's cheeks are yellow. Within two minutes, a team of six people scrum around her. Blood tests. Antibiotic drip inserted into her arm. Oxygen piped into her nostrils. Temperature taken. Suspect an infection. Require two Covid tests to rule out that possibility. Moot that it could be a blood clot as her heart is beating abnormally fast. Very low oxygen. Could be a chest infection. No disguising the panic of possibilities being bandied about.

Made worse when the blood samples taken haven't been labelled, and need to be done all over again. Then the ECG machine falters. Decision taken to move her to the clinical assessment unit in another ward. Wheelchaired over and into the care of an entirely new team of clinicians. All of them calm and solicitous.

"Regret that we're going to have to admit Joan. Please can you return home and bring back whatever you think she'll need."

What I've described in two paragraphs took two hours, which is how long Christine has been patiently waiting for our return. We both express profound relief that Joan is being professionally cared for.

"The moment I saw her, I knew there was something seriously wrong."

Feel like a complete idiot for not realising how bad she was before the weekend. Christine reassures: "Don't beat yourself up. You're not a medic, and being with her all the time means that you're too close to notice what's happening. That's normal." Feel guilt-ridden all the same.

Picked up her tapestry kit, phone, iPad, books, nighties, toiletries, and drove back to the hospital, where she was still in a wheelchair, waiting to be taken off for a scan. Took my hand and whispered, "I'm so sorry you're having to go through all this, Swaz!"

"Don't be silly. I'm sorry that I never clocked how poorly you were on Friday."

Nurse comes to wheel her off and says, regretfully, that

"Your wife is being admitted to the Wilson Ward and no visitors are allowed."

Kiss each other goodbye and watch as she's wheeled to the end of the corridor, then disappears round the corner. Feel stranded, like that moment on a beach when sand and sea swirl around your feet, sinking you down an inch, then washing away all trace of your ever having stood there.

Gripped the steering wheel, trying to get my head around this latest development. Grateful that she is in professional care. Relieved that I don't have to pretend to be a proper nurse any more.

Returning home to an empty house, crammed with everything we've collected together, is . . . I can't find the correct word at this moment.

Unable to sleep properly and walk around the house at 5 a.m., looking at all those things we've collected together. Really *looking*, as if for the first time. Every object memory-charged. Remembering where we were when we discovered something we both "just had to have." The excitement of getting up really early to go to Kempton Park Racecourse antiques market twice a month, or driving around southern France to Béziers, Montpellier, Avignon, and L'Isle-sur-la-Sorgue, in search of more loot. Invariably deciding on the same prized object independently or together. Occasionally we'd do a re-enactment of that *French and Saunders* sketch when one of them says, "Do you really like this?" and the other one concurs enthusiastically, only for the former to reveal that she, in fact, *doesn't* like it, and her pal retorts, "No, I hate it too." Like kids.

When hunting through junk shops and antiques fairs, we always knew precisely what the other was going to want to buy, but she was much bolder and decisive, deploying a thick Aberdonian accent when bargaining. As only an incognito Colonel would.

If we got separated anywhere in public, we'd bird-noise *to-toot-toot-to* until, like penguins, we were reunited. Similarly, if she was bored in company or wanted to leave somewhere, she'd stroke her nose. And if either of us repeated the same old stories too often, we only needed to say "banana" to stop the anecdotals instantaneously!

Wednesday, March 3, 2021

Email from Joan at 7 a.m.

> I love you. Darling, I had a really peaceful night and slept through. Magnificent nurses who checked my blood pressure every hour. Visit from a doctor who said I've developed a few blood clots in my lungs which will have to be removed.
>
> There has also been some shrinkage in my cancer cells which is great but they have left a pocket of air in my lung so this needs dealing with as a minor surgery.
>
> Good news bad news but I feel much better. The ward has ten beds, all separated into blue tents.

I'm in the right place. Have a good happy rest I love you Joan x lol

This is a long email for her as she loathes typing and technology. Profound relief that she's receiving proper care.

Went for a two-hour walk with Julian Wadham in Richmond Park. We met on a film of Orwell's *Keep the Aspidistra Flying* in 1996. He is as garrulous, witty, and empathetic as you'd want any true friend to be.

Midway through our walk, Wanda Cui calls to explain what's happening. "There is good news and bad news. Tepotinib has been so effective in shrinking the tumour on her lung, since she started taking it two weeks ago, that it's created an air pocket, leaking air into the chest cavity. Likely requiring surgery to get the lung to reseal to the cavity wall. There are also rogue blood clots in the lung, which is why her blood pressure was so high yesterday. There's also a bacterial infection in the base of the lung, which we are treating with intravenous antibiotics. So I'm going to suspend her taking tepotinib for a week to allow the lung to repair and heal. Doing a brain scan this afternoon to check if there is swelling around the tumours, since stopping the steroids. Do you have any questions?"

"How long will she have to stay in the hospital?"

"Five days. At least until next Monday. The intensive care unit is on standby in case she deteriorates suddenly, but she is much better this morning."

Conjuring memories of seeing *Fantastic Voyage* (1966)

which only reached Swaziland in 1969. Went to see it as a twelfth birthday party treat with all my friends at the Queen's Way Cinema. It's about a submarine crew who are microscopically shrunk to enter the body of an injured scientist to repair the damage to his brain. Starring Stephen Boyd, Raquel Welch, and Donald Pleasence. Ever since then, all medical terminology seems gigantic in proportion. So, when the doc described an air pocket in the chest cavity, it evokes an image of a child standing inside a vast cave. *If only* I could miniaturise myself and join the doctor's team and enter Joan's bloodstream to obliterate this wretched tumour.

Julian gives me a reassuring hug.

"I'm so, so sorry, Richard."

Turn my head away. It's his kindness that undoes me.

Hospital calls to confirm that I'm allowed to visit for a couple of hours at 2 p.m. Hallelujah!

The ward is large with each of the ten beds screened off by blue pleated dividers. Visual privacy, but you can hear every moan and bleat around you. Such a relief to find Joan sitting up, perky and looking transformed since yesterday. Cheekily joshing with the nurses, completely accepting of her situation and already institutionalised. She imitates every overheard conversation, identifies phonetically where the unseen voices hail from, and, if I close my eyes, she's the woman I fell in love with all those years ago.

Brought her post in and there's a long letter from Ralph Fiennes, whom she's known since she taught him as a student at RADA in the eighties. Boosts her spirits hugely and it's clear that the attention of the nurses, and cast list of unseen patients, has energised her enormously. We hold hands for the two hours we have together, talking in a near whisper, like kids forbidden to do so after lights out. Conspiratorial and colluding.

Makes leaving all the more difficult. Hard not to get emotional when saying goodbye, but that's the last thing she needs from me. Drive home through the rain and into a totally deserted house, where all I can hear is the sound of my own footsteps.

Thursday, March 4, 2021

Face-timed with Binti Velani, a friend who has been so endlessly supportive and patient with Joan, doing reflexology and talking all things meditative and spiritual with her. She believes in an afterlife. Wish that I could. Not for lack of trying, but Darwinian rationalism prevails. Binti was a radiologist whom we befriended on holiday in the Caribbean decades ago, who has retrained as a yoga teacher and become incredibly close to Joan.

Covid restrictions prohibit me from visiting and, when I phone, Joan complains that she's been relentlessly needle-pricked in both arms for blood samples to monitor the efficacy of the blood-thinning drugs, prescribed to combat the blood clots. Uncharacteristically tearful and dejected, compared to yesterday's mood.

"I don't think I will ever feel remotely well again. Only going to feel worse."

Just heartbreaking to hear her talk like this, and do my best to divert and distract with stories and encouragement to imitate the accents and verbal tics of her invisible neighbours. Rallies, but all too briefly.

"I feel fuzzy-headed and can't quite focus properly. Woman next to me moans *all* night long."

As much as various friends have said, "Please call anytime you feel like screaming, or just having a blub," the British reality is that this feels like the *last* thing any of them would want. Resist putting them to the test.

Friday, March 5, 2021

Early morning walk with Oilly in Richmond Park. She always intuits *precisely* where I am emotionally, and we talk the talk and walk the walk. Vigilant about not crossing boundaries.

Wanda calls: "Good news—the lung tumour which was 7 centimetres, has shrunk to 3.5 centimetres, hence the air pocket, and the MRI brain scan has confirmed that there are no new tumours. The existing ones are still shrinking from the radiation treatment. The blood-thinning drugs to disperse the blood clots will be dealt with via daily self-injections, like diabetics administer to themselves. I've put her back on one steroid pill per day and antibiotic pills for the bacterial infection."

Clear, concise, and encouraging. Major relief.

The absence of any *new* brain tumours is mightily welcome news. Impossible to resist the fantasy that if this new drug has managed to reduce the cancer by half in just two weeks, *why* can't it carry on destroying it, until it's all gone, in another fortnight? Doubtless somewhere in the future that medical advance will become an everyday reality. But *not* for us. Fixate on the fact that the tumour was less than a thumb's length, and is now halved, yet seems the size of a submarine when trying to picture it.

When Joan calls, she sounds herself again—hilariously imitating her neighbours and feeling upbeat and positive. How can I quantify just how much I love this woman? Marvin Gaye and Tammi Terrell's 1967 hit "Ain't No Mountain High Enough" earworms its way into my afternoon.

Until instantly usurped by Dean Martin's signature song, "That's Amore," which is what Nigella has called the soup she's sending over today, as she's away for the weekend.

Sunday, March 7, 2021

Drove to the hospital to drop off nighties, her favourite biscuits, and a pile of new books, as Joan called to let me know that they needed to keep her in for *another* week and take chest X-rays every day. *Real* blow for me, but she is completely resigned and accepting of it all—"I don't have any choice in the matter, Swaz."

Despite being double-vaccinated and having a negative PCR test result two days ago, I have to hand over her bag of goodies to a nurse, knowing that Joan is just a couple of metres away, through the wall beside the reception desk.

Called her from the car, to check that she'd received the bag, and she said that she was feeling more chipper today.

Spoke to Pat Doyle, who *always* makes me laugh, and discussed the hierarchy of friends in a crisis. He's survived leukaemia, so understands from the inside exactly where I'm coming from. How do you resist withholding judgement about people you *thought* were close friends, who prove to be distant or absent in a crisis, while peripheral friends claim your friendship through their actions, words, and consistent engagement?

Oilly comes over for the afternoon and confesses that she feels guilty about my being home alone on Saturday. Reassured her that I'm fine and *have* to accept and get used to this new way of living. Boundary issues aside, am grateful that we can share and talk about anything and everything. Feels like a magical invisible ribbon from my heart to hers.

We called Joan and sent her WhatsApp photos of our walk together, trying to make everything feel as normal as possible, when the reverse is our reality. The oncology team have advised her to try to walk as much as possible when she returns home to rebuild her strength.

Our friend Ian Wace video-calls and says, "You may have

narrowly missed winning an Oscar for best supporting actor, Richard, but your supporting role in your domestic drama will be your finest hour."

2017

In late November 2016, I was sent a script titled *Can You Ever Forgive Me?* by my agent and told that I had twenty-four hours to read and decide about doing it, "as it's shooting in January."

"Who's dropped out?"

"Don't ask."

"Who's playing the lead?"

"Melissa McCarthy."

It's the true story of American author Lee Israel, who'd written biographies of Tallulah Bankhead and Estée Lauder, fallen on hard times, and taken to forging signatures of literary greats and inventing letters "written" by Noël Coward and Dorothy Parker among others. She was working in collusion with Jack Hock, a gay coke-dealing ex-con, who died of AIDS—my role. Their love-hate relationship is the heart of the script and the best screen role I've had since my first one, thirty years ago. Months from my sixtieth birthday, and *the* best gift I could have been given, to start the New Year.

Work divide—Joan is in Budapest coaching Russian accents with Jennifer Lawrence, Matthias Schoenaerts, Joely Richardson, and Jeremy Irons, while I'm bound for the

Big Apple, for another little career bite. Customs officer at JFK enquires why I'm here and for how long. Smilingly dismissed with: "Well, good luck, man, 'cos I never seen ya or heard of ya before."

Nothing like a reality check on arrival!

It's Thursday and we begin shooting on Monday, so put in a beg-call to Marielle Heller, the director, requesting a meeting with Melissa for a couple of hours on Friday, to read through the script together and allay my nerves about playing a friendship on screen convincingly having never met her before.

I meet Melissa in the Beekman Hotel downtown and I put my nose to the fabric on the inside of the elevator, prompting her to say, "Oh we're going to get along *just* fine." Any apprehension that she was going to play this role as a comedy star vehicle was instantly dispelled. My sense of her is that she is hyper-emotionally present. Sounds pretentious, which is everything she's not, but it's my stab at trying to convey how emotionally transparent and blotter-like she is. Reacting to everything with absolute clarity. Her delight and inclusivity are contagious, and I instantly warmed to her, and felt that we would become fast friends. *Fast.* And we have.

She works the dialogue over and over, until it sounds and feels utterly real and natural. Every emotional beat is marked and incorporated. She's playing the curmudgeonly Lee Israel, and no matter how unsympathetically the script depicts her, Melissa's gift is that she remains loveable, by bullseyeing where Lee's pain springs from. Instinctively shining her humanity-torch into the darkness of Israel's profound loneliness and career frustration.

I dared ask her: "What is the source of your rage?" To which she laughingly replied, "I don't know, but it's there and I think, 'cos it comes out, that's how I avoid poisoning myself. Once it's expunged I can hardly even remember feeling it. Like I have amnesia. You ask a *lot* of questions and I don't think I've ever been asked *that* one before! Let me tell you about my crazy test. I always try and assess which cast or crew member is likely to be a pain in the butt, and try to excise them before they can wreak havoc on the rest of us. I call it the 'AH test.'"

"Meaning?"

"Asshole test. Avoid if at all possible!"

Putting paid to the movie myth that if you have a happy set, the movie will suffer, anguish guaranteeing a better result.

"I am living proof that the opposite is true."

Being her co-star is about as status enhancing as I never dared wish for. *Everyone* I encounter wants *more* Melissa. Whether it's Glenn Close, backstage after *Sunset Boulevard*, Meryl Streep via email, or Tom Hanks at dinner with Steve Martin, who was at pains to tell me how close he got to her on a press junket in Singapore, actors palpably *love* her.

Tom has not changed one iota since I first met him back in the last century. Boy-Man childlike, with an infectious self-confidence in his ability to hold a room full of people, be they art critics, artists, and a financier, assembled around Steve and Anne's dinner table, or the viewers on a chat show with Graham Norton. Regaling us with stories, snatches of songs, and reminiscences, colluding with and entertaining his "audience," which is what we all are, with complete assurance and the conviction that we are all on side. Delivered at top volume, as his control button clearly fell off at birth. He somehow *is* Woody from *Toy Story* come to life. There is no "side" to him and he strikes me as quintessentially American and as clear-cut as a Norman Rockwell portrait of an "All-round Good Guy."

"Would you like us all to contribute to the Spielberg 'snubbed club' of which you're the founding member, Tom?"

"*What?* Explain, Grant!"

"Well, Mr. Spielberg declared that *you* were his favourite actor, then you were usurped by Daniel Day-Lewis on *Lincoln*, who has likewise become a fellow snubbed member since Steven declared his undying love for Mark Rylance."

Tom guffawed, then mocked up some tears to wipe away—an actor through and through, to the marrow in his bones. He shares with Melissa a likability that convinces audiences; they could be your best friends.

Although *Can You Ever Forgive Me?* is only Marielle Heller's second movie, since shifting career gears from actor to director, she's acutely attuned to what actors need from their leader. In this case, a feeling that we are free to try anything we want, with her full support, knowing that she has an invisible safety net to save us.

It's a big risk when you cast two people whose characters have such a symbiotic on-screen relationship but who've only had a couple of hours to greet, meet, eat, and read through the script once, before starting shooting. But I did feel an instant bond with Melissa, and have to hope and trust that this chemistry will transmit on screen.

And so it proved. The nature of their interdependence was revealed in ways that neither of us anticipated. Lee, despite having maternal feelings only towards her terminally ill cat, inadvertently becomes girlish and maternal-ish towards Jack. Who, in turn, treats her with a modicum of courtliness when trying to impress and ingratiate himself. Two loners. Jack Labradoring up to Lee's less than welcoming "down boy" pats on the head.

When Melissa's husband, Ben Falcone, turned up to play a dodgy book dealer, he described his wife as "all nerve endings, without a second skin." Which suggests someone neurotic. She's not. Just naturally empathetic and humane. He is soft-spoken and withheld in contrast to Melissa's exuberance. Modest, approachable, and an ego-free-range good egg.

Although the entire shoot is only twenty-eight days, I work even less, so have time to catch up with friends—one of whom is Gabriel Byrne. He played my father in my autobiographical film *Wah-Wah* in 2004 and we've continued seeing each other beyond wrap. The cadence of his Dublin accent, combined with an innately soulful, poetic nature, lends his lunchtime musings a Yeatsian quality. Always searching and seeking meaning in everything. He recounts sitting beside Julie Andrews on a flight from New York to LA and how, despite global success, she still seemed insecure. He was similarly taken aback when seeing Barbra Streisand backstage after her concert, who asked, "Was I okay, did you think I was good enough?" when every song was greeted with ovation after ovation. He was introduced to her mother, sitting in a corner, who informed him that it was *she* who was the unrecognised star in the family, and that her younger daughter, Roslyn Kind (Barbra's half-sister), was the *real* talent.

"Right then and there, all was explained. What is it that helicopters over Brooklyn, or Walton-on-Thames or, in Madonna's case, Michigan, and decides that *this* nondescript household and person will have the determination to become Barbra, Julie, or Madonna?" Even when globally famous, there still seems to be a need to get validation from being around famous people.

I wholeheartedly recognise this syndrome, as, like most actors I've ever encountered, you start off your career with everything stacked against your ever succeeding, so whatever fame and fortune incrementally accrue to you, a big part of you still doubts it all. Recognition and validation of people way more famous and successful than you feels like a precarious stamp of approval. Unlike Joan, who is anti-starstruck, I *still* feel like a kid let loose in the Sweetie Shop of Fame.

August 2018

Slow-forward a year and I get an invitation to attend the Telluride Film Festival, in Colorado, for the world premiere of the movie. Not having heard a word or received replies to any of my emails, I had resigned myself to the realisation that my connection with Melissa was a phantom friendship.

Next morning, venture into the lobby of the Madeline ski resort hotel.

Melissa sidles up and coyly says, "Hi." Seems slightly apprehensive. Within no time, we discover that *all* my emails to her have gone unread, as she only texts, and *all* her texts to me never landed, as she'd sent them to the American mobile phone given to me for the duration of the shoot. She had even asked Marielle Heller if she'd offended me in some way, as I'd never replied. This cyber-stalemate made both of us wary of each other. All of which instantly evaporated and it was as if I'd seen her yesterday.

Phew together down the mountainside into the one-horse town of Telluride, where Butch Cassidy and the Sundance Kid allegedly robbed the bank. Gather in the town centre for a group photo with actors in films screening over the next three days. Laura Dern, Hugh Jackman, Nicole Kidman, Joel Edgerton, Sissy Spacek, Emma Stone, Ralph Fiennes, Melissa, and me. The Sundance Kid himself, aka Robert Redford, legends forth into our fray, and the crowd spontaneously applauds. Frail at eighty-two after suffering a fall, he has an astonishingly full head of hair. Wearing signature jeans, T-shirt, and jacket. Here be multimillionaire actors dressed down and cowboying among local film fans. All of whom are within reach-out-and-touch distance, which is the reputed charm of this small-scale festival. No sooner snapped than everyone scatters to their respective screenings.

Ours is at 4 p.m., full house, and Marielle enthusiastically introduces Melissa and me, and asks us both to say a few words. Melissa is cheered to the rafters and effortlessly charms everyone. My turn, and a McCarthy antidote accompanies my deadpan expression. "Please don't be fooled by her comedy-charm persona. It's all fake. Melissa is, in fact, morose, always late for work, never knows her lines, is inconsiderate, selfish, and we did not get along, *at all*."

Big laughs and an even bigger hug for her. Never gotten used to watching anything I've done on screen, so it's a nerve-rack to sit through it. Laughs come in unexpected places, and, when my AIDS-diagnosed character bids farewell to Melissa's, there are audible sniffles all around us. Sustained applause during the credits and enthusiastic endorsement during the Q&A that follows.

Melissa squeezes my hand and whispers, "There's something happening here."

I can sense it too.

Ask Melissa if she feels this disconnect between *real* movie stars and herself.

"I never feel like I'm a member of that club."

Two hours later, during dinner, the trade reviews land—*Variety*, *Hollywood Reporter*, *Deadline Hollywood*, *The Wrap*. Unilateral raves. Each one mooting it as an awards season contender. Receiving this approbation way up in the Rocky Mountains feels truly surreal and the best "dessert" we could have wished for.

Elizabeth Taylor's quip that, "There's no deodorant like success" takes on a whole new meaning.

Something in the air has shifted and, when face-timing with Oilly in London, *her* emotional response to all this has made it feel *real*. Her pride and delight are palpable—"You *so* deserve this, Pops"—and for this moment in time, I dare allow myself to feel that I do.

Land in Toronto and greeted by an online wave of award predictions. It feels like reading about someone else when I see my name tauntingly included in a shortlist of best supporting actor nominations. Although hypothetical, seeing it in print deludes you into thinking it might come true.

Encounter two English actors, who shall remain nameless. One of them is here courtesy of an American studio that's hosting an industry party—in other words, he doesn't have a movie at the festival, and can barely register a flicker of interest as to why I'm here. The other one shamelessly boasts about the brilliance of the film that he's in, due to screen here tomorrow, and just manages to ask when my film is on. I dutifully tell him, to which he gleefully replies,

"Oh, I can't see it as I'm doing press all afternoon tomorrow. Plus, I *never* go to the cinema." And a silent *fuck you too* from me! In neither case had I remotely suggested that either of them might like a ticket. Over and out.

Meet Oilly, who has flown in for the weekend from London. So relieved to be able to share this ride with her, especially as she is mercilessly and hilariously insightful about the whole showbiz shebang of it all. Over breakfast, she sotto voces about how entitled the studio executives and publicists all are, waving their arms, with mobile phones affixed in each palm, talking at top volume, while administering famous names, like sacraments, to the assembled Eggs Benedictus commune.

Film receives the same audience endorsement we got in Telluride.

Breakfast in the airport club lounge (courtesy of the film studio) and the nameless English actor moseys into view and declares, "I just *have* to tell you . . ."—in the pause, Oilly and I think the exact same thing, that he has either heard about my movie or read a review, *but*, true to form, he declares—"I've been partying *all* night after my premiere. Don't let me fall asleep and miss the flight."

Taking our newly assigned alarm-call duties *seriously*, we wait till he's headphoned-up and seated down in a corner, then get on board to hopefully avoid any further encounters with the ego that just landed in our midst!

Gabriel Byrne emails from New York: "You're on the pig's back, these days!" Ralph Brown, aka Danny the drug dealer in *Withnail and I*, messages: "I sense a vigorous renewal, dear boy." And still the good reviews keep on coming, surprisingly from the *Guardian*, predicting a sure-fire Oscar nomination. That "O" word again. That I dare not say out loud for fear of jinxing myself!

Home, and bubble suitably pinpricked by my wife.

"The dishwasher is on the blink, Swaz. Need to get it sorted."

Wednesday, March 10, 2021

Joan calls with the good news that she *might* be able to return home today, as her temperature is normal again, oxygen pipes and drip removed, and she's been walking to and from the bathroom.

Listlessly lope around the house, feeling becalmed—should I go food shopping, run along the river, read the new Stoppard biography, empty out a cupboard? *What?* Or just plonk down and watch reality TV.

Skyped my mother instead.

Frustratingly, Joan has to stay another night. Never went for a run, read, or stepped into the garden.

Thursday, March 11, 2021

Food shopped and spring flowered up the house. In anticipation. In case she's discharged today. Bingo! Calls at 11:30 to say I can come and pick her up. Deluded myself that we could cook together or go for a walk. The reality is that she's too weak to walk to the car, and has to be wheelchaired. Once home, she barely registers anything and heads straight for the sofa to lie down. Her arms are bruised from the multiple blood tests taken. *Very* fragile, poorly, and falls asleep. But am just so grateful to have her home again!

Friday, March 12, 2021

Woken at 5:30 a.m. by the alarm button round Joan's neck. Pelted downstairs to find her supine on the flagstone floor. Just lying there, like a helpless upturned tortoise.

"I didn't have the strength to get up the two shallow steps, Swaz, but I'm not hurt."

Managed to get her upright and standing, with both my arms under her armpits. Shuffled along the hall and then up the stairs to our bedroom. Taking three steps at a time. Then resting. Right behind her, my knees in the back of hers, like a slow-motion pensioners' tango, slowly moving upwards.

After this shocking start to the day, everything progressed smoothly. Plethora of new pills, watched TV together and fell asleep on the sofa. Helped her into the bath, which she has longed for after days in hospital. Asked me to clip her toenails, which I'd never done before. Curiously vulnerable and touching thing to do.

Ruth Kennedy-Dundas and her brilliant assistant, Eleanor

Hickling, have edited, coordinated, and posted the honours application to the Cabinet and Arts and Media Committee. Bruce Robinson has generously agreed to be the nominating signatory on her behalf.

Joan is insistent that I continue to do my 8 a.m. run in Richmond Park, reassuring me that she's not going to move anywhere while I'm out. New routine—sleeps on the sofa at night. After breakfast and pills, she slowly ascends the stairs and spends the morning in our bed, reading, watching TV, and napping. Downstairs for lunch in the kitchen. Scrabble. Back to the drawing-room sofa to nap. Kitchen supper, TV. Then back to her sofa for the night. Increasingly grouchy by the early evening.

Saturday, March 13, 2021

"These drugs make my head feel fuzzy all the time. Do you think I will *ever* feel any better than this? Wonder if it's worth it?" Her question hovers in the air, like the steam from the bath that she's sitting in. She's right—the relentlessness of feeling poorly is utterly debilitating. I have no answer.

Playwright James Saunders concluded that, "there lies behind everything . . . a certain quality which we may call grief. It's always there, just under the surface, just behind the façade . . . It bides its time, this quality . . . you may pretend not to notice . . . The name of this quality is grief."

We are living with this grief, visibly *and* palpably.

Monday, March 15, 2021

Binti is kindly coming to spend the night, as have a one-day cameo role in Stephen Merchant's series *The Outlaws*, shooting in the West Country. Trepidatious about leaving Joan, but she insists that "it'll do you the world of good."

The production team are aware of our situation and agree to do a costume fitting in Bristol at 7 p.m. Feel very odd leaving home and returning to work mode, albeit fleetingly. All the familiarity of "this jacket, or that shirt, and these shoes or those boots" now feels strange and irrelevant.

Met up with my pal Harry Hook for takeaway fish and chips, which we eat under the stars in a Clifton garden square. He was sporting a huge Russian military hat and we sat on a bench shooting the breeze as per, me consciously censoring how much to tell him, knowing that it's *my* burden to bear.

Oilly has suggested that, instead of giving her a daily drip-feed of bad news, I edit myself and relay positive news at the end of the week, so that she is able to cope with her heavy workload and not get mired in the minutiae. Makes total sense.

Tuesday, March 16, 2021

Delighted to work with Stephen Merchant again, as we were on *Logan* together in Mississippi and he kept me from going round the bend during the weeks of waiting to work, when our scenes were on standby "weather cover." The more uptight I became, the more loosely funny was his response.

Fantasised that tepotinib would work its magic, rid her of the cancer and she'd be *the* lottery winner who beat the odds and survived. Returned home in the evening to find that she was indeed on revived form, having upped her steroid dosage and moved back upstairs into our bed again!! Annie Lennox and husband Mitch Besser have sent her stunning flowers.

Wednesday, March 17, 2021

Joan slept through the night. Restored. Walked around the garden for the first time in two weeks. Funny. Affectionate. Herself again.

Honouring the "new normal," which means no over-sharing with Oilly and limiting talking about Joan's condition to the weekends.

Email from my dear friend Taryn Fiebig in Sydney. She played Eliza Doolittle in *My Fair Lady* to my Higgins for the Sydney Opera Company in 2007. She reveals that her ovarian cancer has progressed so far that she is "at the pointy end of this amazing life and I want you to know that I don't think I have *ever* laughed more than being with you!! My life has been enriched by having you in it." Forty-nine years old. Absolutely *devastated*.

Saturday, March 20, 2021

Woken at 5:30 a.m. by Joan having a nightmare. "I'm stuck in a muddy forest, unable to move . . . I'm not sure it's worth carrying on like this, Swaz. Feel so weak and shattered all the time. Feel so sorry for you, having to live your life in the shadow of my illness . . . I'm simply existing."

"I agree with you. If I were in your shoes, I'd feel exactly the same. So let's do a *Thelma & Louise*."

Makes her laugh.

"Don't be daft. Oilly needs you."

"She's all grown up. With her own life."

"She still needs her dad."

"I'm serious. We could just get in the car and drive. Drive until we both feel ready, and then hurtle off a cliff."

Am I *serious* about a suicide pact? Momentarily. *Anything* to escape the pain we're both in.

My tennis partner, Mark Tandy, phones to check in on us, sounding chipper and positive and asking if we'd like to "have supper, or go for a walk in the country?," as though that was the easiest thing to do. How do I begin to convey how circumscribed our lives have become? I can't and don't. Just reply that, "At this moment, we don't have that option, Mark."

Harry Hook texted that he was "astonished by my courage." Puzzling, as there is no courage involved. Only love and loyalty.

Help Joan upstairs and into bed by 8 p.m.

"Are you in pain?"

"No, just exhausted."

Falls asleep in minutes. Majority of her days and nights are now spent asleep, which increases my isolation and sense of entrapment. Since sharing our news with all of our friends two months ago, am finding it difficult not to judge the ones who haven't been in touch whatsoever. No word, text, WhatsApp, email, or call, especially as we're in Covid lockdown. Crystal clear where people are placed in the pyramid of friendship.

How to face *my* old age? That's the question that's pinballing around my brain. The most entertaining insight I've heard came from the octogenarian comedian, writer, director, actor Elaine May, whom I had the pleasure of sitting beside at a dinner at Steve Martin's apartment, high above Central Park.

2013

Ooooooh brother, Elaine is as sharp as they come. Whipper-snappy and as bullseye-witty a delight as you could hope for. Riffing between the pleasures of an electric lavatory seat and flush system to Walter Matthau being such a curmudgeon and Jack Lemmon prompting her to fake a faint "'cos he was *that* boring."

She flings "fuck"s about her conversation like torpedo-confetti. On the state of America, "It's all obese, rigid, right wing, and acting like it's serious and still important.

Democracy is only for the rich. If I was poor again, I'd hire myself out as a prostitute [she's eighty-one] or be a drug dealer, 'cos it's the only way to make a fast buck and who would dare rumble a broad my age?"

All delivered in the most deadpan drollery imaginable. Says she divides her world into Jews and Gentiles. "Every time I meet another Jew, I get a little tingle." Admitted to me at 11:50 p.m. that, "I didn't call you by your name all evening, 'cos I thought your name was Bob, but wasn't sure, so held back. Were you nude in *Girls*? Matthau mistrusted me as a first-time writer-director and made my life extremely difficult. Said, 'I hope you're not gonna try and direct me, Elaine!' which clearly wasn't a question. He was grumpy but also very sensitive and complicated. Knew all about classical music, hung on to a character trait in a role, like you English actors do, and came at everything from the wrong angle, but somehow made it right for him. We became lifelong friends and he cried louder than anyone at my mother's funeral. I'm one of the few, though, who couldn't abide Jack Lemmon. Couldn't do comedy and killed everything with his Midwestern schtick."

Resisted mentioning Mr. Lemmon's sublimely funny performance in *Some Like It Hot*.

Her longtime companion, Stanley Donen, is eighty-nine and claims that he's asked Elaine to marry him 172 times, without success. The fragile director of *Singin' in the Rain* suddenly demands of the table: "So what the hell is rock and roll?" Elaine doesn't miss a beat and replies, "Rock and roll is basically any music that isn't jazz, Stanley."

She plays the entire dinner table, maintaining direct eye contact like a laser beam, sweeping back and forth and from side to side, *all* of us willingly trapped in her sights. Unlike Stanley, who slips and slides in and out of the conversational stream. Never quite able to keep up with Elaine, who ponders out loud, looking lovingly at Stanley, whether it would be worse to go deaf or blind with age? "Having said which, until some truly age-defining moment happens, I have yet to feel old. Only when your body cataclysmically cracks a hip or you lose a precious sense, do you have to face the fact that you ain't thirty-five any more."

Asked if she'd ever consider writing a memoir, her response is pithy: "What the fuck for? Everyone is either dead or forgotten and in our Google age, everything is already available and known by everyone."

What possibly sounds bitter and brutal on this page is dispensed with such perfect comic timing that it's like witnessing a tightrope walker, balancing above the void on a swaying rope, intertwined with irony and a Buster Keaton po-faced expression. Not a man nor woman at *her* table escapes unseduced. I know. Because I asked the smitten lot of them, after she'd left.

Tuesday, March 23, 2021

Marsden check-up. Blood and bone marrow tests are all "good." Lung X-ray confirms that the air pocket has healed itself, obviating the need for surgery. Huge relief. Professor Sanjay Popat tells Joan, "You look transformed" and she instantly started flirting with him. Cheered me up enormously! He urged her to really try to walk around the house and garden as much as possible.

Amazing how his encouragement galvanises her spirits. The tiniest glimmers of good news are grasped by both of us, within the umbrella of the terminally bad.

Sunday, March 28, 2021

Nigella sends us Tuscan bean soup, freshly baked bread, and a lemon drizzle cake. Delicious and generous.

Tuesday, March 30, 2021

Hottest March day since 1968 and have lunch in the garden. Joan only manages twenty minutes, then returns to bed. Am now seriously concerned about her levels of exhaustion and call the lung advice line, who calmly inform that, post her infection and the radiation surgery, this is "to be expected."

Our friend Sarah Standing jubilantly calls to say that she has been given the all-clear from her lymphoma cancer.

Of course we are absolutely thrilled and relieved for her and Johnnie, but it selfishly underlines that this is news we will *never* receive. Joan fixates on how "lucky Sarah is. So, *so* lucky." Her unspoken "if only that was me" hovers between us.

It's the first thing she says when we wake up the following morning. "Sarah is *so* lucky."

"And so are *we*, my angel. We've been together for thirty-eight years, and *counting*. How many people do we know who've been lucky enough to find their soulmate and survive as long as we have?"

"I can't see how I'm going to live till our wedding anniversary."

Hug her close, not knowing how to reply.

"We're in this together, Monkee-mine. *All* the way. This isn't a solo, we're a duet."

She holds my hand tight in the charged silence and gradually drifts back to sleep again, loosening her grip. Feel utterly marooned, becalmed, and impotent as to what I can do.

Chapter Five

April

Easter Saturday, April 3, 2021

Joan wakes at 4 a.m., asks for porridge, honey, and tea. Lying in each other's arms, she asks, "Do I have less than twelve months to live, Swaz?"

"The doctor predicted twelve to eighteen months."

"Is that with or without the drug?"

"That was her assessment *before* it started working."

"So does that mean I could survive *longer* with the drug?"

"Here's hoping! The fact that it shrank the tumour in half after only two weeks is *amazing*!"

"What will you do when I'm gone?"

I burst into tears. So *direct*. So *unavoidable*.

"Don't cry, my darling. We always wondered which of us would go first. And it's me. I'm not afraid"—stroking my face and wiping away my tears.

"If they suggest that I have to have chemo, I'd prefer

not to. As it won't change anything, and losing my hair would be awful."

"Agreed. If it were me, I wouldn't either."

"Agreed."

We just hold on to each other.

Holding.

Holding on.

My heart is breaking.

"Have a bath, and pull yourself together, Swaz."

For her. For me. For us.

The prospect of her not being here any more is *brutal.* No other word suffices.

BRUTAL

Just when the intensity of this living grief is off the scale, she jokes, "Well, Swaz, we all have to go *sometime.*"

"Is there something that you'd still love to do?"

"No."

Her reply is immediate, unequivocal, and I believe her. Then we cuddle up and coast into our day together. Desperate to sleep by 2 p.m. and retreats to the sofa, while I mow the lawn and clear out the rubbish in the garden.

Easter Sunday, April 4, 2021

Feels like Liberation Day, as we've been invited to our friends', the Doyles', for lunch in Walton-on-Thames, and *all* go, as a family. What we've always taken for granted now feels like ChristmasBirthdayNewYear'sEve in one, and might be the *last* time we're ever able to do this.

Despite Joan's puffy face and obvious frailty, they welcome her as if she'd strutted in like a supermodel. Helping her inside, without fuss or alluding to her fragility. *So* poignant, and as they turn the corner, I silently mouth "thank you" for their care and kindness. Pat winks.

Lesley has Easter bunnied the table to the max, and there are Easter eggs scattered *everywhere*. Pat, Lesley, Patrick Jr., Misha, Nula, Elliot, and Abi, *all* may be short on inches, but they're Glaswegian giants of hilarity and hospitality.

Pat is a natural-born storyteller and, even if it's one you've heard before, his enjoyment and self-triggered laughter work their magic *every* time. Lesley laughs like it's the first time she's heard it. Growing up in a three-bedroomed semi-detached house with twelve siblings, his film composing talent has afforded him a sprawling home, with tennis court, pool, and a vast garden. Even though Joan was born and brought up in very different circumstances on the east coast in Aberdeen, their Scottishness prevails, as they Celt and banter, back and forth with each other.

The Doyle laughter box is always so full to bursting with family and show business stories that the hours fly by in a blink and, by 6 p.m., we hovercraft out of there, revived and exhausted. It's been the equivalent of having tea floating below the ceiling with Uncle Albert in *Mary*

Poppins, so memorably played by Ed Wynn, singing "I Love to Laugh."

I was given the LP of the soundtrack when I was nine, and knew every song and lyric, backwards. Or as Mary herself quipped, "Docious-ali-expi-istic-fragil-cali-rupus." Julie Andrews was the nanny I longed for, as I saw *The Sound of Music* and *Mary Poppins* in 1966, when the domestic war between my parents was at its most lethal. The former film inspired me to ask for Pelham Puppets for my birthday and Christmas presents. By my early teens, I had a full-scale puppet theatre built at the back of the garage and did kids' shows in the school holidays, which enabled me to buy books and records. There was no television in Swaziland, so without any competition, these puppet shows proved to be incredibly lucrative! *Less* successful was my attempt, at ten, to Poppins off the garage roof, with just an umbrella to keep me airborne, resulting in a broken arm and much tut-tutting from my father for being such an idiot.

I long for and wish that my father could have known that his son had more than survived a profession which he warily, but tongue-in-cheekily, surmised to be "a life spent in tights, wearing make-up, and avoiding a buggery."

2017

Shortly after we'd wrapped *Can You Ever Forgive Me?*, my agent emailed over a ten-page interrogation scene "for a *top secret* project," which I had to learn and self-tape for. It seems like only an historical blink since we've migrated from video, laser disc, and DVD, to everything being streamed online. Initial auditions now happen without actually meeting another human. The advantage of prepping an audition and filming it on an iPad or iPhone is that you can redo it until you feel it's ready to send, without the nerve-rack of sitting in a waiting room with other actors, and the fear of standing in front of total strangers and tap dancing for a role. However, there is the advantage that once you're in the room, you get immediate feedback and some direction. All of which is denied when you're home alone, and only have the script to guide your choices. And in *this* case, it's a generic scene that looks like it comes from a Second World War movie.

The scene pages describe a "stern-faced Special Branch interrogator who shouts." Opt to go deadpan and soft-spoken instead, as ten pages of ranting doesn't seem realistic. Email it to my agent, assuming that I'll never hear another word about it. Played tennis with Julian Wadham and, when talking about what he'd self-taped for, he described the very same interrogator scene.

"Did you shout?"

"A *lot*."

A month later, my agent texts: "You're still in the loop."

Two weeks after that cryptic missive, I am told that they're sending a car, driven by Mike Bevan, who drove me on my first film role in 1986, to go to Pinewood

Studios to meet with JJ Abrams about *Star Wars*! Despite my barrage of questions, Mike knows nada. Get to the Carrie Fisher Building at Pinewood Studios and bump into Lindsay Brunnock, the art director on *Keep the Aspidistra Flying*, followed by first assistant director Tommy Gormley, with whom I'd done an ill-fated football film called *The Match* in Glasgow, then casting supremo Nina Gold, who cast me as Heseltine in *The Iron Lady* and is the reason I'm now here today. Meeting these four people in a row feels like tunnelling through a time machine, topped off by JJ Abrams, whom I'd met in Los Angeles at a party in 1990, when he was a 24-year-old wunderkind with a three-picture screenplay writing deal, the first of which was *Regarding Henry* starring Harrison Ford. As self-possessed and confident a young buck as I'd *ever* met. He quipped, "You and I are going to work together one day."

Three decades later, that *day* might be *today*. While waiting to go in to meet him, Nina is all reassuring and confirms that this is for a role in *Star Wars*. His vast office is crammed with memorabilia, props, costumes, and Daisy Ridley! He jumps up to greet me, introduces me to Daisy, and then asks, "So, are you gonna do this?"

Room goes upside down, during which he must have described the plot and the role, and *all* I can think is, *You're in, Swaz, you're in, you're actually in!*

"So I don't have to audition for you and Daisy?"

"No! Saw your self-tape."

Remind him that we met in 1990, and what he'd said about working together, none of which he remembered, of course, but he quipped, "Well, I'm true to my word, right? Because now we *are.*"

He speaks at Scorsese-speed, and somehow segues into Streisand stories, as he knows her very well, and, an hour later, am sent downstairs to the costume department. En route, drop to my knees before Nina Gold and her casting partner Robert, to thank them both. *They* are so thrilled, which *ups* my thrilldom, as I'd seen the first *Star Wars* film in 1977, when I was a 20-year-old drama student. Which is *exactly* the age that I feel right now. Inconceivable that I would get cast in the final episode of the Luke Skywalker saga, forty-one years *later*!

Mike Bevan is so pleased on my behalf and, on the way home, we reminisce about all the people we knew on *Withnail* and *How to Get Ahead in Advertising* in the eighties.

Joan is fabulously unimpressed, so when I tell her that I have to keep completely schtum about the film and my role, she says, "Not to worry, Swaz. I've never seen *any Star Wars* movies!"

First time I've ever accepted a job without having read one line of the screenplay. Costume designer Michael Kaplan kits me out in a black and silver SS stormtrooper outfit, with shiny knee-high boots. *Everyone* else seems to know what's going on, except for me. But I'm *not* quibbling.

Monday, July 30, 2018

Cast dinner in the private dining room upstairs at the Ivy restaurant. Joonas Suotamo, the Finnish actor, is playing the giant Chewbacca, because, at almost 7 foot, he is one. Daisy Ridley reveals that her audition process lasted seven *months* and that *Star Wars* fans are obsessive and knowledgeable beyond all measure. "Like an alternate universe of obsession." Anthony Daniels C-3POs up and says that this is his ninth time inside the golden robot suit, and I couldn't help wondering what it must feel like to have spent your entire career being unseen, yet so iconically visible.

Adam Driver wide-shoulders into view and greets me with "Welcome to the madness"—we'd worked together five years previously on *Girls*. Domhnall Gleeson is Dublin-charming and declares, "Your wife, Joan, is *the* best. Funniest. Most brilliant accent and acting teacher imaginable. An absolute *legend*."

"I wholeheartedly *agree* with you, Domhnall!"

Oscar Isaac confirms what everyone has been predicting: "What a great time you're going to have." Almost as if on cue, JJ Abrams excites up. Friendly, intense, and welcoming, and reveals that my character is called General Pryde.

Gorgeous Naomi Ackie and I are the new bugs and she confirms that she hasn't read the script either. John Boyega is equally welcoming. Producer Kathy Kennedy gives a speech that makes *all* of us feel included.

The unspoken *Star Wars omertà* is evidenced by the complete absence of *anyone* taking a photo on their mobiles, or even looking at their phones.

Tuesday, July 31, 2018

Pinewood Studios, and ushered into a conference room that has closed-circuit cameras, two guards at the door, with whom I leave my mobile phone, then sit down to read the script on an iPad. Relieved to discover that I am in more than one scene and have a plot-twister moment with Domhnall Gleeson. Don't understand much of it, other than that Good triumphs over Evil!

Monday, August 6, 2018

First day of filming for me and the entire studio complex is taken up with *Star Wars*. Tommy Gormley has labelled my trailer door with the name STEADFAST, which Joan says, "Pretty much sums you up, Swaz! You're in the *Condiment-ary* phase of your career. Like Colonel Mustard in Cluedo. There to add some flavour—final double episode of *Frasier*, four episodes of *Girls*, two episodes of *Downton Abbey*, three episodes of *Game of Thrones*, final episode of the Wolverine films in *Logan*, and now the finale of *Star Wars*. Each time you get to flirt, seduce, boss, sneer, explode, disappear or die. Colman's mustard for the more spectacular ending, or Dijon mustard for something less violent."

Which results in the following exchange about a Disney+ series:

"Darling, I've been offered a role in *Loki*."

"Dijon or Colman's?"

"Probably a mixture of the two."

"Still, good to get a gig at your age, Swaz, just so long as you cut the *mustard*!"

"Indeed."

Joan's Aberdonian take on *everything* keeps me grounded and endlessly amused.

Flowers, champagne, and a handwritten note from JJ and Kathy generously sit beside my nametag and security pass, with a plastic envelope containing the four red pages of script for today with the bold-lettered warning: RETURN SIDES (script pages) AT END OF THE DAY OR YOU WON'T BE ISSUED ANY TOMORRROW. Fort Knoxed and noted.

Into the make-up trailer and Amanda Knight says that there have been drones overhead trying to snap pictures of sets or actors in costume. Which is why we've all been provided with hooded cloaks to wear between the trailers and studios. Never known *anything* like this level of security before. And I've filmed in Israel! She says that make-up and costume departments have received offers for *any* images or inside info, for substantial amounts of money, such is the global obsession with all things *Star Wars*.

"Ridiculous," says my wife. "It's only a *movie*."

"Agreed, Monkee, but what a franchise to be a part of.

Just thinking about how much has happened since I first saw the original in 1977. Who I've met and worked with. What an incredible ride it's been and is continuing to be."

"Proud of you, Swaz, but it's *still* only a box of popcorn."

The spaceship boardroom set is spectacular, with lit consoles that look so real it's almost impossible to resist pressing a button or twiddling a knob. JJ Abrams is compact, bearded, and as bushy-tailed and energetic as a teenager. Speaks at bullet speed, is enthusiastic, supercharged, and focused and knows *everyone's* name. That's about 300 people! He is concise, clear, and we all know precisely what he wants.

Day before, I'd posted a video on Instagram about how I'd got cast and he came up to me and said, "I *loved* your post. You're so enthusiastic and unjaded and that means the world to me." Phewed with relief that I hadn't inadvertently breached the hyper-security cordon.

Seated beside veteran Richard Durden, who shared his views of thespians we knew or had worked with and opined that "*most* actors are utterly selfish. Albeit sometimes charming, but they *love* the sound of their own voices"—and then shamed and named the most monstrous culprits *he'd* encountered. Which was hugely entertaining.

Monday, August 13, 2018

Domhnall advises that in his experience the scripted lines are easy to read, but difficult to say, in response to my worry that my brain is having problems trying to remember them.

"*Everyone* has had these issues, because we are usually only given them on the day and then they're rewritten, so don't get too hung up about it."

Having drummed a sentence of techno-gobbledy into my cranium for a week, a new script page is issued at lunch, with the *problem* line replaced by something which makes much more sense. You know that you're not working on a low-budget flick when your lunch order arrives in a cardboard carton, specially cooked by a designated chef with a label delineating the calorie/fat/protein contents. Oh, and free use of the studio gym, to keep us all ship-shape. My costume has chest padding to augment the absence of any pectorals.

Ready to shoot at 8 a.m., but actually called to the set at 4 p.m. One of those classic "hurry up and wait" days that is instantly eclipsed when doing a talking/walking scene with Domhnall and Adam in the spaceship octagonal corridors, accompanied by stormtroopers in their iconic white armour and helmets. *Just like in the movies!*

As the scene has only just been rewritten, *everyone* is scrabbling and struggling to remember the new lines *and* walk and talk at the same time. Sounds simple, but *oh boy*, all of us get snookered. Hilarious as Adam Driver is wearing his Kylo Ren helmet, covering his entire head, so we are none the wiser if he's "dried" or not. But he emits a regular "*fuck fuck fuck*," meaning that we all get sent back to our starting positions. If *he* can cock it up, then it makes it easier to bear when I do.

Nothing escapes JJ's laser-like focus. I asked him how old he felt. "Generally about twenty-four, but sometimes ninety." He is inherently childlike and reminds you of that kid from school with a boffin brain, who knows *everything*, without a smidgeon of arrogance, and makes complicated encyclopaedics sound *simple*. Never stops moving. Never stops trying a new camera set-up to shoot a scene in the most interesting way, and his crew follow him loyally, *to the letter*.

In between set-ups, have a moment to catch up with Adam Driver, whose career has gone stratospheric since his big break in *Girls*, and he extols the virtues of directors Jim Jarmusch and Spike Lee. He says that, "Spike has no side *whatsoever*, is completely the same no matter the situation and has worked with the same crew for decades."

Kelly Macdonald pays a set visit with her mum and two little boys. Our paths haven't crossed since *Gosford Park* in 2001, but she's as immediate and friendly as if we'd seen each other last week. After she leaves, JJ declares, "Kelly is like pure sunshine. I love her." Me too.

JJ quietly suggests that being deadpan in my scenes with Kylo and Hux is the way to go. What he identifies as the "normalcy of true evil." Uniformed in jodhpurs, shoulder pads, and striped insignia, we are clearly the spaceship counterparts of Goering, Goebbels, Himmler, Eichmann, and that gang of Nazi psychopaths. Do less in other words.

I've entered my seventh decade of minimalist villainy. Being born with a long, lugubrious face, it makes sense of my mother's query after seeing me in a school play when I was fourteen: "Why do you always play sneery roles?" I've clearly "come of sneer" in my sixty-first year!

At one point Adam/Kylo has to reference Han Solo's admonishing index finger pose. JJ asks his assistant to pull up the original scene on a laptop to precisely emulate it. Surreal and touching to see everyone crowding around to look at a very young Harrison Ford and Carrie Fisher in a corridor set that precisely mirrors where we're all standing decades later. Abba's "Knowing Me, Knowing You" pops into my head. Never been on any movie where there is a back catalogue of eight movies to cross-reference across forty years, giving you the momentary delusion that it's real instead of reel.

Killing Hux/Domhnall on the bridge of the Death Star is a big moment for Pryde, but JJ wants zero evil intent visible, suggesting "concern" while Hux reveals his treachery. Followed by an incredibly casual gun-grab from an adjacent stormtrooper, shooting Hux dead, and calmly informing a minion to "tell him [Kylo Ren] that we found the spy."

Domhnall has to catapult backwards from the blast of my gun. Cue for his stunt double Troy and his team of pulley system and rigid wires to be attached and set up, so that he can be yanked backwards at gun speed. What will last seconds on screen takes ninety minutes to achieve in reality.

Opportunity to slip into the adjacent studio where the second unit are filming coverage of a desert tunnel sequence, with real sand and polystyrene sculpted caves. Anthony Daniels shows me the nineteen pieces that constitute his golden robot costume. "Originally took an hour to assemble, when we did the first movie, and have now got it down to eight minutes." The headpiece only has two tiny eyeholes, cutting out all peripheral vision.

"Is it claustrophobic?"

"Have had my moments, but otherwise you have to go very Zen."

He first played the role when he was thirty, and is now seventy-two, but his golden armour has kept him ageless and timeless on screen, and in incredibly disciplined shape on planet earth.

Thursday, August 16, 2018

Apocalyptic finale scenes. JJ and Tommy Gormley are verbally revved up to keep the day moving as quickly as possible. Action sequences usually take forever to painstakingly plot and shoot, but JJ works differently. Armed with a small handheld screen which is linked to the camera lens, JJ blocks through the whole sequence, which Colin, the camera operator, follows assiduously. JJ is decisive and emphatic, yet always open to trying a new idea or better option.

Script suggests that Admiral Griss, played by Geff Francis,

and I will be standing at a control desk, but JJ isn't a man for static *anything* and transforms it into a steady-camera "ballet" around the entire set. It's a big challenge for Colin, Serge, the focus puller, and Gary, the camera grip, to constantly accommodate JJ's change of plans, moves, and ideas. All of which they seamlessly and brilliantly accommodate and achieve.

At the end of a very fast set of camera moves and changes of direction, JJ leads the applause for a job well done. Patently clear that his crew will walk through fire with and for him. He uses the camera like an extension of his body, meaning that the action is always clearly motivated. Never met anyone with a brain that fizzes quite as fast as JJ's. Smart as a whip of paint, with an opinion and depth of knowledge about almost any subject that you care to mention.

The bridge is peopled up with stormtroopers, technicians, computer workers, and a team of stunt performers, positioned to dive off platforms in response to the squibs and flame-throwers meticulously set up to create the illusion of steam, spark, and fire, exploding in all directions. Constant safety alerts and fire drills until *finally* four cameras are ready to roll simultaneously on a sequence that will last twelve seconds. Beyond the windows of the Death Star, an enormous crane with a remotely controlled camera at the end of it swoops towards the exterior of the ship. This set has taken sixteen weeks to construct and stands above a forest of scaffolding.

We're all invited to watch the playback of the crane shot and it's a collective "pinch, punch, first of the month" *thrill* to be in the finale of *Star Wars*.

Best of all, I get to do something I've longed to do ever since I can remember. Which is to march through those octagonal, sliding, heavy-duty *Star Wars* doors. I expected that they'd be electronic or hydraulic, but no, there is a middle-aged crew member manually pulling two linked cords which open both doors. *Old school!* Rather than distracting, it adds to the romance and glamour of this make-believe world. The budget is rumoured to be around $250 million, and there's an English bloke pulling the ropes! Could not love it more.

Moment I'm wrapped and it's into an adjacent studio to be photographed by 300 cameras in a specially created pod to cover *every* imaginable angle for the special effects team, games, videos, books, toys, and merchandise. A reminder that this is a *huge* industry with schools of pilot fish swimming alongside the mega-movies to supplement the Disney coffers.

You'd imagine that JJ would have *no* time for a natter, but when he does, he's unstoppable. Asked him if he actually knew *everyone* as he has a stream of famous faces visiting his set to say hi and have a look at what he's up to. Spike Lee was yesterday's drop by.

"Do you know Mel Brooks, by any chance?"

"I do, and he told me that the first time he had lunch with Alfred Hitchcock, he ordered a *huge* shrimp cocktail and a giant steak. Followed by a cigar. Mel, unsure whether he was supposed to light it for him, is saved by the maître d', who leans in, to hear Hitchcock proclaim, '*Yes*, I'll have it all over again, please.'"

Which Mr. Brooks discovered was de rigueur for Alfred. He liked to eat twice over during one sitting—hence his girth!

"*Put Chewie's head back on!*" is a command you don't get to hear too often in real life. Well not mine anyway. Poor Joonas gets incredibly overheated inside the furry bodysuit and headpiece and crew members rally around and insert hand fans inside his neck join to funnel cool air to his nethers.

Am taken aback to see that the BB-8 spherical droid isn't remotely controlled, but attached to a puppeteer, whose arms are covered in green felt, which will be removed digitally in post-production. Making sense of why it appears to be so human and all the *more* magical.

Finally manage to speak to Kathleen Kennedy, who reveals that she began producing plays at school in the tiny town where she grew up, was hopeless at maths, and has since become the most successful female film producer in the history of Hollywood. With a box office take of $12.5 billion and counting!

"How do you deal with difficult people?"

"I try to *always* listen, and hear them out."

Vanity Fair shoot with Annie Leibovitz. Dressed top to toe in black, she says "Hey, Richard!" and hugs me with the warmth and familiarity of someone I saw last month. In reality, I was photographed by her for a Gap advert *twenty* years ago. Riveted by her eyes which have seen and snapped every person of living note in the latter part of the twentieth century and beyond. *Privileged* to be her willing subject again. Everything's been set up on the spaceship set, Domhnall Gleeson standing behind, with me seated in front. Expressionless as Mount Rushmore. None of the usual fiddly-bob with lights and lenses and ladders. She snaps away at incredible speed, interchanging cameras, handed back and forth to her by her assistant. Done and dusted in *ten* minutes. *The* fastest shutter gun in the West.

Her strong nose, swept back greying hair, stature, and single-mindedness have the aura of a warrior woman. Zero doubt. Zero hesitation. Prepared. Precise. Perfect!

Star Wars: The Rise of Skywalker grossed over a billion bucks, to which Joan opined that, "While you were very good, Swaz, I confess that I didn't understand a word of it."

Tuesday, April 6, 2021

Back to the Marsden for second Pfizer Covid vaccination, ECG, blood tests and meeting with Wanda. Who admits that she is utterly perplexed as to why Joan is so chronically exhausted all the time. Has spoken to the endocrinologist to see whether her thyroid needs boosting. But is doubtful. Cathy, the resident physiotherapist, did basic strength tests, advised on breathing and very simple exercises for her to do. Very calm, gentle, and reassuring. Pointing out that even getting in and out of the bath is a *major* exertion of energy, and to be especially patient.

While Joan was taking a nap after we got home, I was speaking to a friend on the phone and used the dreaded word "terminal." Unbeknownst to me, Joan had overheard this and went ballistic. "I *never* use that word. *Ever.* To *anyone.* Please just say I have stage 4 lung cancer."

I stupidly tried to explain that most people don't know what the stages signify, which causes confusion and means that they offer "I'm sure it'll all be fine" platitudes. She is having *none* of this and is absolutely furious.

Feel ashamed and wretched, like I did when I hit the ground, umbrella-ing off the garage roof.

"I'm *very, very* sorry, Monkee."

There's no placating her and it's my turn to have a sleepless night. "Terminal" is the word I dread, loathe, and hate more than any other in the lexicon.

Wednesday, April 7, 2021

Just when it seemed safe to dip my toes back into domestic waters, Joan harpoons me with, "What you said is completely *unacceptable.*"

While she knows that she is terminally ill, she's become fixated on my daring to say the word out loud and sees it as some terrible transgression. Maybe she feels that using the word is her prerogative, rather than mine?

Am as helpless as a speared turtle, flailing about, not knowing how to appease her. My lady's *not* for turning, so opt for some diversionary tactics and ask Ryan Sugar if he's willing to bike over and colour and cut her hair. Which he mercifully does. Distracting and cheering her up in the process.

Opt to keep a *very* low profile for the rest of the day. Reply to checking in emails from Eric Idle, Annie Lennox, and Gabriel Byrne from the States, with an abbreviated update—"Stable/Fragile/Becalmed"—rather than chapter and versing, as it feels too much to burden people with.

Supper in Pinter-charged silence, which is finally broken when Joan declares, "I'm still 'ere"—in a perfect cockney accent. The relief of being forgiven is huge. Feel awful for having upset her so deeply and unintentionally.

Our week is marooned by her complete exhaustion, which we try our best to navigate around with lots of sleep, but, frustratingly, this does little to alleviate her continued tiredness. Ask if she'd mind if we had the Mitchells over for lunch. "Just so long as they don't mind if I go to sleep if I get too tired."

Tuesday, April 13, 2021

I *need* company and am delighted to cook for Christine and Stephen, whose Australian gusto and appetite for life *and* seafood pasta is mightily welcome. Buoying up Joan in the process and keeping her entertained and awake until

4 p.m. Like the Doyles, they don't mention Joan's illness and make everything feel normal. It's only when I walk them to the gate that Christine gets overwhelmed and says, "I can't believe this is happening to you both. She is such a *strong* and inspiring woman."

Wanda phoned at 6:30 to report that she hasn't been able to fathom why Joan is so shattered all the time, but reassured that the scans were showing no changes since being done six weeks ago and that the air pocket has significantly reduced and her condition has stabilised. I asked about the efficacy of the drug and she said that it does this miraculous initial shrinkage of the tumour, then plateaus and maintains it at that reduced size. *For a while . . .*

Thursday, April 15, 2021

Joan woke up at 3 a.m., then again at 6 a.m. for breakfast, without any chest pains or headache. Much more chipper and positive. Claims that she had a fantastic catch-up sleep, and feeling very relaxed. No sooner said than I ask if she'd like more lights on to read. "I'm *sick* of instructions. I want to spend the day without *anyone* telling me what to do!"

Felt sideswiped and slapped. Asked myself what instructions I'd been giving her—unless she means my persuading her to go upstairs at 8 p.m. last night, before she was too tired to do so later?

I know I should be taking all this on the chin, but it's

a challenge not to feel a little resentful and unappreciated. I almost say, "If that's what you want, then go ahead and do everything yourself"—but, a second later, *know* that it's her frustration at having to rely on me for everything, which is so difficult for her.

Ironically, my days and nights are *entirely* run according to Joan's instructions—"do this, get that, check this, answer that, order these, cancel them." Nonstop instructions. *Nonstop.* But, of course, she doesn't see it that way.

At 1 a.m., she wakes me up and says, "I'm very sorry, Swaz. I didn't mean to hurt you and am very grateful for everything you're doing for me, but I just get overwhelmed. Can we still go to the country tomorrow? Please?"

"Of course, yes."

Friday, April 16, 2021

And we're in the car by 9:30 and at our cottage in Gloucestershire by noon. Joan had always wanted a country retreat, with low ceilings and an inglenook fireplace, and four years ago went searching online. Found a cottage 100 miles away in a village with a couple of pubs and no shop, and, within five minutes of being shown around, said, "We'll buy it." I bumped my head on every door lintel, until I attached beaded borders above each one, to stop from concussing myself. Five-foot-three Joan sailed through unimpeded! Spirits revived. Energy up! The quiet of the countryside is like balm and there are far fewer stairs for her to negotiate. Oilly and Florian are working remotely from their bedroom.

Lunchtime news reports that Helen McCrory has died of cancer at just fifty-two. We all cried. Both of us had worked with her. Wrote to her husband Damian Lewis. Impossible not to project when this will happen to us.

Saturday, April 17, 2021

Ruth and Bruce Kennedy-Dundas and their son Alfie motor over for lunch in the garden. Ensure that Joan is already out there and seated when they arrive, as she is self-conscious about walking like an old crock in front of them. Am aware of how determined they all are to keep conversation spritzed and pepped up, without seeming forced or too jolly-hockey-sticks exuberant.

Joan rallies and raises the topic of her steroid-swollen cheeks. To which Ruth says, "The richest women in the world drop major lumps of cash for cheeks like yours, Joan!"

Sunday, April 18, 2021

Went for a walk with Oilly and Florian.

"How am I doing on the 'no means *no*' front?"

"Better."

Phew!

Am wondering, at the age of sixty-three and eleven months, if I am *ever* going to be a proper grown-up.

Monday, April 19, 2021

Final lunch date is with Sue Gutjahr and Alex Ciobanu, who both work at William's fish restaurant in Nailsworth down the road. *My* turn to cook and wait on *them* after all their kindness and service over the past three years, since we bought our cottage down here.

Sue is a former nurse, has travelled the globe, treats *everyone* equally, and is one of life's garrulous and uncorkable enhancers. Wickedly funny, irreverent, and adores my wife. As does Alex, whose Romanian warmth guarantees keeping the home fires of friendship burning. They find it funny and hard to resist trying to help me serve lunch.

"In 1982, I was a waiter at Tuttons brasserie in Covent Garden, so I assure you, ladies, I *know* how to plate up my arm, so please behave yourselves and leave me to it."

They're like a pair of excitable schoolgirls and cheer Joan up with their exuberance. Which doesn't preclude Sue asking her if she's sad about her prognosis.

"Not at all. Not remotely. I've had a very fulfilled life."

"But wouldn't you like to travel more?"

"No. I've been everywhere I wanted to go."

"What about Oilly and Richard?"

"Oh, I know they'll be fine."

Her outward resilience and resignation are formidable and being in the country has been hugely restorative. Spring weather sublime, and the love and support of our friends palpable.

Tuesday, April 20, 2021

Taken by surprise when Joan casually suggests that we stop off in Cirencester on our way back to London, to buy a wheelchair. Feels like we're entering the twilight zone and am finding this unexpectedly shocking. The sense that there truly is no going back. Ever.

Heard a bereft woman on Radio 4 talking about how her dog had saved her by being so happy to see her every day. And, like her dog, she's been inspired to wipe the slate clean every morning, to start feeling happy again. Prompting us to code-word "woof" for every time we feel low: new day, new *woof*.

Post-Covid-lockdown traffic jam as we drive to the Marsden. Cars, cyclists, and pedestrians to jangle your nerves. Countered by Wanda's smiling reassurance that the scan results are all stable, steroid dosage reduced to just 2ml per day, and that we only need to return for check-ups every four weeks, rather than *every* week.

Cannot tell you how liberating this feels. Even if we spend every minute at home in London, being relieved of the strain of driving, finding parking, securing a wheelchair, waiting for blood tests, queuing for prescriptions, waiting to see the oncology team surrounded by *very* ill patients, is a *mighty* relief.

Joan is in our bed by 8:30 p.m., leaving me to spend the evening downstairs, in the present, alone.

Friday, April 23, 2021

As we now have a month's reprieve between each hospital appointment, resolve to retreat to the calm of the Cotswolds, where everything is cottage-compact and within easier reach. Stop off for outdoor lunch at William's, where Sue and Alex make a fuss of Joan and cheer her up with a *woof's* worth of their happiness.

Saturday, April 24, 2021

Barbecued giant prawns in the garden for our stalwart neighbours, Nige and Jules Bowsher, who have unstintingly checked in on our cottage for the past four months while we've been in London, picking up our mail and making sure the pipes haven't burst. He is a retired detective, whom we've nicknamed Sherlock, as he's always "on our case, helping to solve *everything*," as well as being a wicked mimic. Jules is a wonderful baker and brings over batches of warm scones or home-made fruitcake, like something out of *The Darling Buds of May*. Their generosity since the day we moved in has been boundless.

My evening ritual, once Joan is in bed, is to soak porridge for her breakfast, prep all her pills, then lay out the tray with teacup, pot, and napkin. Painting her nails is another sweet ritual. Tender and intimate.

"You'd make a good handmaid, Swaz!"

"*Anything* for you, Monkee."

Sunday, April 25, 2021

Leave at dawn for the Malvern Antiques Fair, but am doubt-filled that Joan's going to be able to cope. When I dare ask if she's really up for driving all that way, she looks at me and barks, "*Woof!*"

Slate clean—happiness!

Follow the signs for disabled parking and get the wheelchair clicked open for its first official outing. Catch sight of ourselves in a battered old mirror, shocked by our fragile new reflections. Pushing the chair across the uneven grass is tougher than anticipated and the reality of being among so many people proves too much. We're back on the road within an hour and "never again-ing" back home.

Post-nap, we're back on the road south to have a drink and look-see at Anya Hindmarch and James Seymour's beautiful cottage in Wiltshire, both of whom are "woof-full" of the joys of being new homeowners, then all go together to Mark Tandy and Amanda Marmot's farmhouse nearby, for an early supper. Struck by everyone talking about their summer holiday and future plans, momentarily beguiling us into believing that we, too, might have these options. But we don't.

Wednesday, April 28, 2021

Oilly's come down to stay with us, which is very welcome, as Joan is especially poorly today and has stayed in bed all day. There's no warning or guide as to how to navigate this unknown phase. The dread of waiting. Witnessing. Watching. Knowing that it's irreversible.

Try to remember that today is as good as today is ever going to get, and what's next *will* be worse. Have to adjust and make the *best* of what we *do* have left, together.

Oilly suggests that we compile an album of all the letters, cards, and photos we've been sent about Joan.

"I *see* how heavy your burden is, Pops. I see it. No one tells you how tired this makes you feel, *all* the time."

Breaks my heart. We crawl away to our beds by 9:30 p.m.

Friday, April 30, 2021

Pat and Lesley Doyle come down for a sleepover, and, despite Joan's shortness of breath, Pat makes her *cry* with laughter. He's our unofficial Dr. Laughing Gas, and really ought to be a free prescription on the NHS! The more excited he gets, the faster he talks, until his Glaswegian vowels roller-coaster at such speed that I sometimes lose track of what he's *actually* saying, but this has zero impact on the pleasure and hilarity of his epic stories. If we, his rapt audience, show partiality for a particularly hysterical moment, he instinctively obliges with an encore, amping up the mirth-ometer. Watching Joan delighting in his stories is worth gold bullion to me. She is energised and revived for the twenty-four hours they spend with us. *The* greatest gift of friendship imaginable.

Chapter Six

May

Wednesday, May 5, 2021

My sixty-fourth birthday.

Sgt. Pepper's Lonely Hearts Club Band was the first pop LP I was given, on my tenth birthday in 1967. "When I'm Sixty-four" seemed an impossibly distant, unimaginable age to reach, in the far-off twenty-first century. Yet here I am, sixty-four today, with receding grey hair and lengthening teeth! Oilly asks if the Swinging Sixties impacted life in Swaziland.

"Not particularly. Apart from wife-swapping!" Though I do have an image of my mother sporting a beehive hairdo, kitted out in a paisley pant suit, and swaying wantonly to "Winchester Cathedral" as sung by the Ray Conniff Singers.

My mother is now eighty-nine and Skypes to wish me a happy birthday, noting that I was "born at 12:20 in the morning, at the Mbabane Hospital in black and white, as all your baby photos were taken pre-colour in 1957." We reflect on the staggering cast list of characters we knew in Swaziland, and how so many of them have merry-moled in the interim. She notes that "the world has changed immeasurably since then." Mine certainly has.

I used to play *Pepper* endlessly and pored over Peter Blake's cover art. If you'd predicted that I would actually meet three of the Beatles, decades later, I'd have thought you certifiable. First encounter was with Ringo Starr, who paid a set visit during the shooting of *Withnail*, filming the opening kitchen scene on location in a condemned house in Notting Hill Gate. Very low-key and chatty. George Harrison, whose company HandMade Films produced *How to Get Ahead in Advertising*, likewise paid us a visit with co-producer Ray Cooper, at Shepperton Studios. Told me how much he loved *Withnail*, which threw me, as all I wanted to talk and ask him about was the Beatles. He politely let me gabble away, giving no indication that he must have heard variations of this same old tune his entire adult life.

Met Paul McCartney in 1997, when I'd gone to see Julie Christie in a play at the Wyndham's Theatre. We'd played husband and wife in Dennis Potter's TV swansong *Karaoke*, which was a pinch-me moment if ever there was one, as *Far from the Madding Crowd* was my O-level set book, and she'd been Bathsheba Everdene in the film version, followed by *Don't Look Now*, with that never-bettered, iconic sex scene opposite Donald Sutherland, and then in *Shampoo*, where she disappeared below a dinner table to give Warren Beatty a happy ending. Completing my unofficial screen sex-education curriculum vitae!

Went backstage to see her, and met Paul and Linda McCartney, and their daughter Stella. "Join us for dinner. We're all going to the Bombay Brasserie."

"Why bloody *notsky*!" scrolled across the cartoon balloon above my head as I looked around in disbelief at the dinner guests either side of me. Julie, Paul, Linda, oh, *and* Twiggy and Leigh Lawson, who'd joined our gang. A mini round-up of sixties icons all chatting away with this star-struck Swaziboy among them. Linda instantly took command and pretty much ordered *every* vegetarian dish on the menu. When the feasting was under way, I banged my knees together to remind myself that I was *actually* here, sharing naan bread with *Doctor Zhivago*'s *Darling*, "Hey Jude," "Eleanor Rigby," and Twiggy, while my head went all "Ob-La-Di, Ob-La-Da."

Weird moment when you're talking to people you've known remotely for years, trying to amalgamate the real person with all the memories of their movies and music in your mind. Silent-tap "With a Little Help from My Friends" on my thigh.

Joan gets a bit snappy, ordering me hither and thither. No sooner done one thing, than she has another demand. Tried as diplomatically as possible to explain that I only have one pair of hands and am not an octopus! Makes her laugh and growl out a chorus of "Octopus's Garden."

FRIDAY, MAY 7, 2021

Organise the sale of Joan's sports car, as she concedes that she'll never drive again. Emotional moment beginning this practical dismantling of her life. Piece by piece. Painful.

Joan's moods vacillate, like the cast of *Snow White and the Seven Dwarfs*, between Dopey, Grumpy, Sleepy, Happy, Bashful, and visiting the Doc.

Drive across to Hereford to spend the night with Bruce and Sophie Robinson in their magical farmhouse. Every room a different colour, crammed with books, Sophie's paintings, antiques, and clocks, which Bruce is expert at restoring and keeping ticking. Ironic as his procrastination when completing scripts or books on time is epic.

"Ah, but look at the *results*, duckie!" is his gleeful riposte.

When recounting incidents in his week, each one has the sword of Damocles hovering above every sentence, imbued with his gift for doom-mongering in the most entertaining way. Ask him what time he wakes up. "I get out of bed at 8:20 a.m. and my cock follows at about 10:40 a.m."—*classic* Bruce.

Recounts his recent journey to London in a Mini, which *just* managed to get there, with smoke pouring out of the engine "like the Wizard of fucking Oz," embellished with much scowling and vituperation. Cheers us up no end!

"Have you watched the news, Grant?"

"Given up, but I have a sneaking suspicion you're going to educate me otherwise."

Cue for Bruce to combust about Boris/Trump/Putin/Kim Jong-un/the weather/Blair/global warming/his stepfather/cost of oil/or, when in doubt, Thatcher.

Sophie blithely smiles her way through it all, keeping us warm, watered, and welcome.

"But how does any of this *directly* affect you, Bruce, sequestered here in your gorgeous valley farmhouse?"

Sophie winks and distracts us with a delicious supper. After which Joan excuses herself and heads for bed. Except that the steep stairs prove too much for her and she quite literally crawls up, one laborious step after another. Refuses my help and makes small whimpering sounds like an injured animal. Devastating to watch. Knowing that this is the *last* time we will ever visit this house, together.

Once she's settled in bed, return downstairs and recount how we've been managing. Both of them are stricken and, head-shakingly, murmur, "There is nothing that either of us can say, it's just brutal." And it is. But has to be borne.

Monday, May 10, 2021

Week of cottage calm ahead. No plans. No guests. Quiet.

Joan has taken to keeping a notebook of TV anecdotes that have amused her, two of which are on the subject of hair. A TV critic, reviewing Rula (renowned for her lustrous red curls) Lenska's role in *EastEnders*, declared that "she looked like she was wearing a corgi on her head," while host Lorraine Kelly mused on her morning show that she "always thought that Diana Rigg looks like Cliff Richard in a wig—oops, sorry!" Which reminded me that when Joan first met my mother, she whispered that "she looks just like Roger Moore in a wig." Just as well, because my mother adored Roger Moore. She also loved *The Weakest Link*, as host Anne Robinson was so ruthless with the contestants that they often got flustered into giving an approximately "correct" answer:

"Who was the ex-member of Steps who made his West End debut in Joseph and the Amazing Technicolor Dreamcoat*?"* (Correct answer: Ian "H" Watkins.)

Actual answer given was "Paul Scofield," the late Oscar-winning classical actor of *A Man for All Seasons* renown, clearly intending to have said "Phillip Schofield," co-host of *This Morning* on ITV, who *had* played Joseph. *Both* answers incorrect, but tickled Joan's particular sense of humour no end.

She quoted actor Jim Norton's mantra that "the most important things for an actor are faith, hope, and clarity, and the greatest of these is clarity."

Very touched to find literary quotes she's written down from the wide range of books she's reading:

> *"Keep the heart Awake to Love and Beauty!"* —Samuel Taylor Coleridge
>
> *"That which is only living, can only die."* —T. S. Eliot
>
> *"I measure time as we all do, and partly by the fading body, but in order to challenge linear time, I try and live in total time."* —Jeanette Winterson

Poetry has been for her what classical music does for me—providing sustenance and solace. Prior to falling ill, she regularly read a poem to me before we went to sleep.

Sunday, May 16, 2021

Melissa McCarthy messages about the possibility of Sunday lunch as she is back in the UK to complete on *The Little Mermaid*.

Melissa is astonished at the scale of my Streisand sculpture in the garden and insists that we do a selfie together. Posts it with the tagline: "Secret's out, finally!! Thrilled to announce we are a throuple."

Joan is amazingly resilient and buoyant in company and I don't think anyone guessed just how fragile she is feeling. Confesses after our guests have departed that it was very challenging to listen to everyone talking about work and their future plans, which she could never be a part of. All this social stimulation is too much.

Resolve to keep visitors at bay and on a one-to-one basis.

"When we're alone, I don't have to face the acute divide between everyone else's lives going forward when mine is in stasis."

Seeing Melissa is always a five-star treat.

OCTOBER 2018

Car glides into Claridge's hotel, where all things are bright and beautiful, for the European press junket for *Can You Ever Forgive Me?* All art deco and the kind of place where you'd expect to see Auntie Mame swish around the next corner. My parents took me to see Ginger Rogers playing the role in 1969 at the Theatre Royal, Drury Lane. Her nephew was played by Gary Warren, who, at fourteen years old, was two years older than me, and it struck me that it was actually possible to become an actor. Cemented when we went to see Mark Lester and Jack Wild in *Oliver!* Daydreams that eventually became my professional reality.

Oddly exotic feeling staying in a fabulous hotel on your home turf. Having landed back home from New York last night, just when I'd thought I was King Tut, Joan and I had a monumental argument about something trivial enough to flatten the pyramids of my ego! Today she forgives and joins me for dinner and Claridge's sleepover, and holds my face in both her hands and says, "I'm very proud of you, Swaz! From Swaziland to the Actors Centre to here has been some journey. You deserve it all." Choked me up. Joan's iron-clad belief in me is something I will *never* forget.

In 1985 she was accent coaching at both the RSC and National Theatre, and always insisted that I accompany her to first nights of the plays she'd worked on. I was an out-of-work actor, and there was one legendary casting director who I met multiple times, at these events, over three years. Blank-faced me on every occasion, even though she knew Joan really well, and while I accepted being invisible on the first few encounters, I felt acutely embarrassed at every subsequent blanking. After *Withnail and I* was released in 1987, she came up to me, full-force-friendly, and declared how thrilled she was to see me again and that "we *have* to work together." Never did.

When my career fortunes shifted, it was Joan who had to readjust and accommodate to being my plus-one at premieres and press junkets, which she found understandably uncomfortable.

Lavish breakfast in the dining room, where all the waiters seem to roll in and out on invisible castors. Nothing to sign as Fox are footing the bill for everything. Then it's back to business. Five hours of six minutes per slot, TV interviews with journalists from around the globe. This requires real acting chops, repeating the same anecdotes with enthusiasm and sincerity, as if newly minted. Helped by Melissa, who is as sunny-spirited as ever, laughing at my nonsensicals.

Most especially when a New Zealand interviewer, with a basso profundo voice, prompts me to observe, "It sounds like you've got ten-gallon-sized testicles."

Melissa yelped and asked, "Where the hell does this stuff come from in that head of yours!"

Luckily, he took it in good spirits.

The growing awards noise around our film requires that

Joan and I fly back to LA for more publicity duties. Nothing so grounding as an early dinner at Il Piccolino with our pals Catherine O'Hara (whom I've known since we played husband and wife in *Penelope*) and her production designer husband Bo Welch. Anyone who's seen Catherine's Moira in *Schitt's Creek* will know why we started laughing at "Hello" and say "G'night" on a cackle, many hours later. They provide perspective on all the awards-go-round, Bo having been nominated three times for an Oscar, and Catherine memorably played Marilyn Hack in *For Your Consideration*, Christopher Guest's mockumentary in which she's hilariously deluded that she's going to win.

Bo wisely advises that, "No matter how much you try not to let it affect you, it just does. Even when you know that you don't have a chance, just go for the ride. And Catherine and I are both sure that you're going to get nominated."

Joan squeezes my leg under the table. Being able to share all of this with her is what makes *everything* worthwhile. Writer-producer Mitch Glazer and his wife, Kelly Lynch, intro themselves at the adjacent table and add a spoonful of praise to the proceedings. Come time to pay our bill, and informed that uber-agent Toni Howard has already taken care of it. *That's* a first. I challenge anyone to resist feeling a little light-headed after an evening like this. By 10 p.m. we're the only diners left, with staff standing around like it was already 2 a.m. That's LA.

November 2018: Governors Honorary Oscar Ball

Vast ballroom, somewhere in Hollywood. Meet up with Melissa, as our spouses are not invited.

"Don't feel guilty, Swaz, it's a relief for me not to have to go."

Into the cocktail party fray and the first person we stop and talk to is Emily Blunt, whom I'd met at Jessica Chastain's wedding in Venice last summer. Introduces me to her husband, John Krasinski, who is curiously bashful. Moment he is distracted by another actor, she leans in and whispers, "This is a big moment for him. He was so jealous that we'd met in Italy, as he can recite *every* line of *Withnail and I*." Who knew? Certainly not me, so I reciprocate his unspoken compliments by congratulating *him* on writing, directing, and starring in *A Quiet Place*. "Please assure me that the studio didn't cosmetically account your movie a 'loss'?" Instantly beamed and revealed that the budget was $35 million, and the box office gross $350 million! Nothing quite so satisfying as an actor-writer-director reaping the rewards for a change.

Next it's Lupita Nyong'o, Emma Stone, and Nicholas Hoult. All praise, praise, *praise be*! Can't help feeling that *everyone* is glad to be included on this guest list, and *everyone* is shamelessly rubbernecking everyone else.

"You're both perfect! Perfect. In the perfect movie. Congratulations!!" This approbation, *loudly* proclaimed by

Tom Hanks, who is standing beside Steven Spielberg. I could have kissed him! Both of them, actually. Rita Wilson then chimes in with her husband Tom. *Her* too. The room tilts on its axis. As far as my eyes can see, it's populated with very familiar faces, hob-mobbing in every direction. We are summonsed to our respective tables, for which I'm told Fox Searchlight have paid an eye-watering $60,000, which tallies at $5,000 per head!

First course is a communal plateful of snacks, including Oscar-shaped biscuits with smoked salmon and caviar. Our director, Marielle Heller, producers, and Melissa are no sooner seated than there is an upward swell of guests relaying around the ballroom, for some between-course meet and greet.

Melissa grabs my hand and says, "Follow me." Our tour includes pit stops with Clint Eastwood, slightly stooped, but indelibly Dirty Harry, Thunderbolt, and Josey Wales (seen at the Swaziland drive-in way back when all of *this* was a teenage pipe dream); Hilary Swank, who greets me like we're old buddies; and now it's Nicole Kidman (whom I'd proposed to in Jane Campion's movie *The Portrait of a Lady* in 1995) swanning elegantly towards me, saying, "I hope you win every award coming your way, 'cos you're heartbreaking and brilliant." No denying the sea-change from her polite greeting at Telluride eight weeks ago, before she'd seen the movie. Feels like being given temporary membership of the elite Fame Club.

Next stop, Lady Gaga. Diminutive and enveloped in a

voluminous black dress, with hair/wig the colour of grey-white paint that's been left in the tin for too long. As dead-looking as she is vibrant, immediate, and engaged. Vulnerability comes off her by the megawatt. Generously details how Bradley Cooper surrounded her with the best of the best, and was so collaborative and caring for her during *A Star Is Born*. Chatted for fifteen minutes, then throng back to our table, passing Harrison Ford, Calista Flockhart, Quincy Jones, Timothée Chalamet, Oprah Winfrey, Ethan Hawke, and Spike Lee, for the commencement of the awards.

Cicely Tyson, at ninety-three, accepts her honorary Oscar, forty-six years after she was first nominated. The beauty of the event is that the winners know in advance and there is no time limit on their acceptance speeches, as it's not televised.

Lalo Schifrin, who famously took three minutes to compose his iconic *Mission: Impossible* theme, is introduced by Clint Eastwood and, just as he gets under way, the autocue blacks out. Prompting him to riff down memory lane about their collaboration on *Dirty Harry*. Two old friends bantering back and forth, as if none of the rest of us are here.

Never been in a room full of people standing-ovating as often as this illustrious one. It's like a black-tie and ball-gown workout. Every time we bob up, another familiar face smiles back. John C. Reilly, Kathryn Hahn, Rachel Weisz.

Edith Wharton observed in *The Age of Innocence* that,

"Americans want to get away from amusement even more quickly than they want to get to it."

No sooner had the final honorary Oscar been awarded than there is a well-dressed scramble for the exits. Corralled downstairs to the vast underground car park, which is an instantaneous clusterfuck of limos and town cars, ramming for first position. Uniformed staff wave orange slips of paper, yelling out numbers, like a coat-check for cars. Utter chaos. Under the brutal fluorescent lights, all vanities are bonfired and facelifts cruelly exposed. Takes ninety minutes for my driver to appear around the concrete corner. Time enough to observe the hierarchy in action. The vehicles belonging to Messrs. Spielberg and Hanks and Oprah Winfrey hove into view ahead of everyone else's, despite their arrival way after the rest of us. As befits Hollywood deities.

Somehow satisfying seeing this A-list crowd plaintively waving their car tickets, in between catching up with each other. This has to count as my all-time favourite car park fame game! Fleetingly feels like *everyone* is your friend, as there's nothing quite like the approval of your peers and luminaries to balm your ego. Only heartsore that Joan wasn't with me, to share in all of this.

"I'm too jet-lagged and too short to have enjoyed that kind of bunfight, Swaz."

Flew back to London, followed by a 6:30 a.m. pickup and drive to Pinewood Studios for more *Star Wars*. Make-up team enquire: "Been up to much since we saw you last?"

They've all just returned from a month's desert shooting in Jordan. Being back in the same costume and space station set feels Groundhog Day–like. Hoping that the new dialogue will come out in the correct order. Although I seemingly walk and talk normally, jet lag is playing havoc with my memory department and the words are gobbledy-gooking in every direction.

Our director, JJ Abrams, is button-bright, and as sparky as if it was the first day of filming. His brain is set to permanent overdrive, as he sets up shots, constantly readjusting and trying to find the best and most unusual way to shoot a scene. Amazing laser-like precision and his vast crew and cast follow his lead, to the Moses.

Take one, and the lines all come out of my mouth in the correct sequence. After which they go on a tour of jumble and giddy-up. By take twenty-two, I shamefacedly request paper and a Sharpie to write out the wretched sentence, and stick it beside the lens. Take twenty-three, and it's done. Mercifully, no one bats an eye about this.

JJ declares that "the attack sequence on the Death Star has to be amped up." Meaning that previously filmed scenes are now obsolete. Meaning that JJ is now to and froing between two units, setting up reshoots and new sequences. All of which he manages without *ever* appearing impatient or hassled. A marvel.

Just before the final set-up, notice five missed calls from my agent, and check in.

"You've won the best supporting actor award from the New York Film Critics Circle!" Just when jet lag and publicity campaign fatigue had set in, this news is mightily welcome and surprising.

Wednesday, May 26, 2021

To High Wycombe, for my first day filming on *Persuasion*, which Joan insisted I do. Cast as Sir Walter Elliot, possibly *the* vainest man in literature! Therefore fun to play such a deluded, entitled old snooty-pants. Everything's in a state of haribadari as one of my "daughters" has contracted Covid and had to be replaced overnight. The familiar industrials of filming at odds with my estrangement from the whole rigmarole. Acting as though everything in my life is normal.

Usual moan of actors, already kvetching about the schedule, corset discomfort, and the catering. *Plus ça change!* Feel like an interloper looking in on this goldfish-bowl world, whose big fish is Dakota Johnson, my other daughter, who is charming, flirty, and gilded with youth. I am the *oldest* person in the cast *and* crew and it's a welcome distraction to earwig the young cast talking about their diets, love lives, and career plans.

Feel like a magpie returning to Joan in the evening with some glittery morsels of gossip, while she's been generously kept company by Sue Gutjahr.

After she leaves, Joan murmurs that, "I feel like it's all

over, Swaz, and I'm just waiting. Worrying about my looming MRI and CT scans. Every day just blending and bleeding into the next one."

What can I say to comfort her? Alleviate her angst? Words fail and I just gently hug and hold her.

"I have nightmares that I'm standing on quicksand and being pulled under, then wake up completely panic-stricken."

Rock her back and forth like a baby.

Friday, May 28, 2021

Julie Legrand, who was Joan's bridesmaid at our Richmond registry office wedding, visits and time-warps us back to when we first met at Joan's Actors Centre classes in late 1982.

Julie had worked at the Glasgow Citizens Theatre during its halcyon years when run by the triumvirate of Philip Prowse, Robert David MacDonald, and Giles Havergal, in the seventies and early eighties.

I subscribed to *Plays and Players* magazine when I was a teenager, and religiously read Cordelia Oliver's reviews of their extraordinary-looking productions. Fired further by their full-page ads which featured semi-naked actors sprawled across mirrored tables, replete with a Coke can nestled beside a mound of white powder. Their production images were sexy, violent, and operatic in scale and there was nothing else in the magazine that came close to their distinctive look. Cementing my determination to work there, *one day* . . . in that far-off future that stretches endlessly beyond adolescent reach. The closest I could get in the meantime was to learn the names of all the actors that regularly worked there, as though this would somehow stand me in good stead, so that when I *was* accepted I'd be on first-name terms with everyone. *A teenage boy can dream!*

When I was twenty-four and emigrated to England at the end of April 1982, it felt like a portentous omen that the plane I boarded was called the *Glasgow*, and on landing at Heathrow the first thing I bought before catching the bus was a copy of *The Stage* newspaper. In the classified ads section, there was a distinctive large black box announcing: "Glasgow Citizens Theatre Company. Open auditions at the Round House Theatre" in a week's time. *Surely* this was a sign? I had arrived with a suitcase, Walkman, stash of cassette tapes, and huge hopes. Giving myself five years to get regular-*ish* work as an actor. Failing which, I'd have to return to Swaziland and open up a roadside pineapple beer stall.

What audition speech to prepare? How to make a distinctive impression on that trio of directors who are so particular? In my fevered excitement, I decided that the opening speech of *Richard III* was the perfect choice, especially as I was going to deliver it from a cross-legged yoga position, while using my arms to perambulate myself around the stage, like a crippled beggar I'd seen in

Swaziland. Oh, and wearing an old tuxedo, which I bought from a charity shop.

Got to the Round House on the appointed day at 8 a.m. for the 10 a.m. start, to find that there was already an endless queue and informed that I had no chance of being seen, and to come back tomorrow. What time? Told that today's hopefuls had queued since 2 a.m.! *Ye gads*—truly daunting, as was the sharpness of everyone's cheekbones.

Got there at 3 a.m. the next morning, frozen to the bone, and got chatting with an actor in the line called Valentine Pelka, who had exactly the kind of aquiline face favoured in all their production photos.

Finally made it inside the Round House and given a friendly welcome by wardrobe mistress Trisha Biggar, who quietly assured me that "you've got the look, I'm sure you'll get in." Resisted picking her up for a hug and snog!

Six hundred were interviewed, 150 asked back to audition, thirty recalled, from whom fifteen among us would be chosen for the autumn season. This process took place over a *loooooong* fortnight.

After I'd concluded "Now is the winter of our discontent," balancing on my right knee, crossed legs suspended in the air to the left, while precariously pressing both hands into the stage to keep from toppling over, Giles Havergal diplomatically asked, "And just *how* do you anticipate doing a full-length performance in that position?"

Never occurred to me until this moment, so hellbent

was I on making a strong impression. Gingerly unfolded my legs and contorted my tongue into a byzantine explanation that doesn't bear repeating.

"*Interesting*," was the cryptic response from the trio seated in the dark stalls.

"*Never* seen it done like that before."

Which, in my naivety, I took as a compliment. They appeared curious about my encyclopaedic Citz Theatre knowledge, and asked where Swaziland "actually was." As this was now the third time I'd met them all and had had time to chat up Trisha Biggar while waiting in line, I felt that I was *almost* on my way to Glasgow. During the agonising week awaiting their promised letter, I went to the Criterion Theatre to see Dario Fo's play *Can't Pay? Won't Pay!*, starring Paola Dionisotti, who had worked at the Citz. Waited at the stage door afterwards and invited her for a drink, which she generously agreed to, filling me in on how wonderful it was to work there and giving me hope that, having made it to the final thirty, "you might have a real chance."

Checked the first postal delivery at 8 a.m. Nothing. Then the second delivery at 11 a.m. on Friday, May 21, 1982, and the Citz logo was on the envelope. *Heart pounding.* Tore it open and my legs buckled.

"Many thanks for auditioning, but regret that we cannot offer you any work in the acting company in the Autumn Season, but you are now on our casting list and may use you in the future."

Forty-eight hours of abject misery, moping in my bed of broken dreams, wondering where to begin.

All of which Julie found hilarious when I recounted this after the dialect class with our teacher, Joan Washington. When I reeled off the names of all the Citz actors I could remember, she assumed that I *knew* them all, and indulged my geekery with details about the various productions.

Years later, when I played a supporting role in *The Age of Innocence*, Daniel Day-Lewis told me that he, too, was obsessed with the Citz when he was starting out. Relieved to be in such mighty good company, *neither* of us having succeeded in making it to Glasgow.

And here's Julie, a lifetime later, *still* friends and compassionately keeping Joan's flagging spirits afloat.

Followed by a week of lemony-irritability, where nothing I do is right. Grateful when "Wing Commander" Julian Wadham and Tanya Bird swoop in for lunch. Both so charming and full of cheer that we can momentarily forget how grim our situation has become. He was at Ampleforth with Rupert Everett, where they played all the female roles in their school plays, the stories of which *always* amuse and delight us. Julian willingly obliges with an encore of their greatest hits, making Joan laugh again.

Chapter Seven

June

Tuesday, June 8, 2021

Rupert Everett drives up from Wiltshire for lunch, refuses to use his satnav—"It's not reliable"—opts for a map instead, gets hopelessly lost, and arrives late. Proffering home-grown irises, roses, and freshly laid eggs.

"*All* for you, Munchkin."

He anointed her with this diminutive nickname, from his lofty six-foot-four-inch gaze, many years ago. She has remained steadfastly loyal to him, despite his published self-assessment which reads: "Interior me—devious, superficial and bored."

That this capricious creature should stay for three hours truly surprises, considering his bored-ometer attention span. Regaling her with how his 86-year-old mother has taken to swimming in the river every morning, in the nude. Like everything else he tells you, you can't help wondering how much of it is *actually* true. What he always *is,* though, is witty and entertaining. Which I suppose is his point.

"I've just finished playing a gay stroke victim, so might as well go straight to the Oscars now, darling, as I'm a *shoo-in*."

Texts that it took him three hours to get home, instead of ninety minutes! Hopelessly lost *again*. Whether true or not, he made us laugh.

December 2018

Golden Globe nomination for best supporting actor! Oilly and I are midway through lunch in Nailsworth, Gloucestershire, when this pings into her phone. In twin-time, our mouths emoji "O"s. OMGs back and forth between us, as we try to contain our excitement. This critical wave of good news happily washes my face every day with more wins coming my way from multiple USA critics.

Leaving a Christmas party, a grandee I've known for years bobbed her head and confessed that she and her illustrious husband "found your film rather funny. You know, the *Forgive Me* one. Yeeeeeeeees, we eeeeeven managed to stay awake till the end"—as though this was some kind of miracle of endurance! Managing to be patronising, complimentary, and entitled, in that idiosyncratically British way that joshes and bullies simultaneously.

Prompting me to uncharitably, silently ponder, "So what

the fuck have *you* done, madam, other than target wealthy men and finally bag an old titled badger?"

Dinner with Lord and Lady Bamford and twenty of their friends in the silver room of the newly rebirthed Annabel's club on Berkeley Square. Joan Collins swishes in, surveys us all, and demands, "So who's here?" with the appetite of an anaconda. Couple of guests banter about the Golden Globes this and that, but the majority seem blissfully ignorant of it all. Hilarious!

On our way home, *my* Joan reveals that the man she was seated beside confessed that he'd not been able to get an erection for the past five years. *Never* ceases to amaze me how she manages to get people to reveal their innermosts to her. Squeezes my thigh and says, "Never going to happen to you, Swaz!" It's one of the delights of our marriage, comparing stories on the way home. As delicious as Boxing Day leftovers.

In early January 2019, Joan, Oilly, and I fly to Los Angeles, knowing that I've already won the New York Film Critics Circle award, to be picked up next week, which sweetens the journey.

"You're one of only five actors on the planet, Dad, who's been nominated in your category, and you're going to be in a room full of everyone you've watched and admired your whole career long. Enjoy the ride!" Which I fully intend to do.

Day of the Golden Globe Awards, which I'm so excited about attending with my family. Tuxed up and into a car to join the endless queue of vehicles heading for the Hilton Hotel in Beverly Hills. Our driver declares that our accents are *exactly* like his former client, Roy Harrison. "From Liverpool," brother of George. No kidding. Except that when I google the Beatle's siblings, Roy isn't named as one.

Way before we even get to the red carpet, there is a security checkpoint, with metal detectors, sniffer dogs, trunk of car opened and inspected, tickets and passes examined by the heavily testosterised police presence. Roads closed all around the hotel, making it a vast one-way system. It takes an hour to travel the 2 miles from our hotel to this one.

Finally poured out on to the crammed red carpet, with bleachers of fans raked on one side, looking and sounding like a scene from Nathanael West's *The Day of the Locust*. Screaming and selfie-snapping anyone and everyone they recognise below. Publicists, agents, and managers shuffle and guide their clients along the phalanx of press from across the planet.

Inside, it's like Madame Tussauds for *real*. Everywhere you look, there are actors you've known your entire life, talking to one another, in casting combinations that you've never seen before. The tables are crammed together, and you're shoulder to shoulder, perfume-clashingly close. *No* food! Just sweets and booze. I'm seated beside John Krasinski and Emily Blunt, alongside director Rob Marshall and John DeLuca, opposite Dick Van Dyke (ninety-three) and his wife Arlene Silver (forty-six), Ben Falcone, Joan and Melissa McCarthy. As a Globes veteran, she has wisely brought a bag of ham rolls to sustain our table and generously hands them round. I scoff six of them in quick succession.

Dick Van Dyke looks younger than he did in his old-age make-up as the chairman of the bank in *Mary Poppins*. I have a thousand questions I'd like to ask him, but the noise level makes that impossible. As Joan teaches actors' accents, there's some irony in being seated so close to the man whose cockney in *Poppins* is *the* benchmark for what *never* to sound like. He smiles at everyone, 'cos *everyone* clearly feels reciprocal affection for him, having played such an emblematic role in our childhoods. Two hours into the show, during a commercial break he loudly declares, "Oh, my God. My butt is dead! The only person I recognise in here is Carol Burnett!" Who, at eighty-five, is ramrod thin and upright, palpably moved by the prolonged standing ovation accorded her honorary Golden Globe Award. I spy Timothée Chalamet, who sees me and instantly does *Pulp Fiction* dancing "V" fingers across his face.

The actual Golden Globes ceremony seems secondary to the commercial-break schmoozathon, with people table hopping or bobbing back and forth to the bar or bathroom. *Interrupted* by having to return to their seats for the next round of awards. The level of excitement at reconnecting with people you've worked with before, or fan-dancing with people you've long admired, is like an electric charge through the room, during every advert break.

Realise that the majority of the nominees will all be losers by the end of the night. My category goes by very quickly and, apart from a slight heartbeat bump, it's a given that Mahershala Ali won for his role in *Green Book*.

Having so longed to be invited and included in this hallowed club of the Hollywood elite, it feels curiously underwhelming, and I cannot fathom just why. Guess it's the ego-jostling, attention-seeking antics of it all. Exchange looks with Joan, who is feeling *exactly* the same thing. Even when Julia Roberts, whom I last saw in Paris shooting *Prêt-à-Porter*, twenty-four years ago, leans in for a hug, kiss, and hi, as though we were in touch a week ago.

Oilly sums things up, thus: "I wouldn't have missed it for the world, but having been once, would happily never go again."

In bed by 1 a.m., then alarm-called at 3:45 a.m. for the dawn flight to New York, sleeping all the way, from Californian sunshine to minus-degree Manhattan. Where the New York Film Critics Circle Awards are being presented. Meet Steve Martin on the red carpet, as he has generously agreed to make a speech and give me the award. Incredibly touched and moved by Steve's hilarious and heartfelt tribute to me. That oddity whereby you publicly hear a friend extol your virtues, in a way that never happens face to face. And usually only after you're dead. He quotes from the Bible-thick collection of faxes and emails we've exchanged over the past three decades.

Tuesday, January 22, 2019

Back at home. Slept intermittently, and all morning the internet and my email inbox persistently ping info, odds, and good luck messages, in advance of the 5:20 a.m. PST announcement, aka Pacific Standard Time in LA, when the Oscar nominations will be announced at 1:20 p.m. in London. This is the moment that's been predicted, forecast, call it what you will, throughout the past five months. The "O" word has either been mouthed or mooted in print, without actually being named, for the collective fear of jinxing it all. My mind see-saws between the conviction that my name will *not* make it on to the list of five nominees, and all predictions to the contrary. *Doubt.*

Wonder if all the other contenders are going through the same mental hoops and emotional jangle. No matter how much I try *not* to take it too seriously, it's a deadly serious business.

How will it feel if it *does* happen?

How bereft will I feel if it *doesn't*?

Pick Oilly up and drive to Mediterraneo restaurant in Notting Hill, which we've been going to for two decades. Almost empty and we "will it/won't it/will it" happen, between mouthfuls of pasta. She positions her iPhone against a salt cellar, and hands over one of her headphones to listen and watch the live feed from Los Angeles. My category is usually announced within the first ten minutes. Unsure if that's better or worse. And, within no time, they're naming names, which appear on the screen behind them.

Mahershala Ali

Adam Driver

Sam Elliott

(NO *Timothée Chalamet*?! Means *I'm* toast! In the nanosecond this thought synapsed, my name is announced and appears on the right of the screen.)

Richard E. Grant

Sam Rockwell

We both stare in *utter* disbelief at the miniature screen, look at one another, and simultaneously burst into tears. *Nothing* prepared us for what this would *actually* feel like. For this unreality to become *real*. Rather than the room just turning upside down, it felt like it'd revolved a full 360 degrees, at Mach 2 speed.

Flavio, the maître d', bent over with enormous concern, assuming we'd just heard some tragic news. Reassured him and the adjacent punters that *all was well*! More than! Phoned Joan.

"Oh, my Swaaaaaaz, I'm *so* proud and pleased for you!"

Two minutes later, Peter Capaldi, whom I've been friends with for three decades, called and congratulated, followed by my agent and her office, all on speakerphone, at full communal yell. Phoned Melissa and we were both sobbing like we'd just seen *E.T.* Followed by a never-ending queue of press calls from LA, and a cyberlanche of texts and emails from my friends and colleagues.

I've parked around the corner from where I'd rented a tiny bedsit at 89 Blenheim Crescent, in 1982, after I'd emigrated from Swaziland. Before Notting Hill Gate became *Notting Hill*. The thirty-seven-year trajectory of my life and career struck me so forcibly that Oilly's iPhone recorded my wild-eyed response at having begun my London life here and now landed an Oscar nomination. Posted it on Twitter and Instagram and it went viral, clocking up 3.3 million hits. The positive response was utterly flabbergasting. Complimented left, right, and centre for being so undisguisedly delighted and emotionally open. Being uncool seems to have momentarily rendered me cool. Haha!

"We're all right behind you and hope you win!"

People I've not seen or heard from in forty-five years have found a way to send congratulations, and, by the end of the day, it seems like *everyone* I've ever met has made contact. "You so deserve this" repeats and repeats. Oilly sagely observes that this is the kind of approval you only usually get when you're dead, and unable to appreciate and savour it all. Baked and *bask* in goodwill. For *every* moment that it lasts.

Finally get home and the three of us group hug in absolute jubilation. Am utterly, butterly over the moon and dancing around inside my head.

For the next few days, everyone I walk past or meet is smiling and congratulating—a truly surreal, unparalleled experience and, as Tom Hanks and Pat Doyle pointed out, "You'll always be an Academy Award nominee, to the end of your days."

Been trying to define precisely what the nomination sequence has felt like. And it's this: imagine walking out of your front door and a bunch of strays come and lick your legs. Get to the gate, and bigger pooches appear, get up on their hind legs for a cuddle and stroke, and now you're feeling the love, *big* time. And *then*, you get an Oscar nomination and the entire street is barking at the moon, and, like the Pied Piper, you're happily hounded, followed, wag-tailed, and pounced upon by the friendliest pups on the planet. *Knowing* that this all stops on February 24th. *Woof, woof!!*

Wednesday, June 9, 2021

Picked up at dawn and driven to a stately pile outside Salisbury for the well-worn routine of "hurry up and wait" which characterises *every* film I've made. Sideburns glued on, hair bouffed up, and costumed in Regency splendour to signal the staggering vanity of "Sir Walter." Amplified by huge portraits, on every wall, with my superimposed

"Give me a child until he is seven and I will show you the foundations of the man." —Aristotle

With two-year-old Oilly, kissing it better

REG, Neo, and Joan in Gloucestershire

Oilly and Joan in Provence

Joan and Oilly, two peas in my pod

Incognito and Oilly

Checkmate in LA

Oilly, our supreme and perfect being

Diamond Lil, Scrabbling

Florian, Oilly, and Joan: our final Christmas dinner together

Joan and Oilly, inseparable

Marrying the Colonel—Richmond Registry Office,
November 1, 1986

Paul McGann and I, Withnailing

Chez Uncle Monty's cottage, aka Richard Griffiths and REG

"Old Spice" and his Spice Girls harem

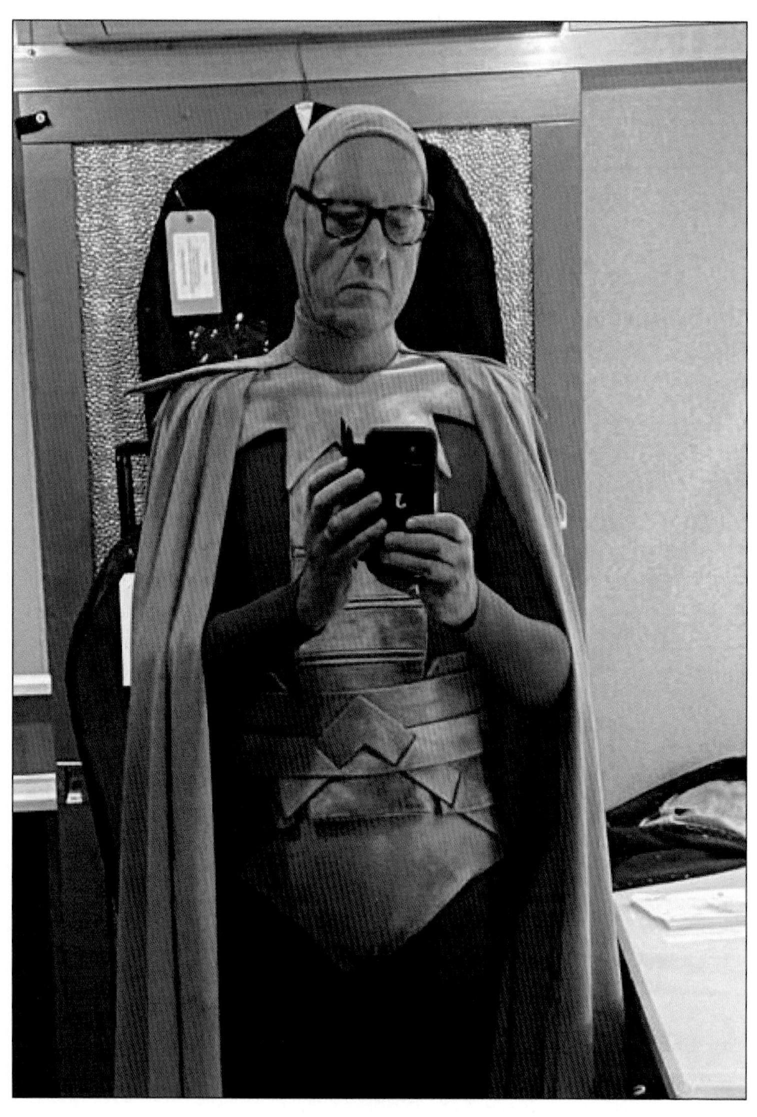

The MMF Loki suit—Miserably Muscle Free

Spot the Stars—shameless Oscars selfies

Oilly and REG at the 2019 Oscars

My new best *Friend*(s)

With Melissa in Palm Springs

Dear Barbra Streisand

I sincerely hope this reaches you personally. You don't know me yet, but I am writing to offer you an idea you might like to consider. My name is Richard and I live in a small African kingdom called Swaziland in south-east Africa. Since seeing Funny Girl we, my family that is, and I have been very big fans. I have followed your career avidly. We have all your records. I am fourteen years old. I read in the paper that you were feeling very tired and pressurized by your fame and failed romance with Mr Ryan O'Neal. I would like to offer you a two-week holiday, or longer, at our house, which is very beautiful with a pool and a magnificent view of the Ezulwini Valley. Which the Swazi people call Valley of Heaven. I think you will agree when you see it. Here you can rest. No one will trouble you and I assure you you will not be mobbed in the street as your films only show in our one cinema for three days, so not that many people will know who you are, so no chance of being mobbed. Please consider this respite seriously. You will always be welcome.

Yours very sincerely,
And in anticipation of a hasty reply,
Richard

PS I am studying Shakespeare's Midsummer's Night's Dream and hope these lines will reassure you: Theseus-'For never anything can be amiss when simpleness and duty tender it', or Puck-'If we shadows have offended, think but this and all is mended. That you have but slumber'd here, while these visions did appear.'

Yours,
Richard

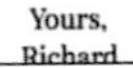

Fan letter to Barbra; beside her sculpture; outside her gates, a fan beside himself!

REG and Barbra Streisand—a fan for 53 years and counting

face. This is theatre director Carrie Cracknell's first film and she has taken to the process like the proverbial duck to H_2O. Her crew are all calm and friendly, and it's as if no time has passed since I last parachuted in for my first day, two weeks ago.

Dakota Johnson is so petite, it's a wonder all of her organs can fit inside her waist. She's all smiles and beguiling charm, and indulges my questions about her father Don Johnson's relationship with Barbra Streisand.

"They were together before I was born" underlines my decrepitude. "Why do you ask?" Prompting me to give her a paragraph's worth about my half-century-long obsession. Makes her laugh and reveal, "I don't hero-worship anyone."

"That's because you're an adult, Dakota, and I'm a 64-year-old adolescent!"

January 2019

If you've ever been a fan of someone, beyond adolescence into adulthood, like I am, then you'll fully understand what you're about to read.

Joan and I are in LA for yet more pre-Oscar publicity duties, and on my one day off I suggest: "Let's have lunch on Malibu pier." Joan agrees and we motor up the coast, under a perfect blue Californian winter sky. "Please indulge me, but as it's early I want to take a little detour." Headed to the former Streisand estate that she donated to the Santa Monica Mountains Conservancy, comprising five houses on 24 acres. Turned off the motorway, beyond Malibu Colony, wound up the hill and down, got lost, and asked someone for directions. "Oh, but you'll need an appointment. You can't just turn up." Drive towards Ramirez Canyon, undeterred. Pull up outside the open gates, where a group of workmen are repairing the impassable road. Either side blackened by the recent catastrophic fires. The foreman confirms that it's closed to the public due to the devastation, but that "miraculously, all of the houses are intact."

"Oh well, it was worth a try."

"I'm sorry, Swaz."

Nose back on to the highway, stop at the T-junction, google her street address, then beg Joan's indulgence "to just drive past."

She looks at me, shakes her head, and smiles. "Well, we're here, aren't we?"

Slow down as my heartbeat speeds up. Round a corner and there it is.

Her gates on the curve of a cul-de-sac. Instantly recognisable. Park up and Joan demands, "What the hell do you think you're doing?" Finger to my lips. She lowers herself in her seat, while I head for the intercom. Press the buzzer.

"Please may I take a selfie outside the gates?"

"Hold on."

Minutes later, a man appears from a side gate and enquires, "Which company are you from?"

"None. I'm a lifelong fan of the owner and requesting permission to take a selfie in front of her gates."

"It's a public road, so go ahead. But thanks for asking."

What was I hoping for? Adolescent fantasy that she might appear or just be returning home? Not even that specific. Just a thrill, being *this* close. Getting *this* far.

"Feel better now?" asks Joan.

I can *feel* the smile fixed across my face. Tweet my selfie alongside the fan letter I wrote to her when I was fourteen years old. Hoping that this would ameliorate my looking like some crazed stalker.

Dear Barbra Streisand

I sincerely hope this reaches you, personally. You don't know me yet, but I am writing to offer you an idea you might like to consider. My name is Richard, and I live in a small African Kingdom called Swaziland, in South East Africa. Since seeing *Funny Girl*, we, my family that is, and I, have been very big fans. I have followed your career avidly. We have all your records. I am fourteen years old. I read in the paper that you were feeling very tired and pressurised by your fame and your failed romance with Mr. Ryan O'Neal. I would like to offer you a two-week holiday at our house, which is very beautiful, with a pool and a magnificent view of the Ezulwini Valley. Which the Swazi people call "Valley of Heaven." I think you will agree when you see it. Here you can rest. No one will trouble you, and I assure you, you will not be mobbed in the street, as your films only show in our one cinema for three days, so not that many people will know who you are, so no chance of being mobbed. Please consider this respite seriously. You will always be welcome.

Yours very sincerely,

And in anticipation of a hasty reply

Richard

PS. I am studying Shakespeare's *Midsummer Night's Dream* and hope these lines will reassure you: . .

Theseus—"For never anything can be amiss when simpleness and duty tender it," or Puck—"If we shadows have offended, think but this, and all is mended. That you have but slumber'd here, while these visions did appear."

Drove back to Malibu pier for a post-pilgrimage, al fresco lunch. By the end of which my Twitter and Instagram posts have provoked an *astonishingly* positive response. Pressing that collective teenage idolisation button in those far-off but never forgotten, poster-on-the-bedroom-wall, years.

Post goes viral and become a news item. Now panicked that this most fiercely private of superstars will be poisoned against me, for impertinently turning up outside her home. At the end of press duties in LA, Oilly phones from

London and asks, "Have you seen Barbra Streisand's tweet to you?"

I can hear her pals cackling in the background and ask if she's pranking me.

"No! I'll read it to you."

I can feel my face crinkling up and eyes spouting.

> Dear Richard. What a wonderful letter U wrote me when you were 14! And look at you now! You're terrific in your latest movie with Melissa. Congratulations and love Barbra

Every word committed to memory. *Instantly*. The timing of this, precisely a week after the Oscar nomination, spins my head off its axis.

She *replied*. Barbra *replied*. Barbra Streisand *replied*!

Within twenty-four hours, it's become a news item all over the place, and being commented on as a "unique awards campaign in its own right." As though it was some pre-planned scheme. Which couldn't be further from the reality. Rather than being trolled online, people are cyber-cheering at the sincerity of my 14-year-old's fan letter. *Cynicism* be damned, for once!

To see my name and face alongside Streisand online feels like the most unexpected prize in itself. Win, win, *win*. Joan earns even mightier love and respect from me for her forbearance of this lifelong obsession, and for gamely attending the Screen Actors Guild Awards, knowing that she finds *all* the hoopla a challenge to keep smiling her way through. She returns home on the evening flight. I fly to New York to meet Rachel Syme from the *New Yorker*, who is taking this Streisand-obsessive on a tour of the key sites of Barbra's former years. In direct response to my viral tweet. First stop is the housing estate at 3102 Newkirk Avenue in Flatbush, Brooklyn. Looks like a prison building, *really* bleak, in acute contrast to the multi-house clifftop estate she's created in Malibu.

Then to Erasmus Hall High School on Flatbush Avenue, where I'm dismayed to find no mention or sign of Streisand *anywhere*. Rachel clearly finds my pilgrimage amusing. Asked the security guard beside the school's metal detector if I could have a look inside. No-go.

No matter—just being in her *actual* neighbourhood gives you a visceral sense and texture of life here that nothing else can provide in quite the same way.

Drove into Manhattan, to the Village Vanguard jazz club where she'd performed. Locked. Funny thing about visiting the places where your idol has lived and worked, unless they're *there*, it's just a *door*. Exactly like Napoleon surmised: "What is a throne? It's just a bench covered in velvet."

Final stop is the Winter Garden Theatre on Broadway where she played in *Funny Girl* for two years. If I *were* religious, this would be my church or temple. Walk around the stalls, imagining what it must have been like to have seen her, aligned with the bootleg audio recording I have of her final performance.

Rachel reveals that she's already interviewed my idol, albeit on the phone, and was smitten. "She's writing her memoirs at the moment and told me that the only chapter that's been easy is the one about her passion for Marlon Brando. Even visited his private island."

Reassured to know that she too feels awestruck by someone else's talent.

February 4, 2019: Oscar Nominees Lunch

Everything has been planned down to the minute, like a military manoeuvre, to process 212 nominees into the ballroom of the Beverly Hills Hilton, via a python's worth of press bites. Everyone is smartly dressed and guided to pose in front of a backdrop of miniature Oscars, then herded into the ballroom for a drink and opportunity to mingle among the fellow chosen folk. Brazenly ask whomever I'm speaking to if they're willing to have a selfie, and mercifully no one refuses. Within no time, I've developed a mild case of "smiling rictus" syndrome, with my first-name-terms compadres—Gaga, Rami, Mahershala, Glenn, Viggo, Spike, Adam, Sam, Rachel, Yorgos, Guillermo, Bradley, Amy, Regina, Chadwick, Marc, Melissa . . . you get the idea. This is getting beyond pinch yourself. More like punch yourself!

There is an unmistakable sense of excitement and ease, as it's not the actual ceremony, enabling us all to feel like winners. See Chris O'Dowd across the throng and beetle up to him to thank him for inadvertently providing me with this opportunity (as he was cast in my role, when the movie was going to be done with Julianne Moore). We'd previously worked together on a BBC costume drama. It's a measure of his grace and generosity that he's able to congratulate me, without baring his fangs!

Lunch is served and the Academy president, John Bailey, makes a speech, with the stern proviso that winners have ninety seconds to get from their seats to the podium, speak, then retreat. Feels like the headmaster giving a year-end review.

There is a six-tiered semicircle grandstand, like half of a giant wedding cake, dominating the room. Each nominee is ushered to an assigned position, with our names announced by Laura Dern and individually applauded as we take our places, like a school prize-giving. Spike Lee is the first name called and, en route, touches the 2-metre-tall Oscar that's positioned in the middle of the half-moon. The AMPAS class of 2019 is duly snapped, followed by a clamber down and scramble off to the next press appointments.

Back to the hotel at 3:30 p.m.

Change of clothes and stylist Barbara Guillaume is back for more primp and paintwork at 4:30 p.m. *Just* in case I've aged drastically since 9:30 a.m. As she's getting paid by the studio, who am I to say no?

The reality is that *this* event, the AARP Movies for Grownups Awards, is affectionately known as the "Old Age Awards," with only guest presenters and winners attending, rather than a clutch of nominees. Even though given advance notice, it's *still* a thrill to *win*. So, for a change, it's Viggo, Spike, and yours truly who get up and receive, rather than sitting back and applauding our younger Usual Suspects.

Catherine O'Hara introduces my award with a sling of plaudits, which feels a bit like hearing your own funeral oration.

Our mutual friend, Martin Short, is the host for the evening, and manages to gleefully insult almost everyone present with a loo-roll length of incontinence and Alzheimer's jokes.

What's odd is that no one gets to *keep* their foot-long, gold twist-shaped award. It's retrieved offstage, wiped down, and sent back on with the next presenter, to "give" to the next recipient! Told in a sharp whisper that "this one's a fake and the real one, with your name engraved, will be posted at some future date." As Alice would say, "Curiouser and curiouser!" Especially as the winners know *in advance* that they're getting one, giving the AARP ample opportunity to have them engraved, *or* is this just in case the recipient keels over *at/before* the event and no point wasting one, *or* could it be that it might to be too heavy for ancient hands to hold on to?

This *somehow* puts *all* awards shenanigans into perspective. They only really mean something to the winners, and, even then, it's a *very* brief moment of glory. *But*, welcome all the same. Don't get me wrong. I'm a lifelong movie buff, but if you asked me who the Oscar winners were for the past five years, I'd pause and struggle.

Got to meet Shirley MacLaine, the twinkly-eyed "broad" of yore, who has metamorphosed from gamine to gravelly grandma, without missing a career beat in between. No disguising my delight when she crinkles her eyes up and recognises *me*. Every movie I've ever seen her in flashes across my hippocampus!

Following the awards, it's a hop and a skip across the lobby to the bar, with Catherine, Bo Welch, and Marty Short, where we park ourselves until the staff finally turn on all the lights. Prior to which, Marty, consummate performer that he is, comedy riffs to the manor born. Requiring no prodding to do an impression, and in homage to the old-age theme of the evening, conjures up Katharine Hepburn in her shaky dotage, followed by his encounter with Bette Davis on a chat show. Catherine matches him, with her impression of Lucille Ball *trying* to sing. One of those impromptu nights, where two talents collude, and like the miracle of the loaves and the fishes it feels like we're in the midst of a multitude. Which becomes *reality*, when hotel guests, emboldened by booze, crowd up and request that she yell "*Keviiiin*" into their *Home Alone* iPhones.

Wednesday, June 9, 2021 (cont.)

"How long have you been married?" Dakota asks.

Trip-switches me to lean in and whisper our situation. Her eyes well up and she hugs me close.

Persuasion filming finishes late afternoon, ahead of schedule, and check into the hotel in the centre of town, which doubtless due to Covid restrictions and the knock-on effect of lockdown feels like *The Shining* meets *Fawlty Towers* with a dash of the Bates Motel. No one in sight and when the receptionist finally appears she struggles to find my booking, like searching for a sixpence in a Christmas pudding. Whole joint feels neglected and abandoned. Tripadvisor reckons that a Chinese takeaway is Salisbury's best option. Mosey up the road to a Côte instead and am their only customer, apart from two drunken Squonkers who've been here since lunchtime, braying at top volume, wearing their customary mustard and burgundy cords.

"So where do *you* see yourself in ten years' time?"

This overheard question neon-lights up the lack of time that Joan and I have left. Call her and she answers immediately. Even though I've only been gone a day, she sounds excited to talk and catch up on my doings and dictates the list of books she wants me to buy.

Am acutely aware that she's *alive* and *there*. Sharing our days, like we've done for the past thirty-eight years. Asks me to discreetly angle my phone in the direction of my squiffy neighbours, to enjoy their ramblings. Identifying where they each hail from. *Attagirl!*

Slept for nine hours. First time in a long while and mightily restorative.

Thursday, June 10, 2021

New scene. New costume. New set. Feel like a *new* man.

The break has given both of us time to clean-slate to "woof" mode. Return home with a bag of new books, and welcomed back like Santa. Social media mania about the Disney+ release of *Loki* last night. Was in just *one* episode and have been "discovered" in my pensioner years by a new generation.

Here's how *my* Marvel Comics cookie crumbled.

October 2020

During that brief lifting of Covid restrictions in October 2020, am flown to Atlanta to be in *Loki*, the spin-off TV series from the blockbuster Marvel movies, starring Tom Hiddleston. We'd met socially many times and joked that we could play father and son as we have a slight physical resemblance. Which I assume is the reason I've been cast to play "Classic Loki," aka the pensioner version.

Despite all the critics' awards and nominations from the year before, am riddled with self-doubt. You'd think that this would have eased up by now, but, like an unwelcome visitor, it *always* comes a-calling at my door. Best get down to the script and memorise my way out of the doubts.

Quarantine in an Atlantan hotel, which is deserted. Staff look like they're on zombie duty. Kate Herron, the English director, attempts to introduce me to the world of Loki, via Zoom, but am blaming my jet lag for only understanding every fourth sentence. Tom Hiddleston, having played the role for eleven years, is a self-confessed *Loki*-paedia and entreats me to call on him "anytime you have a query."

Only human contact is Nurse Tara, who arrives to do a PCR test, describing everything in such forensic detail it feels like we're in an episode of *Grey's ER Anatomy*. Which roughly translates as: "Hold still while I insert a long-stemmed earbud up your nostril, count to ten, then up the adjacent tunnel for ten twiddly seconds."

"Mission accomplished—results in the next twenty-four hours by email or text."

"Where's your next port of call?"

"Oh, *that's* confidential. I'm not at liberty to disclose that"—with all the gravitas of an FBI operative. Which is not belittling her important job in *any* way, it's just the weight with which she answers my query that invisibly marks the cultural difference between Americans and Brits. My lighthearted flippancy met with deadly seriousness. Recalling Oscar Wilde's aphorism that "we should treat all the trivial things of life seriously, and all the serious things of life with sincere and studied triviality."

Finally get to go to Pinewood Atlanta Studios, which is a forty-five-minute drive out of the city. The health and safety chieftain ticks off all my nods to his questions, clearly disappointed that I've denied him the opportunity to test/mobilise emergency forces. *No* disrespect intended, but it does sound like *Movie of the Week*.

Deep breaths and into the costume department where costume designer Christine Wada has me slithering into a Kermit-green Lycra onesie, yellow balaclava, gold helmet with horns, yellow pixie boots, and baggy old-man shorts with a wide belt. Ye gads. The mirror-reflected image is *worse* than I anticipated. I genuinely look like a muscle-free old pixie in a provincial pantomime.

"Why no muscle suit like the Jack Kirby original cartoons, *and* your costume sketch where I *do* have muscles?" I'd hoped that this was my *one* legitimate opportunity to have the muscles I've never possessed in real life.

"You look *great*."

"Excuse the pun, but am I supposed to look *comical*?"

"No, you *look* like Classic Loki."

Resolve to email the director and producers to request a cloak, as per Jack Kirby's drawings, with some shoulder pads to give the *slight* illusion that I have a V-shaped torso. To their and Christine's credit, they agree to give me a cloak and a little chest padding, and to V-shape my baggy pants to look less gramps-ish. Asked Christine who's the most *challenging* actor she's ever encountered, hoping that I'm not top of her list.

"Dustin Hoffman is the most detail-orientated actor I've met. Eight hours for a fitting is not unusual."

Meet Owen Wilson, who speaks in his signature *wow* voice, all convoluted vowels and "hehehe" charm, like someone dope-dropped in from another planet. Albeit an authentically American outpost in the Milky Way. Instantly *bonded*.

Tom Hiddleston friendlies over and says, "Oh my God, you have *no* idea how excited people are going to be seeing you as Classic Loki. I bet you're feeling a little out of it now, but, believe me, it's going to be *immense*."

"But, Tom, I'm only in one episode."

He's having none of it. "Just you wait."

First day shooting and Owen Wilson makes my day, gossips, yaks, asks questions, and reveals that he was a young observer in 1991, when I auditioned for James L. Brooks's *As Good As It Gets* movie in LA, while I was filming *Dracula*. "I remember Jim asking if you were gay as he was casting a gay character and how he got you to improvise for half an hour." Have *no* memory whatsoever of anyone else in that director's office, and am completely taken aback. (Greg Kinnear got the role.)

"You must have been a *child* back then?"

"I was, I was twenty-three."

My turn to grill him about working with Woody Allen and Wes Anderson, whom he was room-mates with at college.

"I was studying English, never thought of being an actor, until Wes wrote a play and asked me to be in it." At fifty-one, he's like a perpetual teenager. Engaged, funny, and fast. On set, he is allowed to improvise and extemporise lines, making it all sound casual and conversational.

Tom, by contrast, strikes me as someone entirely led by his head, rather than his heart. Everything is immaculately prepared and delivered with incredible conviction. Finely sculpted features, aquiline and cut glass in both cheekbone and accent. His discipline is extraordinary—gets picked up at 5:30 a.m., runs 3 miles in the studio gym, then plunges his face into a basin of iced water, to begin his working day. His conversation is peppered with mythology, Norse gods, and cross-referenced with the Marvel Universe. Despite having played Loki for eleven years, in multiple movies, he is as passionate and keen to share his *Loki*-ology expertise as an undergraduate in freshers' week. It's surprising and very endearing.

Sense that playing Loki *is* his life, and his investment in all things *Loki*-centric is absolute. Not like a method actor, but just all-consuming of his attention. Realise that I have *never* felt so single-minded about a role, and admire his singular purpose. He is also the *only* actor I have ever encountered who doesn't have a negative word to say about anyone or anything that he's worked with or on. *Unique.*

Owen zigzags and alters the angle of a conversation in an almost stream-of-consciousness way. Talks very openly about his three stints in rehab to conquer his addiction, lives between Malibu and Hawaii, and, when talking about women, quotes F. Scott Fitzgerald's Gatsby who said that, "I didn't have the top two things—great animal magnetism or money. I had the two second things, though, good looks and intelligence."

All the women I ran this by thought that he had *all* four of those things, *and* he's funny! Back in the make-up trailer, after we'd wrapped, he said, "Fine work today, Richard."

"Thank you, Owen."

"No, I said *find* work, Richard."

This might not *sound* funny on the page, but his delivery is pitch-perfect and really *funny.* Describes himself as being in the sweetie shop of life, with the temptation of new places and faces to explore and discover, *everywhere*. So, monogamy is anathema, whereas his friend Wes Anderson has been married forever. Looked at me with genuine bewilderment when I told him that Joan and I had been together for thirty-seven years, with that expression people usually reserve for discussions about whether dinosaurs *actually* existed.

In his early fifties, he exudes a little boy lost quality, with his shaggy blond hair and pouty lower lip, like an adolescent who's forever on the cusp of adulthood. He has a fluidity and mercurial essence that slips through your fingers. No sooner are you yakking between lighting and camera set-ups than he bicycles off to his trailer. As though there is always something more enticing for him, just around the corner. Making you value all the more what time and witty attention he *does* give you. Completely present, then just as rapidly absent. Like the best magicians, leaving you wanting more.

My father was an addict, as is one of my best friends, Bruce Robinson, so no surprise that I'm a willing moth to the flame of their charismatic company. In my experience, they are hilarious, uncensored in their views, and mercurial of mood, which lends every encounter a particular edginess and danger. Only got to work with Owen for a couple of days, but it's been a 24-carat gold treat. Instant camaraderie and the unlikely hope that we'll get to work together again. He signs off with this juvenile joke:

"Knock knock."

"Who's there?"

"Owen."

"Owen *who*?"

"*That's* show business, Richard! In a nutshell! Here today, *forgotten* tomorrow!"

Tom Hiddleston invites fellow Brit DeObia Oparei, who plays Boastful Loki, and me to his penthouse apartment for dinner at the weekend. Panoramic views of Atlanta and a delicious dinner cooked by Tom. He asks if I've had analysis, which segues into comparing childhoods. Tom was sent to boarding school at seven, and, unlike Rupert Everett's and my wounded sensibilities, it seems to have Teflon-coated him to make the very best of everything. Complimentary about everyone he's worked with and I can't help wondering what he *truly* feels and thinks.

Even though Tom is wrapped by lunchtime, he insists on staying to watch my Classic Loki finale. Which involves cranes, industrial-sized wind machines, and multiple cameras to capture a 63-year-old thespian, Lycraed-up and golden-horned, standing legs apart, Atlas-lifting up an imaginary city, while following the trajectory of a malignant storm called Alioth, which is destroying everything in its path, to which I defiantly bellow, "GLORIOUS PURPOSE!"

Our director, Kate Herron, tells me "how moving this will be for all *Loki*-ites." Tom concurs: "You've knocked it out of the park."

I'm grateful for their approval, but, unlike Tom, am riven with self-doubt and a feeling of having made a complete idiot of myself, shouting at the Krakatoan-force wind machines in my muscle-free Lycra suit!

Mercifully, the dramatic demise of Classic Loki, once they've added all the CGI, music, and sound effects, proves a big hit with both fans and critics, precisely as Tom predicted it would.

Tuesday, June 15, 2021

Feel like a packhorse, getting everything piled into the car for the journey back to London. Joan's breathing is very strained and her chest sounds squeaky. See Wanda at 3 p.m., who prescribes an inhaler to help Joan climb the stairs.

Wednesday, June 16, 2021

Joan is bedbound with exhaustion all day and night.

I at last speak to the guru cancer doctor in San Francisco, having waited four months for this appointment. He talked nonstop for two hours, during which I wrote *everything* down. Sowed doubt in my mind about the treatment being given by the Marsden, claiming that he had stage 4 lung cancer patients who had survived for ten years. Suggested that Joan be given another lung function test. Insinuated that he knew better, or is that just my mind playing tricks? Observed that chronic exhaustion and hair loss were the results of brain radiation surgery, combined with the side effects of the tepotinib drug, confirmation of what I had been told by the Marsden anyway.

Did his analysis give me hope? Nope.

No sooner was the consultation over than his office emailed the financial breakdown for any future calls, which would be "index linked to your annual salary." *Oh brother. Over and out*. Wife and daughter were quite right in refusing to go down this path when I told them my plan, all those months ago. *Ouch!*

Saturday, June 19, 2021

Back to the Marsden for the CT scan. Hospital is deserted. Everything feels calm, and we're in and out of there in half an hour. Back home to mow the lawn, replace light bulbs, chop rogue branches, and order Chinese takeaway for an early supper and respite from my cooking.

The Yen Saan Chinese restaurant opened in Swaziland in the early seventies and, even though my father became good friends with the owner, Joy King, he teasingly referred to *all* food that wasn't familiar, *including* spaghetti bolognese, as "foreign muck." With an ironic wink of course. Declared that the problem with Chinese food "was that the menu always promises edible fireworks, but, in reality, *everything* tastes the same, and half an hour later, you're hungry again."

Sunday, June 20, 2021

Father's Day—my mother Skypes from Africa, a month in advance of her ninetieth birthday, to report that she's won at bridge and is looking forward to watching Wimbledon. When I report that I'm the oldest person on *Persuasion*, she howled with laughter. "What's so funny?"—only prompting further cackling.

Invited to Walton-on-Thames for Father's Day lunch in the garden with the Doyle clan, who are all present and hilariously incorrect. Played badminton, tennis, swam in the pool, and sat around talking as if everything was normal in our world. If only, if only, *if only* it was . . .

I love this woman so, *so* much, but it's as if she's permanently jet-lagged, premenstrual and menopausal, *at once.*

Patience and forbearance.

February 20, 2019

Joan wakes up and says, "I've got something serious I need to discuss with you, Swaz. *Please* don't get cross. I've hardly slept and I *know* how much this means to you, but I don't want to go to the Oscars.

"*Hear me out.*

"I'm five foot three and those American women tower over me, and it's an absolute trial being shunted around like a piece of furniture. It was bad enough at the BAFTAs and you know how I find all that hoopla difficult to deal with, and I *know* that you'll have a much better time with Oilly. So *please* don't be upset, but I just don't have the endless energy that you have. You *know* how proud I am of you and I know how much this means to you, but I promise you, it'll be better without me there."

Am sucker-punched.

"But all three of us are booked to fly tomorrow."

"People cancel all the time. That won't be an issue."

"But it's the one and only time we'll *ever* go to the Oscars."

She hugs me and says, "Please forgive me. But I *really* don't want to go. Try to understand."

"But you've had that amazing dress made specially for you."

Stalemate.

Call Oilly, who is Kofi Annan–calm and diplomatically sees both our points of view, but reasons that what her mum is expressing makes sense and "*you* know in your heart of hearts, Pops, that Mum is right. It's a huge thing for her to admit to, but better that she's upfront with you now, rather than your getting irritated when she doesn't want to go to *every* party we're invited to."

Hangdog my way back upstairs and into each other's arms.

Oilly and I fly to LA at 10:35 a.m. and take sleeping pills to prep for the weekend of *all* weekends ahead. An official greeter eases us through customs and immigration and back to the Four Seasons Hotel. Fruit, flowers, and champagne are set out in the suite, plus the invitation pack to the Oscars. *Still* doesn't seem quite real.

Spend the morning with Oilly doing something that *very* few Beverly Hillbillies seem to do—*walk* around, comparing notes about the two events we went to last night. Then off to the British ambassador's tea party for British nominees, hosted by Consul General Michael Howells.

It's all a little stiff around the edges, including the curly-ended sandwich that I was about to chomp into when a woman friendlies up, with an expression of deepest condolence, declaring, "You must be *sooooo* disappointed going to all these awards and *losing* every time. How does that make you *feeeeeeel*?"

Of course she's a tabloid journalist, who clearly wanted/expected me to wobble and blub, but Oilly chipped in with, "Not at all. He's *won* thirty-seven awards already," and we smilingly shimmied away. Just when we thought we were in the clear, an email pings up with an article in the *Guardian*, with the headline:

Richard E. Grant's Oscar glee:
ingenue or a crafty campaigner?

Taglined with: "Film insiders prefer to believe actor's heartfelt joy is genuine rather than a deliberate ploy."

The article ponders "if, in fact, it is simply the work of a wily old pro." (*You mean the wonderment of this old pro.*)

Charles Gant, writer for *Screen International*, admits that he has never seen such a campaign "that has been so seemingly from an outsider and one so starstruck." (*Charles—if you could see the one-horse town I grew up in, you'd totally understand why, in an instant.*)

"For an Oscar campaign, Grant has broken all the rules," says Charles McDonald, a film publicist. "That is the beauty of what he has done. He comes across as incredibly, unfashionably, enthusiastic. He's loving it. It's fantastic. Why wouldn't you want to win. Of course he wants to win. And he's being disarmingly candid about it, which people are finding very endearing. It's a new approach and he is definitely bringing a very refreshing level of honesty to the proceedings." (*Thank YOU, Mr. McDonald.*)

The PR agent Mark Borkowski describes the campaign as "beautifully uncool." He said, "When everything is so manufactured these days, I think audiences can smell authenticity."

Ye olde tall poppy syndrome comes to mind. Perfectly timed to chop me off at the stalks, two days before the Oscars. Noticeably contrasting with the American *Esquire* magazine headline:

Richard E. Grant's unbridled joy is the best thing about awards season

"The 61-year-old actor is giving a masterclass on how to handle fame and fortune—by doing it like the rest of us would."

As the sozzled old barman in *Withnail* assures, "No man's put me down, yet."

To the beach! For the Film Independent Spirit Awards, which are being held in a marquee on Santa Monica Beach, beside the pier, at 12:30 p.m.

When Glenn Close announced my name as the winner, I practically levitated, fumbled, then *ran* to the stage and into Glenn's welcoming Close-armed embrace. Knelt to accept the award, stood up, then struggled to breathe *and* speak *and* think coherently. I read somewhere that the shock of winning unexpectedly is akin to being in a car collision. Am certainly hyperventilating, and everything is simultaneously speeded up *and* in slow motion. Adrenalin slaloming around my veins.

Nicole and Jeff won their joint screenplay award too, so in the *final* furlong, Fox Searchlight have winners *at* and awards *on* their table! If I were a crate of Coca-Cola, all my ring-pulls would be exploding at once.

The sunny Californian afternoon seems Swazi-brighter, to this son of! Text Melissa and Ben to ask if we can come over to their house tomorrow morning—"We'll bring croissants and eggs and cook breakfast for you all, as we hope to try and *normalise* this completely *abnormal* day for us." They readily agree and, once back at the hotel, we walk over to Whole Foods for supplies.

Long FaceTime call home, and acquiesce that Joan's made the right decision. Much as I'd love her to be here with us, her natural reticence would be at odds with my wide-eyed-in-Babylonics.

Sunday, February 24, 2019: Oscar Day

Really excited. Tried to sleep in late, but no chance of that! Uber over to the Valley with Oilly and scramble eggs for Ben, Melissa, Georgie, and Viv, in their enormous kitchen. Being in their home with children and dogs, rather than a hotel, is *just* what this doctor ordered and needed. Followed by some trampolining in the garden and a quick swim. As we're leaving, Melissa tells me that, "Paul Rudd is an insane fan of yours, so if you see him tonight, be nice, okay?"

"You're kidding me, right?"

"No, it's true. He really is."

Then back to the Four Seasons for our *final* grooming session with Barbara Guillaume, who has been endlessly supportive and encouraging throughout this whole ride. Into our glad rags, and picked up at 2:15 p.m. Truly bizarre to be dressed up for the night in the middle of the day.

Roads are closed and policemen guide, whistle, and gesticulate where to turn and twiddle. Jam of limos and sedans queuing up on Hollywood Boulevard, offloading their starry cargo on the edge of the red carpet outside the Dolby Theatre. It seats 3,400, which accounts for the car-cram. Triple-check that we've got all of our tickets and passes. Cannot quite believe that we're *actually* here. Sharing this once-in-my-lifetime experience with Oilly is *everything*. High-five one another before getting out of the car. The procession through the press takes almost two hours, and is an opportunity to meet and greet your friends, colleagues, and luminaries in between providing sound snippets to the press corps, all of whom are rubbernecking to see who is the starrier scoop coming their way. Accompanied by nonstop screaming fans on the bleachers. Once inside the foyer, we are ushered upstairs to a galleried section, dividing famous faces from the hoi polloi below. It's a continuous cavalcade of coutured, coiffed, and cinched women, the majority of whom look like they last ate a full plateful in 1974.

Ushered/herded into the auditorium for the 5 p.m. kick-off. We're seated just left of centre, a few rows from the stage, with Melissa and Ben to my right, and Oilly and Octavia Spencer to my left. Daniel Craig and Charlize Theron read out the nominees in my category, and there's no denying the thrill of hearing and seeing your name announced, applauded, and cheered by *this* audience. Mahershala's serious and sonorous thank-you speech is delivered with the calm and assurance of a foregone conclusion, and all of us are on our feet to reward him with an ovation for winning his second Oscar in three years.

During the commercial break, am tapped on both shoulders, turn around and see Tina Fey, Maya Rudolph, and Amy Poehler, *all* flashing the "L" sign with their index fingers and thumbs, chorusing, "*Loser!* Welcome to the Losers' Club!" Hilarious! And I'm not kidding either. Amy leans in and teases, "Admit it, Richard, you *must* have thought you had a 99 percent chance of winning, right up until the last second?"

None of this trio are buying my *genuine* retort that this was *never* even a remote possibility, and thoroughly delight in their impromptu joshing session. They're like the female Three Stooges. But *much* more attractive than Larry, Curly, and Moe!!

As we're seated on the aisle, every presenter comes past us, including Paul Rudd, who *kneels* in front of me and says, "I can't even look you in the eyes, I'm in such awe of your talent."

Adopted a stentorian tone and declared, "You're misinformed, young man. Now get up and look me in the eye." Melissa leans in and says, "I *told* you, didn't I?"

Almost every winner follows the set-in-stone pathway of previous awards. With one exception. Glenn Close has been nominated for the seventh time this year, is the bookies' favourite to win, wearing an Oscar gold dress with a long train, and seated in the middle of the front row. Olivia Colman, seated much further back and to the right, is announced the winner, and seems genuinely discombobulated that it's her, and not Glenn, clutching the gold.

My greatest surprise *and* reward is when Barbra Streisand comes on to introduce the best picture nomination for *BlacKkKlansman* and is given a standing ovation just for being here. And I am now hoping that she will attend the Governors Ball afterwards.

After the awards, there's a celebrity cattle-crush to get into the ballroom, to finally eat something, as there's been no food available *anywhere* for far too many hours. Unbeknownst to me, Oilly spots the sequined black beret that Streisand is wearing, some distance ahead, alerts Melissa, who then *grabs* my arm and frog-marches me to meet my idol.

"*Barbra, meet Richard.*"

Well, Swaziboy, you didn't win *that* little gold guy tonight, but *this* is the golden moment to top *all* of your goldens. My iPhone aloft and flashing before I've even secured her actual permission, while thanking her for replying to my 47-year-old fan letter tweet. Melissa is hilarious and tells me to breathe. Manage to string some sentences together, and pose for a formal photograph between Melissa and Barbra. Win. *Win.*

Then speedily down dinner at our assigned table, wondering if I can get back in there. Oilly warns me to, "Calm down, Pops, you've met her now. You look like a crazed madman."

"But I *am* right now, Oilly. Stay here. I'll be back."

And am up and off to the bodyguarded enclave, where she is in cahoots with my awards circuit buddy Spike Lee.

Nudge the bodyguard and, just as I'm about to try to blag my way past, Spike looks up and beckons me to join his fellow Brooklynite, Barbra, who asks, "You two know each other?"

Spike saves my bacon. "*Yeah*, sure. We go *waaaaaaay* back." And am laughingly included in this triangle. Talk revolves around feeling like eternal outsiders. During which she notices that the large art deco, lozenge-shaped brooch, strategically placed in the middle of her chest, has come unfixed and is now futzing to get it reattached. "Need my glasses."

"May I help?"

"Sure."

Swaziboy is now on his knees, before his lifelong idol, leaning in and taking his sweet time to get his fingers dexterously around that rogue pin, and making sure it's reattached. Veeeeeeeery. *S l o w l y.* No prizes for guessing that *this* is *far* closer than I ever dared imagine getting to her. Scent close. *Steady the Buffs, boy!*

"Thanks. You're very polite."

Stay another ten minutes, then excuse myself and retreat to find Oilly, who just shakes her head and says, "Just as well Mum's *not* here!"

A British journalist moseys up and asks why I'm looking so happy, having lost.

"Depends on how you define winning! I'm having the time of my *life*."

Clearly not what she was hoping for and beats a hasty retreat.

Marc Shaiman, multi-Oscar-nominated composer (including *Mary Poppins Returns*), has been staying in the hotel room across the corridor from us, at the Four Seasons, for the past month and become an instant friend. He suggests that I check my selfies.

"I photo-bombed you with Barbra."

And he *has*!

And with much ha-ha-ha, we all head for the *Vanity Fair* afterparty at another venue. On the way out, I see Barbra, way ahead of me, and just as I'm about to Streisand-sprint, Oilly grips my arm and stops me.

"Dad, you've had *two* meetings with her this evening. If you try for another, you'll blow it and she'll set the bodyguards on you."

"But this is my *last* chance."

Her common sense prevails, and we throng off to the next celebrathon—the *Vanity Fair* Oscar Party.

The guest list includes Melissa McCarthy and Ben Falcone, who've quick-changed into matching black track-suits and trainers, in prep for the party-thon ahead. Smart move. And *Barbra Streisand*.

Waiters dressed in white uniforms circulate with platters of In-N-Out burgers and booze. Glenn Close has exchanged her gold dress for a black number and is giving her all on the dance floor. Olivia Colman whispers up with a note and says, "Amy Adams and I are having a lock up later. Please come."

Try stopping me! It's only 10 p.m., but already feels like

4 a.m. Caffeinate up on Diet Coke and doubtless embarrass Oilly with some dad-dance moves. Feel like a toddler that's been let loose in a playpen of the famous. Wolf down four burgers, pay and receive compliments, acutely aware that, come midnight, our ride in this crystal carriage will pumpkin-bump back to reality.

Hand over Ms. Colman's slip of paper with the address to our driver, and take stock of everything before the next party. Park up and no sign of anyone, anywhere on this empty street. Worried that we're at the wrong house. Buzz the door and invited inside for some intimate mayhem. High heels are off, dresses hoicked up, and it feels like being a student again! Olivia's Oscar passed around, posed with, and noted for how surprisingly heavy it is. Amy Adams is doing karaoke and there's a cram of us queuing to make fools of ourselves. Mic in my hand and belting out Bowie's "Life on Mars?" with abandon, I clock that Oilly has her head in her hands, signalling that what I *actually* sound like *might just be* at odds with the *fantasy*. To have been able to share this ride with my daughter—the good, the bad, and the ugly vocals—has made all of it unforgettably worthwhile. Like her mother, she has a much more grounded and grown-up sensibility than I ever will. Dawn by the time we crawl back into the hotel.

And with that, it's over. Going to sleep for seventy-nine hours, having been awake for more than I can count.

Monday, June 21, 2021

Haematologist calls to say that Joan's blood test results look good. He is jovial, positive, and reassuring, which feels like a welcome injection of good news.

Tuesday, June 22, 2021

Joan is very antsy about her scan results, due this afternoon.

"I've seen everyone I want to, grateful for all the cards and messages, flowers and food parcels. Don't need any more. I thought that I'd feel normal on the tepotinib treatment, but I suppose that was being too optimistic."

Depressed, tetchy, and irritable.

"Feel like I'm fully retreating from the world. I'm sorry that you're having to suffer all this, Swaz."

Escaped into the garden while she napped, to mow, weed, plant, *anything* to divert myself until Wanda's promised call. Rang once at 3 p.m., answered on speakerphone, and knew in a nanosecond from her tone that it was grim news.

"I'm so sorry that I'm having to tell you this over the phone, Joan, rather than face to face, but while the brain lesions are under control post–radiation surgery, I'm afraid that the CT scan confirmed that the cancer has spread throughout the lungs and is now very aggressive. Tepotinib is no longer working, and I'd suggest that you come off it, as it's increasing your fatigue. The only option left is chemotherapy, which I wouldn't advise pursuing—"

"I won't have chemo, under *any* circumstances."

"Understood. I'm just *so* sorry that tepotinib has stopped working so much sooner than we thought it would. The palliative care and hospice advisor will be in touch shortly. Do you have any questions?"

"Yes. Will I be in pain?"

"We will do *all* we can to alleviate any. Are you in pain now?"

"No. Just very breathless."

"I'll call again at the end of the afternoon to confirm the radiologist's report, and again in a week's time, to discuss what we do next. I am *so*, *so* sorry, Joan. I didn't expect to be telling you this so soon."

"Thank you for everything that you've done for me, Wanda, and for always being so clear and honest."

Joan is outwardly calm and quietly says, "I expected this, as I knew the tepotinib had stopped working. I'm so sorry, Swaz. Please help me across the garden and up into bed."

We shuffle together in an intensity of silence. Completely *poleaxed*. The news feels devastating, having truly thought that this dreaded call was at least a couple of months away. Feel so stupid.

Yet, we've known the prognosis all year, why should today's news be so traumatic? Because tepotinib had given us *hope*—

Hope that it would extend her life expectancy.

Hope that it'd give us some normalcy.

Hope that is now hope*less*.

Called Oilly, who is astonishingly calm and says that she anticipated and had prepared herself for this moment. Feel profound failure as her father, incapable of protecting her from this brutal news.

Wanda calls at 4:30 to confirm the radiologist's report that the cancer has spread throughout her lungs, with no sign of further brain lesions or metastasis to her bones—"Meaning that she won't suffer any pain."

"How much longer do you think she will live?"

"As it is spreading so aggressively, I think six months, at most. I'm so sorry, Richard. If it spreads in the brain, it'll be less."

Count the months off on my fingers, which end in December, *this* year. Called Nigella as, more than anyone I know, she *knows* what this is like, having tragically lost her mother, sister, and husband to cancer. Her response is immediate and practical, putting me in contact with palliative care specialist Dr. Kathryn Mannix. Phone her and she quietly recounts a case study of someone whose diagnosis most closely matches Joan's. Offers to send me a copy of her book *With the End in Mind: How to Live and Die Well.*

Lie next to Joan as she sleeps. Listening to every breath she takes. Overwhelmed with longing. *Longing* that she won't have to suffer. Longing that none of this is actually happening to us.

L o n g i n g . . .

Wednesday, June 23, 2021

Aftermath and fallout. Having lived in daily dread of this news, there is a weird sense of relief and calm, now that we know. That there is *nothing* left to try. No more "is it working, or how long will it work for?"

Joan is very serene and sanguine this morning. "You know that I'm not superstitious or given to psychic notions, Swaz, but I predicted a year ago that I wouldn't live longer than 2021. I've known for a month that the drug had stopped working, as I felt so shattered all the time. Please promise me two things: that you will stay with me all the way to the end, and to let me die at home."

"I promise. On both counts. Till your last breath, Monkee-mine."

Called Oilly, who said that she'd phoned Joan earlier and they'd talked very calmly and clearly about everything.

Find myself sitting in front of the TV, iPad, and iPhone, alternating between three screens, absentmindedly seeking distraction until midnight. Finding none.

Thursday, June 24, 2021

Woke up feeling *very* depressed. Joan is having none of it and snaps, "Pull yourself out of it!" Obeyed and called the Longfield Hospice in nearby Minchinhampton, who advised that I firstly need to register Joan with a local GP in order to secure care with them in the weeks ahead.

Amazing difference between a London health centre and its country cousin. Get through almost immediately, without five options to figure out, or any obfuscation. Sorted very quickly and compassionately.

Joan has no appetite and is in bed by 7:30, leaving me downstairs to idle my evening away watching TV or trying to read. Neither holding my attention properly. Reappears at 10 p.m.—"Am having nightmares about dying. Can we talk about it?" We do for two hours.

"What do you think happens when you die?"

"I think it's like asking where you were before you were born. Or what it feels like once you've fallen asleep. We don't *know*. Have no memory, whatsoever. My father always told me that he found this very reassuring. That we *only* have the here and now. Nothing beyond. And nobody's ever come back."

"But you live on inside someone. You leave your mark."

"Well, you certainly have. You'll always be in me. In *everything* we've done and talked about, chosen and collected together. You've embroidered cushions in every room of our house and cottage."

"I suppose Oilly will auction all our stuff off at a fraction of what we paid for it, as Florian is a minimalist?"

"Well, neither of us will be around to worry about that!"

"Who do you think you're going to pair up with when I'm gone? I bet they'll be lining up and knocking themselves over like dominoes to get you. But I can't really see you with anyone else. They'll *all* drive you nuts. Except for . . . hmmm . . . then again, no. Her accent would annoy you after a while . . . Oh, *I* know, whatshername in Swaziland. *Yes!* Ideal for you. Then you could go back and live there in your dotage!"

She systematically goes through an extensive list of all the single women we know, in the most *loving* terms imaginable, while stealthily pinpricking each of their "prospects." She is on such funny and feisty form that it's as if the finality of all medication having failed has liberated her. At *this* moment, she doesn't seem terminally ill, *at all.*

Would never have guessed that talking so openly about death and what I might do after she's gone could be so funny and forthright. She has *always* surprised me throughout our marriage, but never more so than now.

Sunday, June 27, 2021

Emma Thompson and her Rwandan adopted son, Tindy, come over for tea and stay for four hours. She has the gift of making you feel like you've known her all your life. Warm-hearted, inclusive, with an unwavering moral compass. A warrior woman. Manages the tightrope act of accepting faults in her friends, without being two-faced when talking about them. Prompting me to ask: "Were you born fearless?"

"I think so, yes. Definitely."

Asserting this without a scintilla of arrogance. Just a statement of fact. Would gladly trade a limb to live my life free from fear! Talked about the late, great director Mike Nichols, whom Emma worked with many times, and she said that he defined people as either metallic or porous. She seems as steely strong as she's emotionally porous, but is essentially the latter.

Tindy sits beside Joan, holding her hand, like he's never going to let her go.

Tuesday, June 29, 2021

Joan asks if she can read Kathryn Mannix's book, which takes me aback. "Why don't you go to Kempton this morning, and I'll read it while you're out."

"Are you sure?"

"Absolutely."

It's the first time I've been to the antiques market this year, and my first time without her, but as she quipped as I was leaving, "My eye is in yours, so please bring me back something I'd have chosen." Done deal!

This may sound odd, but there's a lightness and buoyancy in her mood since being told that all treatment has ceased, which feels bizarrely life-enhancing. Somehow *not* knowing how long the tepotinib would work was more torturous than the certainty of it not. Acceptance and resignation.

For three decades, we spent our summers in the south of France, in a converted *pigeonnier*, which we bought when Oilly was six weeks old, and every Monday we drove down to Nice from upcountry, for the antiques market. I remember one morning, at the end of a successful shopping trip, we'd just got into the lift with all our booty to go down to the underground car park, when two substantially upholstered tourists attempted to get in with us. Like that scene from *In Bruges*, when Colin Farrell announces to three tourists that they can't go to the top of the clock tower "'cos you's a bunch of fucking elephants," Joan gave them the once-over and brightly declared, "Oh no, this is *never* going to work. You won't fit in," promptly pressing the close-door button, to the consternation of teenaged Oilly who admonished her with, "*Muuuuum!*"

"What?"

"You can't say that to total strangers. It's fattist."

"I had no choice. They would have squashed us to death!"

Scurried into the car and scarpered in case we were steamrollered four floors below!

Oilly came over after lunch, working remotely on her laptop from our bed, while Joan shared her thoughts about Kathryn's death manual and how we enthusiastically prepare for birth and marriage in the West, but daren't talk about death, for fear of it "catching."

"Just so long as I'm not in any pain, I'm genuinely *not* frightened."

Watched Wimbledon while waiting for Wanda's call, which rang in at 6:30 on speakerphone.

"I'm truly devastated, Joan, that the miracle drug stopped

working after only four months, instead of eighteen. It's been an honour to treat you and we all appreciate how open and honest you've been throughout the whole process."

"When's the next time I need to come in for a scan?"

Oilly and I exchange glances as Wanda pauses, then reconfirms, "You won't need to come in for *any* further scans, Joan. That's it."

"Well at least I won't ever have to return to the Marsden."

That's my girl. Diplomatic to the last!! Oilly and I can't help chuckling and we *all* chime in and thank Wanda for her expertise and care, as she signs herself "over and out."

"What?"

"*Mum!* Wanda *works* at the Marsden."

"So?"

"Sounded a bit blunt saying you'll never have to go back there."

"But it's true!"

Kofi Annan she's not, but her no-shit-Sherlock honesty is *vintage* Joan Washington.

Wednesday, June 30, 2021

5:15 a.m. pick-up for *Persuasion*, and driven to Ammerdown, south of Bath, an amazing country pile stuffed with covetables. It's light relief to play dress-up again and do a funny scene with Dakota, Yolanda Kettle, and my on-screen "crush," Lydia Rose Bewley.

During the relighting set-ups and camera track changes, we compare notes about the most selfish/cruel actors we've ever had the misfortune to work with, which makes for a very entertaining and informative confab. If I gave you the list, we'd all get sued, of course, but rest assured the usual suspects cross generations. The common denominator being a level of self-absorption that gobbles up every molecule of oxygen in a room, as though everyone else is superfluous.

Check into the Francis Hotel in Bath for the night and go out for solo dinner, as all the other actors are staying closer to the location. As I turn the corner off Queen Square and head towards the Theatre Royal, am reminded of the shock at seeing Joan walking towards me in 2005, when I was touring in Simon Gray's *Otherwise Engaged*, prior to the West End. She hadn't told me she was coming, hoping to surprise me and *did* so. I only had half an hour before I was due at the theatre, grabbed her, and we U-turned back to the Francis for some pre-show honeymooning!

Presages what lies ahead. *Everywhere* that we've been together, ghost-charged. But *right now*, she's alive, Swaz. Savour that. Gratifying to remember her when she was well. *Must* hold on to that.

Chapter Eight

July

Thursday, July 1, 2021

Mid-breakfast, text pings announcing Covid shutdown on *Persuasion*—a new PA who'd been in contact with Henry Golding, "Mr. Elliot," has tested positive, so I'm being sent home until further notice.

Race back to London and read out letters sent to Joan. First is from Miriam Margolyes:

"I adore you, Joan, and am crushed to realise what you're both going through. My fondest love. If I can do anything, just ask. But I imagine all you want is to be left alone. You are magic people and Joan will always be my hero. How lucky I am to know you. Arms around you. MM."

The second is from Emma Thompson:

> Dearest, darling Joan
>
> Now I've *seen* you, I feel able to write a proper letter with pen and ink and everything that's necessary

to convey what you mean to me. I thought Domhnall's message was spot on—cancer is a life-stealing BITCH and this is the worst news and no more can be said about it than that it is the worst. It can and must be the opportunity we all need to tell a person how very precious they are and this can only be a good thing.

When we did *Alone in Berlin*, you revealed such a loving heart during that job and to have you there was the most immense privilege. Not only because of the work, but also the opportunity to discover more of you and share so much as we did. I shall forever be grateful to you for your skills as a professional and your generosity as a friend.

But the thing I can never possibly thank you ENOUGH for is your unparalleled kindness to Tindy. He loves you, Joan, so much, you *gave* him so much, again way beyond the work, but deep into his soul your kindness and interest reached. You were and always shall be one of the *pillars* of his recovery from all the traumas. He will carry you with him forever.

The tendrils of love that connect us all cannot be uprooted by death and wherever this journey takes you, we will remain connected to you in the tenderest and most profoundly meaningful and sustaining way until it is our turn to follow you.

Ever with love and with you in my heart then, darling Joan,

Emma

"Until it's our turn to follow you" reverberates throughout the rest of our day. Reminding me of the scrawled note handed to me by a *very* old Swazi mourner, after my father's burial, which read: "Goodbye Baba Mathlaganipani. Do not forget us." (His Siswati nickname meaning "the man whose brain ran faster than his feet.")

The inversion of the usual "we will never forget you" precisely pinpointed the feeling of being left behind among the living. Death had somehow been given the aspect of a destination to which we were denied entry.

I was nicknamed Mondlwani—"the man whose head is in the clouds"—which is pretty much how I'm feeling at this juncture. *Trying* to keep my feet on the ground and *not* go spiralling off into the sky, projecting into the future.

Monday, July 5, 2021

Return to the Cotswold cottage and, while watching Wimbledon, Joan nudges me and asks, "If I run out of breath, Swaz, will I have to be in the hospital?"

"I'll do everything in my power to prevent that happening, Monkee. We'll get an oxygen tank for you, if needs be. Okay?"

She nods and looks up at me with her large, green eyes, like a five-year-old seeking reassurance. Sense that when these questions bob up, they're just the tip of her iceberg of anxiety.

Sophie Robinson video-calls to report that their daughter

Lily has Covid, and Bruce has gone into mega self-protective mode, roaming around the house in full Zorro mask and high dudgeon. So convinced was he of imminent catastrophe some years ago, when avian flu was threatening, despite the fact that "only in rare cases can it affect humans," that he shot all fifty doves in their dovecote "as a precaution."

Negotiating how to handle Joan's mood changes requires diplomatic skills beyond my reach. *Too* much enthusiasm and she gets irritated. *Too* little and she accuses me of being glum. The evening's menu options prompt a negative response.

"Don't want soup.

"Don't want pasta.

"Don't want pudding."

Leave her to snooze and, an hour later, she texts wanting soup.

"Why are *you* looking so glum?"

"Don't mean to, darling. Just feel like I've failed you today, unable to give you what you want."

"Not at all. Don't be silly. I've been very tearful and melancholy all day. Nothing to do with you."

Hold her hand and stroke her head, till she dozes off.

Tuesday, July 6, 2021

And it's still raining. And Joan spends all morning in bed. Scrambled eggs and Marmite toast for lunch, then Wimbledon. For such a fiercely energetic and independent woman to be immobilised and becalmed like this is palpably frustrating for her. Always self-reliant, but now having to beck and call her every whim via me.

Oilly calls and details her incredibly stressful work schedule and how low she feels about her mum, but when I hand the phone over to Joan, she is all positivity, sweetness and light. Genuinely staggered by this young woman's resilience and compassion. *Staggered*.

Wednesday, July 7, 2021

Skype my mother, who is ninety today. Already been to the hairdresser, thrilled to receive my flowers, and is about to drive off and play bridge, chain-smoking her way through our entire chat.

Gabriel Byrne drives across from Cardiff to have lunch, as he's not filming today. Asked if he could sit beside Joan, on our bed, and stays put there for the next ninety minutes, plate-spinning philosophicals, anecdotage, and ruminations about life. All delivered in his lilting Dublin accent that bears *no* trace of his past thirty-three years in Manhattan.

When he played my father in *Wah-Wah*, he was *always* to be found, both on and off the set, surrounded by women, of *all* ages, transfixed by his storytelling skills. So involved does he get, that eating seems like an unwelcome distraction, and I don't think I've ever seen him consume an entire plateful, preferring to share an earful instead.

Joan signals that she's flagging and needs to nap. Gabriel and I retreat into the garden and he asks how I *really* am.

"It's a *real* challenge trying to remain buoyant and positive with her, when the dread of what's fast approaching is so all-engulfing."

"How angry are you?"

"I am not angry really. She smoked thirty years ago and I think about that and naively wish that she'd never started. But then I Skyped with my 90-year-old mother this morning, who chain-smokes, so what do I know?"

"Not fair, is it?"

"Nope."

Friday, July 9, 2021

Joan slept well and apologised for being so grumpy and negative this past week. Managed to dress herself and insisted that we sit out in the garden, beyond our bedroom doors.

"I feel like I'm fading, Swaz. Just getting weaker and weaker every day. Really don't want to see anyone. Feel so unattractive and unentertaining. I feel like I need to retreat, completely."

Totally understand, but it's very isolating, especially as she's now asleep more than awake. Compounded by the lifting of Covid restrictions, which has *everyone* scrambling to go abroad for some summer sun, while we sit here beneath solid grey skies, with only the odd peep of sunshine every other day.

Have to return to London for the weekend as filming

Persuasion at Osterley Park in Isleworth and hoping that a change of geography might help her in some way.

Sunday, July 11, 2021

Wondering how best to navigate around Joan's melancholia and hypersensitivity to *everything*? Just hang in there, Swaziboy. Just hang in there. Remember your vows: "in sickness and in health."

Live so close to the location that I'm given permission to go home for three hours while they're filming another scene, meaning that I can watch the Wimbledon men's final with Joan. She is immeasurably revived by Matteo Berrettini's arms and charms, about whom she declares, "I'd like to take a bite out of *him*! Let's have pasta for supper."

While I can't offer her the former, the latter is a pleasure to cook for her! Fresh crab linguine. *Viva Italia.*

Wednesday, July 14, 2021

Oilly works remotely from our house, as am doing the press junket for *Everybody's Talking About Jamie* in central London. Sound-biting all day about what it was like to play a Sheffield drag queen.

Reminded that this was the final role which Joan coached me for, and how we fell back into our real-life former roles, of teacher and pupil, when we first met in 1982.

Whereas she was professionally patient with me, way

back then, this time she's as intolerant as one family member foolishly trying to teach another how to drive. *Very* impatient and *very* strict.

"You'd make a fearsome dominatrix!"

"*Concentrate!* I'd forgotten how *irritating* you could be. Now do it again, and *stop* flirting with me."

"Worked first time around!"

"You better get this right, because I can't have people thinking I'm no good at my job if you sound like Dick Van Dyke."

Truth is, I'm terror-stricken attempting a Sheffield accent, shooting *in* Sheffield, and *in* drag. Spent two months working with Joan, and grilling drag artist David Hoyle about every aspect of his life. Aided and expertly abetted by Jonathan Butterell's direction, Guy Speranza's costumes, Guy Common's make-up, and Nadia Stacey's Thatcherite wig, which, combined with the leopard-print heels, elevated me to a lofty 6 foot 7 inches, while trussed and tucked uncomfortably below. *Plus,* singing coaching from Anne-Marie Speed and dance and high-heel-wearing classes with Shaun Niles.

Getting ready for filming felt like being a vintage Ferrari pulling in for a pit stop, to undergo a total transformation in three seconds, except this ol' crock took three *hours.*

My father's concerns about my becoming an actor ringing in my ears: "Do you *really* want to spend your life wearing make-up and tights?" His crystal-ball-gazing, verified by my dragging up as "Loco Chanelle" and subsequently getting kitted out in Kermit-green Lycra, playing Classic "Old" Loki.

Joan and Oilly giving giggling encouragement when I practised tap dancing around the kitchen, wearing vertiginous platforms.

The *joy* of those evenings now feels like a lifetime ago, as we all sit eating takeaway fish and chips on our bed. Oilly tells me later that she'd helped her mum take a shower, and how traumatic that was. Experiencing how breathless, fearful, and incredibly vulnerable she's become.

"I think you're doing a wonderful job, Pops, 'cos I see that it's *really* difficult."

Her compliment wobbles and undoes me, with her recognition of just how challenging *caring* has become.

Thursday, July 15, 2021

Paid off, as Joan has the courage and fortitude to shower and wash her hair *on her own* this morning, dresses herself, and asks if we can go to Gloucestershire earlier than planned. This *sounds* like such a simple day-to-day routine that you'd never think twice about doing, but it near exhausts her severely depleted energy reserves.

"Oilly was absolutely brilliant with me yesterday. Brilliant. *Much* more patient than you are."

Ignored the sting in her tail, *grateful* that she's on semi-restored form.

"You're absolutely right. Oilly's our supreme and perfect being. *Much* more patient than I'll ever be."

As we drive down the M4, she says that she has pain in her left lung, for the first time, and that it "feels deep." Pull into the nearest motorway services and call the GP in Nailsworth, who is incredibly kind and patient, and, even *more* incredibly, advises to get paracetamol or ibuprofen over the counter.

"Will that seriously be sufficient, in her condition?"

He tempers my incredulity with reassurances that "if the paracetamol doesn't work, call me back, and I'll prescribe something else." Neither Joan nor I believe him, and can't help wondering if he's even read her medical files. Lo and withhold our scepticism, but by the time we get to the cottage, the pills have totally obliterated her pain. The dread of when it will return now hovers invisibly.

Once settled in, I take both her hands, look her in the eyes, and beg her forgiveness for "being impatient" and tell her that I love her "completely and utterly and am here for you, *every* hour of the day and night. I *know* that when you get crabby and irritable with me it's because you have to rely on me so much, so I'm asking *you* to be a little patient with me, especially when you ask me to do five things in a row. This is *not* a criticism, just trying to do my best for us."

Worked! She stroked my arms and, possibly prompted by my close proximity, segued into stories about her teenage boyfriends, imitating their assorted accents and chat-up lines. Or lack of.

Sassy Joan is back! She *never* ceases surprising me. I've *never* heard these stories before, and I thought I'd heard them all. She's certainly heard all of mine.

Phoebe Nicholls popped in for tea, plonked herself down on a low chair at the end of our bed, and has been doing so regularly on an almost weekly basis. Very low-key and calm. Just the way Joan likes it. Someone we have both known peripherally forever, but who has expressed her love and friendship with such steadfast devotion that we have become unexpectedly close. She instinctively knows when to leave and never requires more than a cup of tea to keep the conversation flowing.

Elizabeth McGovern texts a message that Joan asks me to read out loud:

> I'll never forget a period in my life when I was first in the UK, and I was sent to Joan to work on my English accent. I was driven to a magical house in Richmond. I was immediately enveloped, cosseted and lifted by the beauty you two had created together there. There were doll houses everywhere. Oilly was playing sweetly in the background. You were kind and understanding with me about being from somewhere else. Joan was nurturing and intuitive. You were an artist. It might not always have seemed so easy or magical to you. But Joan, and your partnership with her, fortified my vision for all that is possible.

We are both profoundly moved by her generous view of our marriage. Reiterating the same message we keep hearing about Joan's acts of kindness that haven't gone unnoticed or unappreciated. What's so poignant is how amazed she genuinely is by these affirmations. Especially when she's feeling so melancholic. Her gift for instilling confidence in her pupils and clients is something that cannot be taught, and, once experienced, is *never* forgotten. *Faith*.

Held each other's hands. Exchanged how much we loved each other, "for thirty-eight years and counting . . ."

"Now go downstairs and make me a cup of tea, Swaz."

Tuesday, July 20, 2021

Mercifully, the paracetamol continues to keep her chest pains at bay. Very aware that the maximum time she can meet friends, or go out, is an hour.

Sense that this will be the last time we go out for lunch together at William's fish restaurant. Ten-minute drive, two delicious courses, during which she casually says: "I'm genuinely *not* afraid of dying, Swaz. Just don't want to be in pain. *That's* what I'm most frightened of. Now I'd like the sticky toffee pudding, please"—segueing as casually as a jazz singer changing tune, then back to the cottage for a snooze.

Sounds so simple, described like this, but the reality is that it takes enormous willpower and effort for her to get out of the cottage and into the car, and to walk the few metres to the outdoor tables. Sue and Alex welcome her with open arms and help her settle in, then bring our food order out, *pronto presto*.

When she's asleep, take a stroll around the garden, trying to imagine my life without her, knowing that her voice will always be in my ear and her love always beating steadily in my heart.

Wednesday, July 21, 2021

Virginia Carrington emails from Buckingham Palace to ask if Prince Charles can drop in on Sunday at 12:30 before he departs for his summer holiday in Scotland.

Regretfully, we have to be in London that day. An hour later, she replied: "The Prince wondered if he could drop in today at about 2:30 instead?"

"Of course, yes."

Joan worries that she won't be able to stay awake. Compounded when we are visited mid-morning for the first time by palliative nurse Susie Baines, who has to ask very difficult questions, one of which is: "If you collapse and have a cardiac arrest, would you choose to be resuscitated or not?"

Her answers are clear, resolute, and pragmatic. Listening to their exchange is extremely confronting and upsetting. Understand why it has to be done, but that doesn't make it any the easier to hear. Moment Susie leaves, Joan confesses to feeling *very* depressed and overwhelmed and retreats into sleep.

Security officer calls at 2:40 p.m. to alert me that HRH "is five minutes away." Meet the Prince, who's dressed in a beautiful cream linen suit and carrying a bag of mangoes and a bunch of highly scented roses from his Highgrove garden. Instantly at ease, and complimentary about our cottage and garden, hugs and kisses Joan, then sits beside her on the sofa in the pergola, which we've nicknamed the Taj, as it's decorated with Indian panels, doors and lanterns.

"How are you, Colonel?"

"Thank you so much for the mangoes. They're my favourite fruit," and they chat nonstop for the next half hour. At one point, taking her hand and saying, "It's been an absolute *honour* to have known you, Joan," to which she quipped, "I'm *still* here!" which made us all laugh.

Talked of the spiritual journey ahead, the "armoury" of true love, full of empathy and tenderness. Intuited when she was beginning to flag, and, before taking his leave, asked, "Would it be okay if Camilla dropped in next week?"

Before he got into his car, he said, "I hold you both very dear in my heart."

Having held it together through his visit, and the upset of Susie Baines's questions earlier, I could hear my voice quiver when I quietly said, "Thank you."

Stood watching as he drove away, struck by Joan's gift for speaking to *everyone*, whether prince or pauper, in exactly the same way. Rejoin her in the Taj to find that his impromptu visit has galvanised and lifted her spirits immeasurably.

"Am truly touched and flattered by his visit, especially after I had to sign that palliative care form, giving my consent *not* to be resuscitated, 'in the event of.' *Bloody hell!* Do you think the Prince knew about your bloodied undies?" Made us both laugh at the memory.

Sunday, July 25, 2021

Joan gets dressed but decides to stay upstairs, reading in bed, rather than coming down for lunch with Emma Thompson, Greg Wise, Tindy, and the Doyle clan.

"Can't cope with that many people at once. Ask them to come up and see me in pairs, like Noah's Ark."

Which they do, arriving laden with flowers, chocolates, champagne, Scottish tablet (sort-of-fudge), compassion, and bundles of good cheer. Felt weird having a celebratory lunch together, knowing that Joan was upstairs, alone. They all stayed until 5:30, then two by two went to say goodbye to her. Suspect it's the last time any of them will see her. Sense that they feel this too, when they return downstairs.

Once they've all left, she asks me to sit close by her and softly says—

"I feel like I'm dying, Swaz. Feeling weaker and weaker every day. Please let me go. Don't fight it. Don't try and organise anything for me. Let me do it in my time. In my way."

Wept. Just held her hand and *wept*, engulfed and *utterly* overcome with grief.

Living grief.

Raw.

Savage.

Oilly and Florian returned from a wedding in York in time for a late supper. Hearing the wedding vows had knocked her sideways, knowing that her parents had lived *theirs* to the letter, acutely aware that when and if *she* gets married her mum won't be there to witness it. We have an incredibly honest and painful heart-to-heart. Told her what Joan had said to me, and how, as much as I didn't want to, I *have* to accept that we must *let her go*.

Monday, July 26, 2021

Joan slept through the night and is determined to begin the week as revived as she can possibly muster. Doesn't get up, though, and sleeps most of the day. Oilly came over after work and says that our talk last night had wiped her out. Feels incredibly raw and vulnerable, but has been hugely supported by her friends, who've reassured her that having bad days is a necessary purge. Kathryn Mannix wrote that terminal patients asking to be "let go" is a common phenomenon, near the end of life.

Tuesday, July 27, 2021

Lynda La Plante visited for ninety minutes and didn't draw breath once! Hilarious, passionate, opinionated, and full of impressions and asides. I first met her in 1985, during my nine months of unemployment, when I determined to try and gain a stone in weight and muscle, with the help of her then husband, Richard, who did bodybuilding. I'd read an article which claimed that if you're 6 foot 2 inches tall, you ought to weigh 12 stone. Convinced myself that my career prospects might significantly improve if I was the "correct" weight, hence gulping down weight-gain powders and pumping iron. She'd recently segued from actress to writer and gained instant success with *Widows*, followed by her landmark *Prime Suspect* series.

Apart from saying how well Joan looked "in the circumstances," she avoided *all* talk of illness, happily diverting us with the one-woman show that she is.

There's something of the Restoration comedy about her—"a flamboyant display of witty, blunt sexual dialogue, boudoir intrigues, sensual innuendo and rakish behaviour." Her formerly flame-coloured hair is now bright blonde at the front and Elizabeth I red at the back. Arrives and leaves in a theatrical swagger as if walking through her own invisible swishing curtains. As we descended the stairs, she Mrs. Malapropped, declaiming, "You *must* have this house recorded on film, *for prosperity*!"

Joan overheard her, and endlessly repeats it with the

relish of rolling a Werther's Original around her mouth and an "I *love* Lynda" smack of the lips.

As do *I*, for being such a good friend and cheerleader at this bleak moment.

Wednesday, July 28, 2021

Vanessa Redgrave, fragile at eighty-four, and her daughter Joely Richardson arrive mid-morning with country flowers and a cooler bag crammed with tubs of ice cream and sorbets from a farm shop in Hampshire. Impromptu feast on our bed. *Anyone* eating ice cream becomes a kid again, and it's instantly celebratory. Feels like *family*.

Vanessa quotes Dylan Thomas's "Do not go gentle into that good night" poem, which asserts that, "Old age should burn and rave at close of day; / Rage, rage against the dying of the light," asking Joan how she is able to be so calm and accepting.

"I don't have a choice, Van, nor the energy for anger."

Hard to reconcile that great Amazonian beauty of *Blow-Up* and *Camelot* with this frail, snow-white-haired octogenarian, *until* you look into those ice-blue eyes, which retain their mesmerism. Her idiosyncratic throaty voice is now fluted with age and immense vulnerability, but her unique and passionate viewpoint is as intact as ever. Adores Joan and we snuggle on the bed, talking together for two hours.

Later that afternoon, Joan calls the health guru whom

a friend of hers has generously gifted to talk to for an hour. Casting doubt on Western medicine and science, promoting a list of supplements and bath salts, all of which she politely nodded to, without the slightest intention of following through with. He also claimed that he could diagnose and begin the healing process *just* by looking at a photograph of her.

She is first and foremost an Aberdeen doctor's daughter and, after hanging up, asserts that "*nothing* is going to cure me, Swaz, so what's the point in pursuing *any* of this?" Agreed!

Oilly pointed out that *her* female support trio, comprising acupuncturist/reiki practitioner/counsellor, all sublimate their egos and offer empathy and practical help, in contrast to the males we've encountered on the alternative/second opinion circuit. All of them egocentrically sowing doubt and making claims that they have some secret solution. *Do it my way, and you'll be on the highway to recovery and salvation*.

Thursday, July 29, 2021

Our bedroom has become like a boudoir-salon, with visitors paying their respects and sharing memories with Joan. Staying in bed conserves her energy, enabling her to rally and be as uncensored and undiplomatic as she ever was.

Cooked roast chicken for Oilly and Florian and distracted

ourselves watching YouTube compilations of people falling over. Feels so good to laugh, which we do, like 5-year-olds. On the way to bed, an email pings in from Los Angeles.

"A message from Barbra Streisand."

This *must* be a hoax. *Surely?* But it has her name across the top and signature below, clearly a letter, with a note from her assistant: "Hard copy is coming in the mail."

Dear Richard

I'm sorry to hear about your wife, Joan. She was a wonderful addition to my *Yentl* team.

I can only imagine what the two of you are going through. But please know that I'm thinking of you both, and hope you can find some comfort in all the memories you share after almost 40 years together.

Richard, you're still the first (and only) person who has ever commissioned a statue of me, to my knowledge. I'm not sure what I've done to deserve your devotion, but I love your devotion to your wife.

Please take care of yourself, and each other.

Sincerely

Barbra

Barbra Streisand

Read and reread *many* times. Bittersweet that our profoundly sad situation is the reason for her message.

2019

What you're about to read below is headlined "AN ASTONISHMENT OF A DAY AND NIGHT."

Two summers ago, on Friday, July 26, 2019, I was in Philadelphia, filming Jason Segel's TV series *Dispatches from Elsewhere* and invited Sally Field to lunch at a brasserie. Just ordered when my phone pinged, which Sally insisted I look at, "as it might be the production office, 'cos they're *always* changing the schedule." I was due to night-shoot this evening.

"I can't, Sally, it's rude to look at your phone when eating."

"'Cept we just ordered. Go ahead and *look*." Acquiesce.

Text message: "Overrunning. Night shoot delayed till Monday. Apologies for late notice. Have a good weekend."

Levitated, slapped a $100 on the table, and said, "Forgive me, Sally, I *have* to go. Will call and explain." Then *ran* a dozen blocks in as many minutes from Rittenhouse Square to the Amtrak train station on the other side of the Schuylkill River.

Managed to board the fast train to Penn Station, called Trudie Styler, and told her that I was now free this evening, and how was she getting to the Hamptons to visit her grandchildren, as I now urgently needed to get there too. We've known them since 1984 when I was in a play with Freddie Jones and Annette Crosbie at the Lyric Hammersmith, and Trudie was acting in a Doug Lucie play downstairs in the studio theatre. It came down half an hour after ours, so Freddie introduced me to Trudie's husband, Sting, at the bar, which he propped up most evenings, to wait for her.

"Going on a friend's helicopter. Hang on before you book the Jitney, which won't get you there in time on a Friday evening, and I'll call you back in five minutes"—which she does.

"Ron Perelman has invited you to fly with me on his 'copter at 5 p.m., and is offering you one of his guest houses for the night. Can you be here by then?"

"*You bet!*"

Call Andrew Saffir, founder of The Cinema Society marketing company who's described by the *Hollywood Reporter* as a "top movie premiere strategist, who provides a vital link between NYC's chattering classes and the studio execs who need their Manhattan rollouts teeming with boldface names," and breathlessly ask "if it's still all right to go to the Hamptons tonight, as the night shoot got shifted?"

"Yes!"

He's invited me to a screening of a new Julianne Moore movie, at Donna Karan's estate in the Hamptons *because* Barbra Streisand is the guest of honour. Which is why I was absolutely *gutted* when scheduled to do a night shoot—the *only* one in a three-month-long job—*tonight*.

Call Sally, who is completely flummoxed by my story, doubtless because I'm telling it all back to front, upside down and sideways, reflecting my current state of mind and erratic heartbeat. She laughs and says, "You're a *nut*!"

Suddenly aware that I have *no* clothes, other than the drenched shirt and pants I'm wearing, relying on the carriage air-conditioning to combat the incredible summer humidity, to dry out. Woman across the aisle smiles, eyebrow-raises, and asks, "*Boy,* you look happy. Get good news?"

My head smilingly imitates one of those dashboard nodding dogs in reply, and stays like that for the remainder of the journey.

Scuttle my way through the Penn Station crowds and walk fifteen minutes to Sting and Trudie's apartment. Time to have a shower, catch up, *and* get to the heliport in time for 5 p.m. take-off, incredibly grateful to her for organising all this at zero notice. "Don't thank me, thank Ron. All his doing. He's invited you to join us for dinner tomorrow night, *if* you can bear to pull yourself away from *Barbra*."

"*Tease* me *all* you like, Trude, I'm *Teflon*-coated!"

Taking off on a perfect New York summer's evening from the Lower West Side and 'coptering across Central Park, towards East Hampton, feels about as close to a *magic* carpet ride as I'm ever going to get.

All courtesy of multibillionaire Ron, whom I have *yet* to meet. Thirty-five minutes later, we land in the land of the uber-rich. Lushly forested and populated with deer and hidden houses. Met by a driver who looks for my luggage, then asks if I want to drop by the guest house before going to Donna Karan's. Opt not to and, twenty minutes later, pull up to her all-white, clean-lined, spa-like, beachside retreat. Thirty guests that number Calvin Klein, Cuba Gooding Jr., Brooke Shields, Julianne Moore, and, and . . . apologies, but no matter *who* I'm talking to, I can't stop my eyes over-shouldering, east and west, scanning for *you know who*.

Donna takes my arm and says, "I *totally* get it, I've known her for *years*, we're like sisters, but I'm *still* awed by her. She and Jim are staying in my guest house next door and I *promise* I'll come get you when she appears."

The pool is surrounded by double bed–sized loungers, to watch the movie on the *vast* screen at the deep end. Buffet table, drinks station, and servers everywhere. See her, before Donna does, and have to bide my time till Donna honours her pledge and brings me over.

"*You* again. Are you *stalking* me?!"

Manage to *coherently* explain how and why I'm here, which makes her laugh, and then I *shamelessly* attach myself to Mr. and Mrs. James Brolin for the evening.

"May I sit with you both?"

"Sure."

Offer to get her a plateful of food, which she accepts. Now for the moment that feels *truly* surreal. As the movie starts, I'm lying back beside James Brolin, who promptly falls asleep, and his wife, Barbra, who is *less* than a stretched arm's length to my left.

Swaziboy, you're in "bed," albeit on a pool lounger, beside Brolin and Babs.

All I can hear is Shirley MacLaine belting out "If My Friends Could See Me Now" from *Sweet Charity*, seen through windscreen wipers on a rainy night at the Swazi drive-in in the last century.

Majority of the guests stood around for a drink, then peeled away after the credits rolled, and I asked Barbra if we could have a chat.

"Sure."

Seat myself on her left side, as it's her preferred profile, then fire my opening salvo:

"Do you think that the burgundy-coloured sweater that Mrs. Toby Berakow knitted for you when you were a little girl is the reason why you've loved that colour ever since?"

She looked at me, *quizzically*, and said, "You're *very* direct. No. I've *never* made that connection before. Makes sense, though." And we were off and chatting for the next *ninety* minutes! Perfectly interrupted by Brooke Shields, who knelt down beside us and proceeded to tell Barbra, "This man is *brilliant*."

"How d'you know each other?"

"We've slept together, which resulted in twins."

Beat, just long enough for her to register that we were kidding. She clearly likes Brooke, so receiving this thumbs-up from her proves to be my seal of approval. Brooke *got* what this opportunity meant to me, and graciously withdrew. (*I'm still paying her in monthly instalments for this generosity!*)

What was discussed between us is something that I

memorised word for word and will hold dear till my dying day. So, what *can* I say—well, if you subscribe to the theory that people get emotionally arrested at the age that they become famous, in my view this broadly applies to Barbra.

I *know* that's facile, *but* hear me out. At seventy-seven, there is *still* a palpable sense of that driven teenager who went on to win a Grammy award for her first album at the age of twenty-one, and has been famous ever since. Throughout our lengthy conversation, I'm struck by her restless need to prove herself. *Still* striving. *Still* yearning. *Still pursuing the dream*. No sense that she's ever likely to just put her feet up and watch the world go by. Too many plans and projects to pursue.

"Seems to me that you've been *farbrent* all your life." (Yiddish for "on fire.") She laughed and corrected my pronunciation.

"Not *faaaaarbrent*. It's *farbrent*."

Am *more* than happy to be corrected! Told her that when I was filming *Prêt-à-Porter* for Robert Altman in Paris in 1994, I'd bought tickets to see her perform in London, which was the first time she'd toured since playing *Funny Girl* in the theatre in 1966.

I had cleared the date with the producer, and been given permission to go. Knowing all this, Altman came up to me the day before I was due to fly home and said, "I'm *really* sorry Eeeee Grant, but schedule changes mean you won't be able to go tomorrow."

Fell for his ruse completely and spluttered, "Well, Bob,

I *am going*, no matter what, and you're just going to have to fire me." He laughed.

"And here I am *again*, dodging filming schedule changes to see you!" Adding that I had commissioned a 2-foot-tall sculpture of her head in profile, which is now in pride of place in my garden. This earned a head-shaking pause—

"You're crazy."

"I know."

"No, you *are*, *crazy*."

Saturday, July 31, 2021

Pouring rain. Cool air. The British summer.

Julian and Isabel Bannerman, garden designers extraordinaire, drop in for tea in the Taj at 11:30 a.m. He chain-smokes so conscientiously that he uses his shirt pocket as an ashtray. Worry that when Joan wakes up, he'll find it hard not to smoke in our bedroom. Mercifully resists, and gets his fix from Diet Coke instead. Both are so garrulous and full of stories about their huge gardening projects for illustrious clients that time does a merry jig in their company. Platefuls of improvised sandwiches and cups of tea, with "Mayor Juliani" taking smoke breaks outside, fuel away the hours in their delightful company.

Chapter Nine

August

Wednesday, August 4, 2021

Come downstairs and discover Joan in the living room saying, "I'm dying. I'm dying."

"You're not, my angel, I can see that you've just been asleep at an odd angle, which is why you're so uncomfortable. Have you been here for long?"

"Came down in the middle of the night. Couldn't sleep."

Encourage her to come back upstairs to bed, but she is too weak to climb more than five steps. Florian suggests that we take her in the wheelchair, which she agrees to, and go via the front door, up the garden steps, through the gate and round the side of the cottage, into our bedroom. Once in bed, she takes the first dose of low morphine liquid, which calms her down and regulates her breathing.

Surprises me an hour later, asking, "Who's coming to visit us today?"

Mark Tandy and Amanda Marmot drop in mid-morning and gather in our bedroom for "An Audience with Joan," vicariously diverting us with their summer holiday plans, which involve tripping the light fandango between various friends' villas in the south of France and Tuscany, and sailing around Turkey on their friends' luxury "tub."

When Joan wakes up from her afternoon nap, Oilly calmly insists that she wear her panic button *all* the time, and that she doesn't venture downstairs on her own, in the middle of the night, "as it's way too distressing for *us*." Of course, Joan argues back like a Trojan, leaving Oilly in tears. "I'm just trying to *help* you, Mum."

Joan amps up the strained atmosphere, like a sulky adolescent, and says, "I want to be alone." Painful as it is for Oilly to insist on this panic button boundary, it has the desired effect. An hour later, she presses the alarm and, when we reach her, is full of apologies and they both hug it out. This simple boundary pays dividends as she sleeps through the night, doesn't move, *and* takes the new morphine medication.

FedEx delivers the promised hard copy of Barbra Joan Streisand's letter in a burgundy-coloured folder which Oilly sagely advises *not* to show *my* Joan.

"Mum doesn't need reminding of your phantom one-way love affair at this moment, Pops."

Thursday, August 5, 2021

Go for a 4-mile run with Florian at 7 a.m., which helps clear my head. When I return, Joan claims that she's seen "green monkeys dancing on the garden wall. Maybe it's the morphine, Swaz?"

"But you haven't had any yet, Monkee."

"My biggest fear is that the brain tumours could be back."

"Don't know. Maybe you were dreaming?"

"Possibly"—the doubt hangs worryingly between us.

She asks me to prop more pillows up behind her, to alleviate the pressure on her chest, then drifts back to sleep, semi-upright. When her head slumps forward, her hair pitifully resembles an old doll found in the attic.

Monsoon deluge and, at 10:30 p.m., we hear an incredible crash, momentary flicker of the lights, then complete blackout. Rush downstairs and into the lane to discover that a tree has fallen across the power lines. Emergency services arrive within ten minutes, close off the road, and we're told that, "It might be a few hours before it's on again."

Mighty relief that Joan is not relying on a ventilator. We read together using our iPhone torches, reminding us that we'd both sneaked torches and books under the covers as kids, after official lights out. Swaziland had regular power cuts during summer thunderstorms, so we had candles in every room, just in case. There was such a distinct smell and atmosphere of excitement whenever this happened, huddling around candles and paraffin lamps, grateful for being indoors, but also fearful that the roof might blow off, or a tree collapse across it. Everything felt heightened and laughy-scary, until the electrics were restored, which instantly dissipated the high jinks and meant having to go back to bed.

"Remember that storm in Swazi when Oilly was seven? We were having dinner with the Donaldsons, and it was the first time I'd ever experienced an African thunderstorm, that you'd always told me about. Everyone carrying on as if it was the most normal thing in the world, while I was terrified that we'd get struck by lightning."

It seems like yesterday and five lifetimes ago.

Sunday, August 8, 2021

"Don't argue with me, Swaz, but I *insist* that you go to Theo's birthday party on your own today. Oilly agrees with me. Be good for you to get out and you can come back with some stories. I'm just too weak and don't want to be pitied and pushed around in a wheelchair."

It's Theo Fennell's seventieth, so they've gone the full monty and erected a huge marquee and set it up like a garden fete, replete with bunting and food stations. Theo and Louise are *the* most loved couple we know, and have legions of friends, ranging from thorough-blue-bloods to Janet Street-Porter, and everyone else in between. Get there early as am anxious about people asking, "And how's Joan?" Or, "Where's Joan?"

Great pleasure to congratulate him on clocking up seventy *and* fathering an Oscar-winning daughter! Emerald wrote and directed *Promising Young Woman*, fulfilling her own title's prediction by bagging the original screenplay award.

Clodagh McKenna, the warm big-hearted Irish TV chef, bursts into tears when I give her an update on Joan's condition, and have to comfort her, as she so adores my wife and says, "I just can't believe that this is happening to you both."

No sooner said than a *very* good friend of ours, whom we've known *really* well for twenty-five years, shared holidays with, regular lunches, tennis, Christmas parties, you name it, joins us and, choking back her tears, says, "I just have to tell you how incredibly moved I was." Uh-oh, here we go, I thought. "We saw *Singin' in the Rain* at Sadler's Wells last night and it was *incredible* being back inside a theatre again after Covid restrictions lifted. Standing ovation. *We* were all crying and the *cast* were all crying. *Soooooo* moving!"

You're kidding me?

She then mock-berated me for "being on TV *all* the time." *Write Around the World* (in which I travelled around France, Spain, and Italy, interviewing writers or following in the footsteps of long-gone authors) has just shown on BBC Four so my mug featured on the cover of the *Radio*

Times. "*And* you looked absolutely *ludicrous* in that awful green *Loki* costume! What *were* you thinking?"

Best I don't tell her what I'm thinking right now.

Not a *single* word about Joan. Clodagh diplomatically took my arm and said, "Excuse us, please, we were just heading for the ice-cream station" along with my averted gobsmacked face. Clodagh asked: "Who *is* that woman? Doesn't she know about Joan?"

"She most certainly does, which is what makes it all the more hurtful, but I suppose you can't predict how people will react. I stupidly thought I *knew* her. Not heard a single word from her partner, either."

Left immediately and received an afterthought text, four hours later: "And, of course, love to Joan," followed five minutes later by, "and to Oilly."

Over and out.

Gabriel's advice *not* to judge friends echoes up. Call me old-fashioned, but I find it difficult *not to*.

Of course, didn't breathe a word of this to Joan, who wants the detailed lowdown about the food/the flowers/the marquee/who was there/who said what to whom/what they were wearing/who you avoided, and "did anyone ask after me?"

Felt out of body when I was among the birthday throng, and feel similarly "third eyeing" in the recounting, acutely aware that our lifelong habit of sharing *every* detail of our days is drawing to an end.

Wednesday, August 11, 2021

After an horrendous night, Joan having taken two lorazepam instead of half a pill to quell her panic at being breathless, *everything* goes tonto. At dawn, she is still delirious. Can barely stand. Instead of *calming* her down, she is poleaxed.

Cancel Louise Fennell's morning visit, and call the palliative nurse for advice, who says to keep monitoring her, but that she will "likely sleep all day until the drugs wear off."

Sat with her and tried to read, but got waylaid by a nagging thought that rattles around my brain like a marble: "If she were a dog or cat, a vet would mercifully end her suffering with an injection . . ." It feels utterly *inhumane* to make her endure this drawn-out dying.

By 11 p.m., there is no sign of improvement whatsoever. Even though I am sitting beside her, she suddenly jerks and falls out of bed. Discombobulated and incoherent. In desperation, I call 111 and, after twice having to describe *every* detail to two different people, they finally agree to send out an ambulance, treating it as an overdose. "Could take a minimum of two hours, or more."

Oilly is amazingly together and advises me what to do. "One step at a time, Pops." Our night and day and night has tilted into a canyon of unease, doubt, and acute anxiety.

Waiting.

Waiting.

Waiting.

Ambulancemen arrive four hours later, at 3 a.m., and are calm, kind, and pragmatic. Blood tests taken, heart rate monitored, and, midway through, Joan miraculously wakes up, coherent and compos mentis! Concluded that she didn't require hospitalisation, but that I should inform the district and palliative nurses that we need a "Just in case" emergency medical kit for the cottage.

Mightily relieved and reassured. All hail the NHS!

Thursday, August 12, 2021

Joan slept all morning, but when she wakes up, she is pretty much her normal self again. "Bloody hell, Monkee. Thought you'd done a Janis Joplin on us!"

"I'm still 'ere," she quips back in perfect cockney, with pigeon-head movements to match. Whenever she taught an actor to do a cockney accent, she always got them to imitate the jerky head movements of the bird, and, daft as this must sound, it *always* worked and got their bodies to match the vernacular.

The *relief* at having her back on form cannot be overestimated. She has no memory of what happened in the last twenty-four hours.

While coaching Christian Bale, he asked her, "Do you always equate speech rhythms with dance? If so, how do you deal with English? Is that like Morris dancing?"

"Probably. You twiddle around in every direction, then

surreptitiously throw the baton to someone else. Nothing about English is straightforward."

She had a theory that landscape and climate *directly* affected accents—flat Norfolk parallels with the flat Midwest in the USA. "Both sound like sheep." In contrast to the up-and-down rhythms of mountainous Wales, or the nasality of New York and Liverpool, "both port cities, polluted and congested with sea air."

Jo Grenson, the no-nonsense palliative nurse, visits at 4 p.m. and is going to put in an application for an NHS nursing care package for "when the time comes" and order a hospital bed, so that Joan can button-press going up or down, and also be safe from falling out of the bed in the middle of the night.

At the front door, I asked how long she thought Joan was likely to live.

"Are you quite sure that you want me to tell you?"

Nodded.

"It's not an *exact* science, but I think weeks, rather than months. Four weeks. She won't be strong enough to return to London."

Oilly asks me to share everything that Jo has said and am reluctant to do so. It feels like a terrible betrayal of Joan to tell her, but she's insistent that I do. Sit together, *reeling*, as this information ricochets in every direction imaginable.

We have to be grateful that she won't have to linger on, in such a poorly state. Both Florian's parents are doctors and he urges me to get a second opinion, so email Wanda Cui, describing Joan's condition and what Palliative Jo has suggested.

Friday, August 13, 2021

Wanda calls first thing in the morning and concurs with Jo's prognosis, confirming that she feels that four weeks "is the maximum, and to prepare for the likelihood of only three weeks left. I'm so, *so sorry*, Richard. Joan has been so strong, clear-sighted, accepting and inspiring in the way she's handled this all."

Silently wept as she said this. How do I tell our daughter that her mother has even *less* time left?

Ruth Kennedy-Dundas visits for an hour, sitting at the end of our bed, diverting and entertaining us all with tales from the Big Smoke. Joan flags after half an hour and falls asleep, and we quietly file downstairs. Share our news with her and she suggests getting all the honours list application letters collated and printed up into a book, which we can give to Joan. We're both incredibly touched by her offer to get this done and sent.

Oilly and I find it difficult to concentrate on anything, as *everything* feels like it's sliding off the table, in

s l o w   m o t i o n.

Joan sleeps all afternoon and, when I check on her at 6 p.m., asking what she'd like for supper, she says, "Piece of plain grilled salmon. *Nothing* else. Salad sticks in my teeth. Come here . . . *Please* don't be sad, Swaz, but I'm *so, so* weary. I feel like I'm dying. I don't think I'll live more than another two weeks."

Absolutely devastating. Just when I think I've got a handle on things and can control myself, the living grief is all-engulfing. An *agony.*

Saturday, August 14, 2021

Karen "Gin" Jones, the gorgeous script supervisor from *Wah-Wah*, visits, overflowing with flowers, gossip, and good cheer, bringing us news about all the films she's been working on and people that we know in common. Like being lowered into a warm, bubbly bath in her company. As a first-time writer-director on *Wah-Wah*, I found in her a brilliantly patient guide and mentor, quietly advising what extra shots and coverage I needed for scenes, informed by her wealth of experience. Gave her that nickname, as she always looked forward to a libation at the end of a long shooting day in Swaziland.

She's in pieces when saying goodbye downstairs, *knowing* that this is the last time she will ever see Joan. So grateful that she made the long journey for such a short time.

Back upstairs and ask her to read out Roy Croft's "I love you" poem, which I've been asked to read at Harry Herbert's marriage to Clodagh McKenna this afternoon. Joan is a supreme reader of poetry, and I know of no one better to shamelessly imitate. Record it on my iPhone and play it on repeat all the way to St. Michaels and All Angels Church on the Highclere estate, where they're getting married.

Deluging rain all the way and, just ten minutes before turning off the motorway, the skies cleared, as if on cue, and the sun blazed through. "Luck of the Irish" reiterates through the top-hatted, tailed, and fascinator-affixed throng. *The* picture-postcard image of an English wedding, including the bride and groom's dogs, who are beribboned and leashed at the church door. Country flowers inside the Victorian church "with Tudor bits," and a feeling of *real* celebration, minus any mutterings of "this will never last" that I've overheard at countless other nuptials. Imelda May singing traditional Irish songs as we enter.

Nervously waiting to read the poem, knowing that "in sickness and in health" will be part of their vows, a heart-rending reminder that *our* vows are now in reverse order—*in health and in sickness.*

The newlyweds climb aboard a horse and cart after signing their names as husband and wife and all 150 of us walk in their wake to the house, Broadspear. Three long trestle tables inside a vast marquee in the woodlands and, this being Clodagh's wedding, the food is utterly delicious. As is the music. Another Clodagh-ism is that the bride makes a speech in between the groom and best man, and references Joan's absence, which is unexpected and touching.

She's also created an Irish pub in a restored "shed" complete with a fireplace, bar, and Guinness on tap. Imelda May sang and fiddled, everyone danced and spilled out into the lantern-lit woods, and the heavens twinkled without a drop of rain. *Magical*.

Joan would have loved it, and asks for a detailed download of it all when I get home at 11 p.m.

Sunday, August 15, 2021

Joan is experiencing intermittent chest cramps on her left side, relieved by morphine opioid and paracetamol, which doesn't entirely succeed in numbing the little attacks.

Feeding her, helping her wash, and loading her toothbrush with paste all feels intensely intimate. All so difficult for her to achieve. Everything a struggle now.

"Weird this, Swaz . . . me just lying here, waiting to die."

Cannot fathom what to say and just hold her close.

The night ahead becomes the night I've anticipated and *dreaded* from the day she was diagnosed. Awake every hour with chest cramps which are now continuous. None of the meds we try can alleviate her suffering.

Monday, August 16, 2021

District nurse Amy arrives at 8:30 a.m. to inject Joan with pain relief and she falls asleep almost instantly. Plan to have an intravenous slow drip attached to her arm.

Covid restrictions mean that the usual next-day delivery of a hospital bed will likely be a week. Palliative nurses Katie and Tracey, from the Longfield Hospice in Minchinhampton, visit for the first time in the evening, to be followed by two nurses in the morning, and again in the evening.

Am astonished that this is all coordinated and offered at *no* cost whatsoever, and think back to the moment I was thrown off a horse during the filming of a chase sequence in *Dracula* in LA in the early nineties. First thing I was asked: "Are you intending to sue Sony Pictures? Do you have private healthcare? What credit card do you have?" This *before* any medic would so much as glance at my injured knee.

The two nurses cheer Joan up, remake the bed, tend to her every request, and even though present for only twenty minutes, alleviate our anxieties with their expertise and bonhomie. Feels like a true measure of what a civilised society we *do* live in, despite the national penchant for a good old moan.

Joan's love of custard and sweet delights shows no sign of abating. That she at least has *this* pleasure is *mighty*.

Tuesday, August 17, 2021

District nurse Louise advises that we get a prescription for slow-release pain pills, obviating the need to go through the palaver of requesting a district nurse twice a day, to inject her morphine dose.

Tracey and Katie visit in the morning and evening for fifteen minutes each time and Joan responds to her audience, imitating their Gloucestershire accents and being a nosy parker about their personal lives. All of which they take good-naturedly. Have told them that she is a dialect coach and isn't sending them up in the slightest. No offence is taken! Am amazed and delighted to see her rallying when they call.

Can't work out whether it's the low-dose morphine or cancer affecting her brain, but she suddenly verbally sprints and segues, albeit coherently, between the present and a friend's boyfriend fifty years ago, leapfrogging back and forth, without missing a beat. (Not *unlike* this diary, come to think of it. So what's *my* excuse?)

It's as if she's stumbled into Eddie Izzard's stream-of-consciousness schtick. Very entertaining, but also gobbledygookish.

Most significantly, the slow-release pain pills have stopped *all* her chest cramps and enabled her to sleep for hours at a time. Having an uninterrupted night's sleep feels completely rejuvenating, as does having the Longfield carers twice a day.

Joan is so revived and palpably excited about Sue Gutjahr's morning visit that she paints on some lippy and brushes her hair. Sue pops in with home-grown sweet peas, a bag of books, and her irrepressibly grinning positivity.

Jules and Nige Bowsher come over with freshly baked

soda bread and tomato soup, while I painted Joan's fingernails as she and Sue sorted out the world's problems with a hey-nonny-no gusto.

In the midst of Joan's fragile state, the *kindness* and compassion of our Cotswold clan is as pure a moment of pleasure as we ever thought possible at this time. Oilly tells Joan how proud she is of her mum being top of her profession, reporting that every agent she speaks to holds her in the highest regard.

As she's leaving, Sue comments on just how much Joan has deteriorated since her last visit, and it's my turn to comfort *her*.

Thursday, August 19, 2021

Finally get through to the hospital bed supplier in Gloucester and assured that, "It'll be there between 10 and 4 p.m. tomorrow. Will call you half an hour in advance of our arrival."

Progress!

Nurse Matt, the only man on the palliative team, and Nurse Zoe arrive to give Joan a bed wash, and help her to the loo. My domestic duties resemble the list of a fifties housewife—shopping, washing, ironing, cooking every meal, tidying up, paying every invoice, answering the mail, both cyber and postal, and the front door, and taking delivery of the flowers and gifts that arrive for Joan. Going to the pharmacy *every* day to try to get the fully comprehensive list of her medication. Always seems to be missing at least one item which "should be in tomorrow." Patience-*challenging* for *this* impatient Handmaid Grant!

Phoebe Nicholls drops by for an easy hour of bedside nattering, always buoyant, positive, and welcome.

While I'm cooking supper, Joan presses her alarm bell and I rush upstairs to find her breathing very rapidly and saying, "Let me go. Let me go. I just want to die."

Give her some calming medication and sit stroking her hand until her panic subsides and she dozes off.

Friday, August 20, 2021

Joan is speaking sense, *but* not making any. Individual words aren't gibberish, but when strung together they sound it. Random and repetitive. District nurse Chrissie visits to assess her and privately explains that, "This is part and parcel of the degeneration of *everything*. Confusion and displacement."

Gabriel Byrne arrives just before the delivery of the hospital bed, and helps us carry it up the garden stairs and assemble it in our bedroom, in front of our double bed, so that Joan will have the exact same view of the garden, just a couple of metres further forward than she has been. Plugged in and we can now heighten or lower the bed to suit her needs, with the remote control. Without having left our bedroom, when resettled in the hospital bed she asks, "Am I in the hospice now?"

"No, Monkee, in our bedroom, and Gabe is here to see us."

Masterful actor that he is, he talks as though there's *nothing* amiss and she happily vagues and meanders with him down her own Lewis Carrollian rabbit holes.

Only an Irishman White Rabbit runs across *my* brain. I will *always* love him for this. Gabriel reports that the bed-deliverer said to him with a quizzical look, "I think we've met before?" then shook his head. We ruefully laughed about the fact that no matter how many movies, series, or awards come your way, there is always a daily reminder that you're never more than a blink away from being blanked or asked, "Don't I know you from *somewhere*?"

Mercifully Joan now has no pain at all, and Palliatives Matt and Gilly prove themselves to be very patient and attentive when they check in on her in the early evening, allowing me to drive Gabriel back to the train station. Like Sue Gutjahr, he expresses how shocked he is at Joan's deterioration in less than a month. As I'm in such close proximity to her all the time, I have no third-eye perspective.

"I think that you're lucky in a way that Joan is somewhat confused, 'cos she didn't resist moving from your bed to the new one, *at all*, whereas it could have been very traumatic for her."

"True, but traumatic for me, Gabe, because it means we will *never* share our bed *ever* again."

He bearhugs me at the station, shakes his head, then my hand, and walks away, waving without looking back.

Joan is asleep by the time I get back and Oilly manages to finish her calls at a reasonable Friday hour, for once. She's wholly consumed with casting 400 young actors for Spielberg and Hanks's Apple TV+ series *Masters of the Air*, amid endless Covid setbacks and actors changing availabilities and new schedules. Her working hours extended, due to the producers being in LA, and having to respond to their demands after hours in the UK.

Makes us an omelette and puts on some trashy TV to distract ourselves, while I'm ironing sheets, and says, "I'm so proud of how you're handling all of this, Pops, and how tender you are with Mum."

"*Thank you*, but what *else* would I be, my angel child? You're *unbelievably* strong and supportive, dealing with everything here *and* remotely getting all your casting work done. Take my hat off to you."

"I can't *actually* believe that this is happening, sometimes. Just seems completely *surreal*."

Saturday, August 21, 2021

Oilly sits with Joan, while I rush off to Stroud market for bread and croissants, and then do a massive supermarket shop as Nikki and David are weekending with us, along with Oilly's school pal Imogen, her partner Pete, and their nine-week-old son Frankie. Amazingly uplifting to have new life in our midst. Everyone Noah Arks in pairs to visit Joan, who is completely lucid and herself again this morning. *That's* what's so cruel and unnerving about this disease.

"Bring me your iPad, Swaz—I want to watch your *Write Around the World* series, please."

Watches two hour-long episodes without a break and is as sharp about my mispronunciations as ever she was when well, and asks which of the people I've interviewed I fancied *or* fancied *me.*

Vintage Joan questions! She is complimentary and critical by turns, as she always has been about *all* of my work, and it's an unbelievably upsetting realisation that this is the *last* time I will ever have the benefit of her opinion.

Am so grateful that Oilly's friends have made the journey down here, to divert, distract, and support her.

By 7 p.m., it's as if Joan's lucidity supplies have run dry and she is discombobulated and *very* distressed. Medication has zero effect. No sooner has she fallen asleep than she wakes up and asks, "Why have you locked me in a cupboard?" Followed an hour later with, "Have you packed the car to go back to London, yet?"

Sunday, August 22, 2021

All through breakfast, she talks in fluent gobbledygook, so follow Gabriel's lead and agree with or demur to wherever her jabberwocky leads us. Nikki and David have to leave for London and get very emotional when saying goodbye to her, as Joan has been like a surrogate mum to Nikki.

Consult with the palliative nursing team and they quietly confirm that this "in and out lucidity is normal at this stage."

Joan sleeps through most of the day, and I sit reading on our bed, behind hers.

Completely compos mentis in the early evening, *yet* has no recall of Nikki and David saying goodbye or the nurses giving her a bedbath. Manages to complete the crossword and then asks me to remove her nail varnish. Been trying to work out *just* what it is about touching each of her fingertips that feels so tender and delicate. Sideswipes me by asking: "Do you remember when we went to Rome and saw the Sistine Chapel, with Michelangelo's painting of God reaching out his finger and *almost* touching Adam's?"

"*Yes*, and we got the giggles when you whispered that Adam's winky was *tiny* compared to the rest of his body, and we had to leave!"

It's a moment of pure unalloyed *happiness* to laugh together at the unexpected memory of this. She then seamlessly starts quoting the opening scene from Bernard Shaw's play *Saint Joan*:

> No eggs! No eggs!! Thousand thunders, man, what do you mean by no eggs?

Sir: it is not my fault. It is the act of God.

Blasphemy. You tell me there are no eggs, and you blame your Maker for it.

Sir: what can I do? I cannot lay eggs.

Where the hell does *this* segue come from? Or is it the "God" connection?

She then recounts playing the title role in her final year at school and how her father left at the interval, embarrassed. I google the play and she has quoted it *verbatim*!

Goes to sleep at 8 p.m., without taking any sleeping pills, and sleeps and *sleeps*. Crept downstairs and had toasties with Oilly in front of the TV, who sweetly advises me "not to fixate upon whether she's lucid or not, but rather to take each moment and day for what we can. Flow with whichever way *she* flows."

WEDNESDAY, AUGUST 25, 2021

Grey, Groundhog of a Day, feeling grumpy and tired. Joan has been intermittently awake all through the night and has zero energy left and struggles to feed herself. She looks like a little vacant-eyed, half-feathered bird.

No sooner does this state seem fixed than she's suddenly *all present and correct*, reaches for our daughter's hand, and sweetly says, "I love you *so* much, Oilly! I'm *so* proud of you! *Why* are you crying?"

"Because you said you're *proud* of me, and you don't say that a lot."

"That's 'cos I don't want you to get a big head."

Just like *her* mother never did to her. Feels like a seminal moment.

Her mind wanders between Michael Jackson and someone from her childhood she's never mentioned before called Plummy.

"Why Plummy?"

"'Cos she looked like a Victoria plum."

All of it makes sense, separately but not consecutively. Her spirit and wit still intact. Just in piecemeal form.

Yet.

Yet, when Joely Richardson and her daughter Daisy Bevan train down with a cooler bag of ice creams and sorbets, Joan is spirited and completely coherent with them. Cannot get over how much trouble they've gone to, coming all this way from London just for an hour and then back all over again. Vanessa was too fragile to make the journey this time.

Thursday, August 26, 2021

Oilly asked me what I feared most, and, after a long pause, dared tell her that it was making funeral arrangements, "as it feels treasonous even talking about it *in advance*." Saying it out loud made it less frightening and we agreed that it should be a small-scale service at the crematorium. Wicker casket, covered in flowers, and wrote out a guest list of local friends and lifelong compadres.

Palliative nurses Helen and Zoe must have reported back about my obvious lack of sleep, because Liz called from Longfield Hospice to say that Lynn, a night nurse, would "babysit" Joan from 10 p.m. till 8 a.m.

A kinder or more compassionate person you couldn't wish for.

Friday, August 27, 2021

Miraculous to have slept in the adjacent guest bedroom almost all through the night, apart from an emergency bell at 2 a.m., when Joan woke up while Lynn was downstairs making a cup of tea. Sleep deprivation is so cumulative and exhausting that, having had almost eight hours, I feel like I've been given a transfusion of energy and hope. *Ready* for anything.

Lynn determinedly told me *not* to feel guilty about her staying up all night with Joan, instead of me. Still do, though. My middle-class manners silently muttering "it isn't gentlemanly."

It's one of those grey, late summer days. Temperature has dropped to 11 degrees and it's *still* August! Immeasurably brightened when Sue Gutjahr drops in with garden roses and the last of her sweet peas and insists that I take the opportunity to go and shop for weekend groceries. When I returned, they were both nattering away in German!

Sue's late husband was "an *Eisbein*" and Joan learnt hers from a long-ago German boyfriend, whom she affectionately called the "Kraut."

"I've told Sue that I think I'm going to die tomorrow."

"Well, to quote you, Monkee, you're *still 'ere*!"

After two hours together, Joan declares, "I've had enough of you, Sue. *Go!*"

Though glassy-eyed and vacant of expression, she is stiletto-sharp with intent. Sue sportingly obliges, and I walk downstairs with her. Hasn't taken umbrage as "this is what happens near the end."

Palliative nurse Matt arrives and notices the sharp decline in Joan's coherence since seeing her four days ago. *Yet*, Sue confirms that not only has she been completely coherent for two hours, she's done so speaking *German*!

Oilly finishes work in time to join me at Joan's bedside for supper. She suddenly says how cold she is. Blanket. Duvet. Another bedcover and her hands are very clammy. Breathing erratic. Increased tempo, then *really* slows down. Shallow breaths.

Oilly googles and is convinced that this is the final approach. Holds her mum's hands and silently weeps. Joan falls asleep and her breathing becomes regular again.

Saturday, August 28, 2021

Night nurse Christine comes down at 7 a.m. and reports that Joan was "completely coherent" in the middle of the night. Sleeping pills had no effect, whatsoever, "but she quizzed me in detail about my Northern Irish accent and family background and is a very interesting and *interested* woman."

Joan drifts incoherently in and out of sleep all day, then surprises by asking "was it Lana Turner or Marilyn Monroe in *Gentlemen Prefer Blondes*?" So clear. So sharp. *So* unexpected!

Cue for me to read her a snippet that's gone viral on social media about a Dublin car mechanic, who sent a customer called Mary an invoice for €73, after he: "Found dildo belonging to customer jammed in rails that the seat slides on. Unwilling to carry out repair due to hygiene concern. Instructed customer on repairs required."

Poor ol' Mary had "innocently" returned her car to the mechanic because "ever since we fitted a new wing mirror, the driver's seat will not move back or forward."

Joan chuckled, didn't say anything for a while, and then, in a pitch perfect Dublin accent, murmured, "*Dildo*." Intermittently throughout the afternoon.

By the early evening, her panic levels have risen dramatically and she's fearful about *everything*. No carer this evening, so decide to go to sleep at the same time as she does, which is at 7:30 p.m., in our bed behind her. Wakes up at 9 p.m. and says, "I want a cup of PG Tips, with *proper* milk. Like cows make."

Whether she is intentionally being funny or not doesn't matter, as am just grateful to have *any* of her true self *present.* She now has almost no interest in food of any description.

Sunday, August 29, 2021

Bruce and Ruth Kennedy-Dundas visit for a bedside hour and give a masterclass in how to act as if the four of us are still having the time of our lives, when we went to Portofino together for a long birthday weekend, two years ago. She has brought the book of printed letters about Joan, which she nicknamed Operation JoanStar*, and when she handed it over to me, *I* knew that *they* knew that *I* knew that this was their farewell visit.

Told Joan about Christine Mitchell and Ruth's campaign to put her name forward to the honours list application committee, and that we now had a book of all the letters of recommendation, with a green cover, "to match your beautiful eyes."

"Would you like me to read you the letters, Monkee?"

She shakes her head and says, "I know how sad you are, Swaz, but you and Oilly are going to be okay. I truly want you and Oilly to try and find a pocketful of happiness in every single day. Will you do that for me?"

My turn to nod and blink back tears.

Monday, August 30, 2021

The palliative nurses had told me all about night nurse Marianne, whom they hold in the *highest* esteem and respect, and Marianne lives up to her golden reputation. Small of stature and enormous of heart, she has the most empathetic and compassionate nature imaginable, and recounts her night with Joan.

"She fell asleep at 10 p.m. almost as soon as I sat down with her, then awoke again at 1 a.m., *absolutely lucid* and asking to see the book of letters with the green cover. I thought this might be a fantasy, but gave her the benefit of my doubt and looked around the bedroom for it. She then asked me to go downstairs 'as it's likely to be on the hall table,' which I did, and indeed it was, brought it up to her and she put on her glasses and read it from cover to cover.

"Joan told me who had written some of the letters and expressed how appreciated, admired, and loved she felt by her peers. Then promptly fell asleep. Woke up again at 4:30 a.m. and was completely incoherent. In my opinion, this is not drug-related behaviour, but the brain tumours playing havoc."

What utterly undid me was knowing that Joan *had* been lucid enough to read her paean of praises and just wished that I could have been with her when she did this. That they have all *registered* with her is reward in itself. For her to know the impact she has had, both personally and professionally. Whether her application was approved or not will sadly remain unknown, as they are not awarded posthumously.

Marianne suggests that I put in a request for more slow-release pain medication, to ease her agitation and increase her sleepiness, until the Big Sleep of Sleeps.

Bedside vigil all day long, with brief respite when the palliative carers come in for ten minutes, morning, noon, and at dusk. Hours pass by in a Zen-like mode of total acceptance of our situation. It's a relief in itself just to be with her, to hear her breathing, calmly . . .

. . . B r e a t h i n g . . .

Oilly has had her Bedalian school "besties," Zoe, Ben, and Liv, to stay, who each dropped in to say hello, then retreated to the Taj for a BBQ, and it's magical to hear their intermittent tinkly laughter in the distance, beyond the garden doors. Life going on. Am so grateful for the boundless love and support they're giving her.

Jo Grenson, palliative supremo, calls to say that Joan's agitation is caused by the brain cancer and that she is exhibiting signs of "terminal palpitations," which is what the body does when trying to hold on. She says that the slow-release sedative will allow her body to relax and release.

Chapter Ten

September

Wednesday, September 1, 2021

Lynn has returned to sit through the night, which enables all of *us* to sleep, and reports that Joan is no longer interested in eating or drinking *anything*.

Felt very emotional that the last thing I cooked for her was chicken soup. Her last meal.

She sleeps most of the morning and, when she does surface, we sit stroking her hand and hair, to try to keep her calm.

District nurse Serena arrives to assess all the medications that she's taking and calls Dr. Latter at the local health centre, who comes to the cottage an hour later and gives his approval to "double all of the sedative dosages" to try to ensure she is peaceful and asleep.

"I've *rarely* come across anything like this level of determination before. Do you mind my asking if your wife is a very strong-willed person?"

"*That's* an understatement!"—makes me really laugh.

"I can tell. Even when she's asleep, or struggling to get up, I can see that she's *very* determined."

On leaving, Serena noticed that her breathing had changed significantly since lunchtime and had become much shallower and "closer to the end. She might die tonight."

"What do I do?"

"Call the out-of-hours district nurse, and one of the team will come out to certify that she has died, then it's your call to get in touch with a funeral director."

She manages to tell me all of this in a steady, unpatronising tone, simultaneously pragmatic and compassionate. As she drove away, I started shaking uncontrollably. It's one thing to be very grown-up and practical when a stranger is giving you instructions, but another feeling entirely when the *impact* of what they're advising hits you with *such* meteoric force. Returned to Joan's bedside and held her hand with my left, while scrolling through local funeral directors on my iPhone with my right.

Unquestionably surreal, but truly feel that *my* Joan has left us in spirit already, and it's only her body that is struggling on beside me.

Call James Showers at Family Tree Funerals in Stroud and tell him what Serena has advised me to do. He is incredibly reassuring and has the bedside manner of an old-fashioned GP in Swaziland. Request that the cremation take place at Westerleigh, near Bristol, in the smaller chapel as anticipate there will only be thirty people, since it's not in London. Oval-shaped wicker casket to be *in situ*, in order to avoid the horror of following a hearse. He says that it's possible at a push to organise it all in a week. Am surprised to hear my voice insist that, "It *has* to happen in a week, please, James." The prospect of everything being protracted and delayed fires my resolve.

"I'll do my very best."

Oilly joins and we sit either side of Joan, each holding one of her hands, in the same positions and attitudes of every painting and sculpture depicting the bedside vigil—

A pietà.

It's a real privilege to be able to do this together as a family—having said all we wanted to one another when Joan was still conscious. And continue to tell her, when she's not. Knowing that hearing is the last sense to go.

Palliative nurse Christine checks in at 10 p.m. and we request that, "If it sounds like Joan is dying, to please wake both of us up."

Thursday, September 2, 2021

Wake up and am relieved to hear from Christine that Joan has slept through the night, doubtless due to the doubled-up sedative dosage. Nikki and David drive down from London and spend time sitting with her, talking to her and holding her hands. We're incredibly moved by their profound love for her. They're both very emotional as we reminisce about all the good times we have had together. Nikki reminded me about the time we were all staying at the Coral Reef Club in Barbados and I'd rushed into the ladies' loo, as it was the closest, and how Joan had followed me in, then barked, "*Who's* in here?"—in a perfect Bajan accent.

My feet shot up off the floor, desperately hoping that they'd not been seen.

At noon, nurses Susie Baines and Sharon arrive to change over the slow-release syringe pump.

Joan doesn't wake up properly at all, apart from the odd eye flicker. Sit stroking her hand and talking softly about some of the daft things that we've done together. She loved collecting old papier-mâché carnival heads from the south of France and tried to bring one through Nice airport as hand luggage. A very officious customs officer (are they ever *not*?) informed her that this was strictly *interdit*, and that it would have to be packed in the hold.

"But it would get damaged, Monsieur!"

He wasn't having any of this and indicated that she was holding up the queue. Joan being Joan promptly put the papier-mâché head over *hers* and asked if *this* was permissible? He threatened to arrest her for being "a potential hijacking security risk" and strong-armed her off to the side and suggested that she buy a case to pack it into. Which we duly did.

At 7 p.m., her breathing slows down quite suddenly. Stroke her hand and keep repeating, "It's all okay, my angel. It's *all* okay. Don't hold on. We *all* love you so. So, *so* much."

After each intake of breath, the gap until the next inhalation gets longer and longer. At 7:25, I thought that her hand felt like it was *cooling* in mine.

Was I just imagining this?

No, it *is* getting colder.

Do I let go of her hand and call Oilly to come?

Can't let go now.

Then another breath, and count the seconds before the next one.

None comes.

Her hand is noticeably colder. Lean in and listen.

Nothing.

She died at 7:30 p.m.

Let go of her hand and called out for Oilly to come quickly.

She came running over with Florian, Nikki, and David. All of us holding her lifeless hands, kissing her forehead, sitting around her and talking to her.

Weeping.

Her body is still warm and we each in turn express how grateful we are that her suffering is over. Whereas *ours* has only really *just* begun.

Feels like my heart is going to explode out of my chest, such is the intensity of this grief. Our hearts are *truly* broken. Relieved that she's finally *released*, but profoundly shocked and overwhelmed by her loss.

Even though we had warning that this was imminent

Even though we knew that her time was terminally measured out in months, weeks, and days

Even though we knew *all of this*

NOTHING can properly prepare us for *this* moment.

I fixate on slipping her rings off her fingers and their limp, unresponsive *lifelessness* will haunt me forever. Felt so mercenary, but they're the most tangible keepsakes of our life together. *Her* engagement ring and wedding band measured to precisely match the width of *my* wedding ring. We are sixty days short of our thirty-fifth wedding anniversary on November 1.

Phoned her brother David and sister-in-law Suzanne—who are boarding a plane in Aberdeen, heading south to see her tomorrow—to tell them that it's too late. Unbearably brutal.

Informed the district nurses.

Called James Showers and asked that he come as soon as the nurse has been.

Oilly is *inconsolable.*

Hug her, with the intensity of imagining never being able to ever let her go.

When we finally do unlock, we email and text the thirty friends who have been the most vigilant and present throughout the past eight months and twelve days, with these ten words, three numerals and four emojis:

💔💔 Joan died at 7:30 this evening.
Our hearts are utterly broken 💔💔

Christine Mitchell phones immediately and is so distraught that she can barely speak, but manages to say how much she *loved* and admired Joan, and how lucky we are to have been such a tight family unit, especially during the past eight months.

We sit with Joan for an hour until two young district nurses arrive to officially confirm her death and tell us that the doctor will issue the death certificate in the morning and that everything will be done online.

James Showers and his business partner Jane Diamond arrive half an hour later. He is wearing a Henley Regatta–style striped jacket, is courteous to an olde worlde degree, and asks if it's all right to speak to Joan. Nodded my assent and he knelt beside her and gently told her that we were all going to help wrap her up in a winding sheet and then take her away, after which she would be very well looked after. This *sounds* bizarre, but it's *the* perfect thing to say and hugely comforting. Talking to her as if she's *still* here, while indirectly conveying to us what was going to happen and what we needed to do to assist.

Nikki took Oilly downstairs to console her, while Florian, David, James, and I wrapped the sheet around Joan, then gently lifted her body on to a stretcher and carried her out into the garden, left down the side stairs, and into the back of the station wagon. Stood watching as James and

Jane slowly drove away with her, down the lane, until the red tail lights disappeared around the corner.

Cannot get over how steadfast Florian is being, coping with the maelstrom of our grief. *And* poor David, who is not only grieving the recent death of *his* father, but now Joan too.

Oilly lies on the wet grass in the dark, for a long time, unable to move. "I have an overpowering urge to be as close to the ground as possible."

We then all retreated to the Taj. The *unreality* of our new reality is acute. Talk our way through what's just been, in forensic detail, while answering texts and emails before finally peeling away to our separate bedrooms.

Me to "ours" that is now "mine." After an hour of trying to get to sleep, give up and go downstairs and clear the substantial stockpile of medicines and assorted gubbins. Compile lists of what needs to be done in the morning, then replay every video I have of Joan on my iPhone.

Alone in our bedroom.

Alone.

Fell asleep at 5 a.m.

Friday, September 3, 2021

Moment my eyes opened, was hit by a tsunami of grief. So overwhelming, I felt like I *would* drown.

Her handbag is next to our bed. As is her tapestry kit, with the needle and thread waiting for her next move.

Make-up on the chest of drawers with a lipstick that's no longer needed. *Her* pile of bedside books. *Her* bottle of Jack Covent Garden perfume. *Her* handwriting in *her* book of crossword puzzles.

All *hers* and yet no *her* here any more.

The unfathomable enormity of her loss ricochets throughout the day, off every wall, *every* object we've collected together, every call, and every message of condolence we receive. Stops me in my tracks. Aching lungs trying to breathe in enough air to process it all. Feels like an accordion that's been squeezed shut.

It's the *kindness* of people that is so utterly *undoing*.

Condolences come in from everywhere. Kevin Kline and Phoebe Cates call from New York—"We've only *just* heard. *How* can this be?"—joining the chorus of disbelief from people we haven't heard from or seen for ages.

Posted, on Twitter and Instagram, a tribute of us dancing to The Platters' version of "Only You" (videoed in May 2020, during lockdown):

> @richard.e.grant ♫ONLY YOU♫ Joan—Love of my Life, giver of Life to our daughter Olivia. Our hearts are broken with the loss of your Life last night. 35 years married and 38 years together. To be truly known and seen by you, is your immeasurable gift. Do not forget us, sweet Monkee-mine 💔💔💔💔

Astonishingly, it garners messages from across the globe—actors she has coached, friends flung far and wide and *total* strangers. We are consoled and heartened by *every* message.

Florian and Oilly organise the funeral arrangements, suggest hiring a marquee for the wake tea in our garden and draw up a guest list. None of which I'd given any thought to. When I suggested cooking and baking and doing it ourselves, they rightly told me I was bonkers and that we needed to hire a caterer.

Called Isabel Bannerman to ask if I could hire their tent, but it's already been loaned out. She gives me the number of Toti Gifford, founder of Giffords Circus, whom I'd met a few times at the Hay Festival and coincidentally again at the Woolpack pub in Slad last summer, when Joan and I were having lunch and I asked him in detail about the tragic death of his young wife, Nell, from cancer.

Toti confided that, "*Nobody*, not even my closest friends, have dared to ask and discuss what you two just did. I cannot tell you how grateful I am to be able to talk about Nell like this, with you." He reminded me of this conversation when I called him, and said, "The tent is yours. No hire charge. Name your date and time and I'll get my lads to pitch it. Just pay them for their labour." Flabbergasted.

Now to find a caterer. Oilly suggests asking Clodagh McKenna. Call Clo and she recommends a friend of hers called Annie Hudson, who instantly agrees to do it.

Florian looks after Oilly and me, cooks lunch and dinner,

answers the phone, and takes in the flowers and cards that avalanche through our front door.

"*A pocketful of happiness*" is the mantra Joan charged us to live by and it has resonated with whomever we've told it to. *Generosity, love, and kindness* reciprocated.

Saturday, September 4, 2021

None of us can quite compute the thousands, *literally* thousands, of messages we've received and the plethora of flowers that have accumulated on every available surface and outside the front door.

Funeral director Jane Diamond arrives with the forms to complete for the crematorium and returns Joan's two gold bracelets I'd inadvertently neglected to unclasp.

Karen "Gin" Jones had admired Joan's bracelets when they worked together on a film called *Stage Beauty* in 2003 and asked where she'd got them from, and she'd casually replied, "Oh, Richard E. Grant gave them to me."

"*What?* For coaching him to do an accent?" Clearly wondering why *she* hadn't been similarly gifted after script supervising on *Hound of the Baskervilles* with me, the year before.

"He never gave me *anything* like that!"

"Probably that's because I'm married to him."

Still makes Gin Jones and me laugh, because it somehow captures her deadpan, sleight of hand delivery.

Messages flood in from actors she's worked with,

repeating how generous she was and how she always boosted their confidence and belief that they could do it.

The weather is as sunny and warm as we'd almost forgotten to hope for, and Oilly sits in the Taj beside me, writing a tribute on her laptop for the funeral service and encourages me to do one as well.

"But I'll never be able to hold it together enough to read it out loud."

"Then ask Julian Wadham to do so on your behalf. I'm going to ask Ruth to read mine out, and I'm adding some Joan-isms to Henry Scott-Holland's poem 'Death Is Nothing at All,' which I want Anya Hindmarch to read, if she's willing. Do you think Pat Doyle would be the MC?"

Video-call Pat and he readily agrees. The service has a strict time limit of thirty minutes *all in*, so we have to work out precisely how long each reading should be, and how many music choices we can fit in between. Gives us something to focus on.

Our neighbours Joe and Rachel leave a loaf of warm home-made bread and a card at the door.

Called Alex Ciobanu at William's restaurant, requesting takeaway fish and chips for supper, which she flatly refuses to take any payment for when I pick them up. Too emotional to even speak, and adds a box of chocolates and a card with a photo of Joan, Sue, and herself, taken the last time Joan was at the restaurant.

Oilly has organised the funeral service booklet to be collated and printed, as well as ordering a set of photographs of Joan, for the cottage, and written up a tribute page from actors and directors to be read out "in case the service runs short." Thinking of *everything*, whereas I'm lurching around in a daze, feeling stripped of five layers of skin, *funeral shopping*. How does anyone get their heads around that concept? *Coffin. Cremation.* Could there be any more horrible words than these?

The cool damp of autumn is palpable, prompting us to light the Chesneys outdoor wood-burning stove in the Taj and spend the evening replying to emails and typing up the RSVPs to the funeral service, which now number seventy. Oilly reveals that while I was out, she sat on the hospital bed in our bedroom and "talked to Mum, even though that must sound silly, it really comforted me."

"I've done *exactly* the same." (I can't help thinking about her body, lying in a cold drawer a few miles away.)

She looked at me for a long while then plaintively asked: "Can you *ever* run out of tears, Dadda?"

Tuesday, September 7, 2021

Matt in the Gloucestershire registration office calls to go through all the legalese details of Joan's life to complete the death certificate and green form, which gets emailed to the funeral director, in order for the funeral to go ahead. Required to then fill out an online "one for all" form, which is sent to every government department to officially shut her life down. The bureaucracy of death.

Then to the printers with Oilly to pick up and pay for the photos of Joan, plus copies of the praise sheets for the service. Kev gives us complimentary doubles of every photo and a discount on the whole job.

On the way home, a number comes up on my phone located in Slough.

"Don't answer, Pops, we don't know anyone there and they'll be cold-calling, trying to sell you something."

"Might be to do with the online government form I signed earlier, as they required my number. Hello?"

"Hi, it's Elton."

"Sorry, but you're on speakerphone as I'm driving, and the line is bad. Please say your name again?"

"It's *Elton*." As in *you-know-who*! "I'm so sorry to hear about Joan. Let's get together when everything's settled down again, okay?"

"Sure. Many thanks for your call."

Last time I saw him was at a charity fundraising dinner in November 2014, for Ruth and Bruce Kennedy-Dundas's son Louis, who tragically died from a brain tumour at the age of four.

We first met Elton backstage at the Albert Hall with Ray Cooper, his percussionist, who was also a producer on *Withnail and I*. Taken up briefly into his unofficial Windsor court and invited for lunches, his fiftieth birthday extravaganza, pre-Christmas dinners, and always lavished with incredibly generous gifts. We both liked him and David Furnish enormously, and saw them in the south of France with the Fennells a couple of times. Then, in the warp and weft of show business friendships, we never saw them again. Yet today, he checks in as though *no* time has elapsed in the past seven years. Am surprised and touched.

The cottage resembles a florist's shop as there are flowers *everywhere* and they keep arriving every hour. Peter Capaldi phones to check, "How are you doing, Don Ricardo?"

"Well, Don Pedro, it's a bit like organising a wedding, *except* that instead of having two months to plan it all, *everything* has to be done in less than a week—invitations, venue, chapel, order of service, music, MC, marquee, caterers, guest list, parking, flowers, and a dress code. Oilly has done almost *all* of it and immaculately. Florian has taken over all shopping and chef duties and is cooking us Austrian specialities."

"How is Oilly coping?"

"Amazingly. I cannot begin to properly express how wonderful she's being and how *strong*."

"That's Joan in her."

"I know, I *know*."

Wednesday, September 8, 2021

Woke up at dawn to help with the delivery and storage of all the catering kit—tables, crockery, cutlery, glasses, teacups, and urns—to feed and water eighty guests.

Mowed the lawn, then drove over to the Market Garden

in Cirencester and bought Ian's entire stock of lilies to cover Joan's casket, as she loved them so. Back at the cottage, a huge bouquet has been delivered from Moyses Stevens Flowers in London, from the Prince of Wales and Duchess of Cornwall, with a four-page, deeply empathetic, handwritten letter from Prince Charles, posted in Scotland.

Oilly and I read it together sitting on a bench at a carwash in Brimscombe, like a pair of *teuchters* (Lowland Scots word meaning "uncouth/rural/yokels") compared to where the future king composed his letter, at Birkhall in Scotland! Joan loved this Scottish word, along with *oxter* (armpit) and *doup* (bottom).

Whenever we found ourselves in lah-di-dah company, she'd always quip, "How the hell have a pair of *teuchters* like us ended up on our *doups* among this lot?" *Always* grounded and unintimidated, with an unwavering moral compass. As we've both spent most of our careers employed on a freelance basis, we've never dared live beyond our means for fear of being in debt.

Oilly teasing both of us for opting to use our Freedom Passes on the bus and tube, even late at night, rather than jumping in a cab "when you can easily afford to do so." Reminding us that we don't think twice about spending money on "antiques and those papier-mâché heads!"

True, but both of us have always had the *exact* same attitude to money. Joan had waitressed at the Washington café on the seafront in Aberdeen when she was a student, and I'd done six months' waitering at Tuttons brasserie in

Covent Garden. We both knew what it was like to not have much money, making both of us *wary* of profligacy.

Toti Gifford's team arrive at 1:30 to pitch the marquee, managing to fit it in between the trees, and it's all set up within a couple of hours. Decorate it with Indian garlands from Artique in Tetbury and lay out the tables for drinks and tea. More flowers keep arriving every half hour, including a vast flat pannier crammed solely with gardenia plants, our favourite scent, from Cate Blanchett and Andrew Upton.

Nikki and David arrive from London and instantly start tidying, cleaning, unpacking, and moving whatever is needed, without any fuss. They've also brought down our visitors' book, which we've placed in the entrance for people to sign tomorrow, surrounded by candles, flowers, and a triptych of Joan's photos.

How can this be? How can we be preparing a tea party in her honour and she's not here to enjoy it all?

Find myself statued in shock while in the middle of doing something. Poleaxed *but* perpendicular. In the evening, while Oilly, Florian, David, and Nikki are having a BBQ in the Taj, I've retreated to our bedroom to read all the emails, texts, and condolence cards that have poured in. Unreal that everything about Joan is in the *past tense.* Rationally understand that she's died, but cannot comprehend it emotionally.

Thursday, September 9, 2021

How can it be a week already? Pull back the curtains and it's *bucketing* down. Scrambled outside and found tent side panels to attach to the marquee and then, with David and Florian's help, laddered up and improvised a cover corridor from the marquee to the Taj, where Annie Hudson and her team are laying out all the food. It's an insane rush: we're due to drive to Westerleigh at 1 p.m. and at 12:50 a.m. soaked and yet to get dressed. Would have amused my memsahib enormously.

Houdini into dry clothes and cleaned car, with Zoe, Ben, David, Nikki, Florian, and Oilly, who says, "I *hate* the word crematorium. Surely there must be something *better*?"

Thirty-five-minute drive through torrential rain which luckily stopped just as we did outside the chapel. The funeral service ahead of Joan's was attended by a Hells Angels chapter, all leather-clad with their pack of bikes, prompting *our* guests to quip that they never knew about Joan's secret affiliation with them.

Precisely at 2 p.m., I Pied Pipered in with everyone filing behind me to the accompaniment of Pat Doyle's haunting piano suite from his *Wah-Wah* soundtrack. Her wicker casket is covered in white lilies and a giant white-flowered crucifix from Lady Carole Bamford, atop the catafalque. Pat begins his celebrant duties with great solemnity, but within four sentences is swearing his eulogy off, like *only* he can. Irreverent, funny, poised, and moving.

Back and forthing between Joan and the congregants. Followed by Ruth's reading of Oilly's piece, tracing Joan's career. Then my pal Julian delivered my tribute to Joan, far better than I ever could, knowing that I'd be incapable of doing so myself.

Julian concluded with the closing words of my tribute:

> Joan's gifts as a teacher were legion—making you believe that you *could* achieve the accent and characterisation that she was coaching. Always pragmatic and clear. None of that "lie on the floor, spread your pelvis, breathe through your anus, and think of a breeze in Finland" claptrap.
>
> Loved poetry and could quote Shakespeare, John Donne, T. S. Eliot, and Robbie Burns at length. Brilliant and inventive cook, adored custard, cheese, and chocolate, and deemed me a freak for loathing all three.
>
> Oilly and I are profoundly grateful for everything that you've gifted us with, and we're relieved that you no longer have to struggle for breath.
>
> Our loss is incalculable.
>
> Your love is immeasurable.
>
> Goodbye, Monkee-mine.

Followed by the Scott-Holland poem read perfectly by Anya Hindmarch. Pat Doyle wrapped up with, "The final piece of music is by Abdullah Ibrahim, titled 'The Wedding,' and a favourite of Joan and Richard's. They've pledged to play it at both of their farewells."

The four minutes that follow are *the* most intensely pain-filled of my entire life. As the music crescendoed, I got up and stood beside her coffin, held on to it, then moved up to the head and wept my final farewell to the woman I have loved *unequivocally* and *completely* for almost four decades.

Despite the rain, everyone trooped back to the cottage, signed the condolence book, ate, drank, reminisced, and celebrated her life.

Chapter Eleven

Solo Sailing

Day that Joan died,
I lost my meaning,
My compass.
No mast,
No rudder,
No sail,
No wind.
Becalmed.

Once you've stepped off the running machine, it's suddenly clear where you're actually standing and who is standing with and beside you. And who *isn't*.

It's the sheer aloneness of being alone. Wherever you go, whoever and however many people you meet and play with, you return alone.

Change the sheets on our bed. How can it be that she's no longer here? *How* can that be? Our favourite work of art is *The Bed* by Toulouse-Lautrec, painted in 1892, and the two heads of the occupants not only look like we did when we first met in 1982, but the feeling of intimacy, lying together in the feathers and yakking, is perfectly captured. The reality of *never* being able to touch or talk to one another, ever again, is unfathomable.

Everyone warned us that we would feel profound emptiness, but Oilly pinpointed that we've been in a state of grief for the past eight months and that the funeral felt like a full stop. Mercifully releasing Joan from any further suffering.

What we do feel is bone-deep exhaustion. Which no amount of sleep seems able to assuage. Wake up as exhausted as the moment we went to sleep. Is this the brain telling the body, "We need to go to sleep together. For a thousand years." Like being inside an aquarium of grief, looking out at the world with a silently gulping mouth.

Oilly returned to work and, at the end of her day, automatically speed-dialled her mum to tell her about her doings, then realised that she would never be able to, *ever* again. It's the *stealth* of grief. Creeping up and through everything.

Sitting solo in the Woolpack pub for Sunday lunch, knowing what Joan would have ordered, her murmured commentary on the clientele, identifying their accents, *that* person's clothing and *this* person's speed of eating. I *never* succeeded in eating slowly enough for her. All of this going through my mind, in total silence. The absence of her feels blinding. How do I find that pocketful of happiness in each day that she asked me to?

"I'll always be inside you, Swaz," is what she said many

times over in her final weeks. "Of course you'll be sad, but I *know* you're going to be all right."

Two weeks after her funeral, James Showers kindly drops by the cottage with her ashes and says, "I find it oddly reassuring that a baby is approximately 7 pounds at birth, and Joan's ashes weigh about 7 pounds."

Her body left here two weeks ago, in a bag, and here are her ashes in an oblong box, returned in a hessian hold-all. She requested that I bury them beside the cherry tree in the garden, but can't bring myself to do so. Not yet. Feels too final.

Return to London and begin going through all her papers and clothes. Oilly and I are astonished to discover that Joan has kept *everything*—all of Oilly's kindergarten drawings, paintings, school reports, prizes, photos, and birthday cards, hidden in a wooden trunk.

"She really *is* proud of me, Pops."

There's a stash of close-typed aerogrammes that I posted to her from various filming locations, before mobile phones and video calls replaced the need. Here's a sampling of my purple-prosed adoration:

> I truly dote on you like a fig before it's plucked;
> hanging ripe for you. Sweet and yours. I love you so
> much puddle duck. We are so lucky to have found
> the pancake mix and flip together. Jam and syrup
> times we've had here./ Your voice is like Christmas-
> pudding-dark, sixpences and all. Your Holly to my Ivy.

We love each other so wonderfully and I pity anyone who will never know the sheer exhilarating miracle of being IN love and LOVED. It is flying, skiing, and swimming simultaneously./ You have made Human of me and given love back to me, where before I had denied its very existence. Given faith to me, fill me up like Joni sings "I could drink a case of you."/ Being in love with you is the complete re-discovery of the time and feeling of being 5 years old, playing hide and seek, and being able to fit snug inside a drawer or the floor in the back seat of a car, safe as a pillow in its case, warm and wrapped. Living with you is like playing House and Doctors and Nurse Fondle, Murder in the Dark and K.I.N.G. spells King, and when I look to see, it's you who are always there. You, for me to play with in my Life. Mirror, mirror on the wall, *we* are the luckiest of them all!/ We cup and saucer one another./ Take care when crossing the road, for me, take care not to walk in the dark alone, for me, take care to save some smiles and your laughs, for me./ You have engulfed me with your life and your love, and banished whatever gaping shadow there was./ I love you so, it's an ever beating thing, that hovers between us like a wave. Every time I speak to you or talk silently in my head with you, it ebbs and flows and always returns. Even if I get dumped now and again, sure as sunshine, you will lift me crest-wards again. May the Gods please ensure that when

> we go, we leave this earthly Life, TOGETHER. I don't mean to be morbid but I couldn't bear not being able to have you, know you, love you and cherish you. Swaz xxxxxxxxxxx

Oilly takes charge of sorting through all her clothes and has the brilliant idea of asking her oldest friends Zoe, Imogen, and Carmela to help her, for moral support. What we'd anticipated as being a morbid, agonising thing to do transforms into a celebration of Joan's style, with women who adored her. Joan *loved* clothes and had a treasure trove of them. Oilly gave each of them clothes that they loved, so that we can feel like she's still with us. Like a resurrection. Life-enhancing and invigorating.

Pat and Lesley Doyle call daily to check in on me, and invite me over for supper once a week. Mark Tandy organises tennis and Helena Bonham Carter arranges sleepovers, to be with her family and have a mini-break in north London.

Oilly books and pays for me to have a reiki session. "Give yourself over to it, Pops, and leave your scepticism at the door, and it'll work."

I do, and it does. No clue as to how, but it did. Lay down, eyes shut, and Lauren calmly explained what she was doing—no actual touch, but can feel the heat of her hands all over my body and, a few minutes later, can feel both my ears fill with water. Then realise that they're tears. I could swear that there are multiple hands hovering over me and, by the end of the session, I couldn't stop smiling and then started laughing. Couldn't believe it. Left feeling energised and profoundly grateful.

Monday, November 1, 2021

Posted a video on social media: "Today is our posthumous 35th wedding anniversary. What's so incomprehensible is that we can never touch or talk to one another ever again. We just have to count on the feeling that the love goes on."

Accompanied by this text: "I married Joan Washington 35 years ago today. Best decision I've ever made. We were together for 38 years and our daughter @oliviagranted is the lifelong gift of a Human that we are blessed with."

Heartening to read the *thousands* of messages from people who have lost and loved or who *long* for love.

Returning to our country cottage, where we'd spent the past eighteen months together, in one another's pockets, is bracing.

It's utterly country-winter-night silent here. *Silent*.

No distant urban hum. Just a kind of white noise in your ears.

Sophie Robinson video-chats for half an hour and says, "It's just something you've got to get through." Know what she means, and how compassionately she says it, but the moment our call ends she's still got Bruce to talk to.

Joan's embroidery bag is hanging on the corner of the chaise where she used to sit and sew. Her ashes stored in a box below, labelled and dated. No matter how many lunch and dinner arrangements are made, calls, texts or emails received and sent, nothing can protect you from this silence.

How to get through it, after our thirty-eight-year conversation where we covered everything and nothing was too trivial to talk about: Who said *this* and what do you think was meant by *that* and how much did *this* cost and can you believe what he did to her and why the hell did those two ever get married and why is it that, with some couples, you love one of them but *loathe* the other and did you see what *he* ate, has *she* had a stroke or is that Botox and do you reckon they *still* have sex? Where shall we go tomorrow or shall we just stay at home, get takeaway or have our beloved beans on toast, with Marmite instead of butter, or shall I just scramble us some eggs?

Us.

We.

Let's.

Now it's solitary.

Single.

Solo.

Alone.

In Gwyneth Paltrow–speak, we've now been de-coupled by death. Amputees talk about phantom limb syndrome. That's me without Joan. Legless *but* walking. Tongue-tied *but* talking. Limbless *yet* lugging myself here, there, and nowhere. Looking but *not* seeing.

How often is *too* often to call your friends? Without wanting to impose or intrude?

"Just call us, *anytime*."

"You must come over."

"Don't hesitate to ask if you need anything."

Steering-wheel talk on the way home, where you cross-hatch about where you've just been, what you've eaten and who you've talked to, now no longer an option. To share with, calibrate, defend, disseminate, or discuss.

Return home. Key in the door. Outside light to switch off. Curtains closed. Keys hung. The sound of *every* habitual action is amplified. Footsteps. Mine. Light switch, click on. Teeth brushed. Click off. Clothes off. Climb into a cold bed. Reach out and touch. Amputated. How long will this last? Wishing her here *cannot* bring her back.

Epilogue

Oilly had done a brilliant job of sorting through Joan's clothes but I still had to face dealing with all of her papers. My dread turned to delight when I found a cake tin containing all the aerogrammes we wrote to one another when I was filming a TV series in Israel in 1987. I had completely forgotten I had them. Forgotten too that, when not required to type or text, Joan was a very lively, handwritten correspondent. Re-reading them instantly resurrected her voice, which couldn't have come at a more perfect, longed-for, moment. Especially the postscript to her last letter:

"My love for you is total and forever, Swaz, and I really believe that, although we're mortal, our love is immortal."

In April 2022, I travelled to Australia to film.

Posted the following text/video message, walking along a beach on the Gold Coast:

Beautiful as this beach is, I feel and look like an old turtle without my shell, trying to navigate the world on my own, having lost my loving "compass."

Feels like a whole new world, navigating solo, after 38 years together, but as Joan so wisely asked me—Find a pocketful of happiness in each day . . . I'll try my best.

Tributes to Joan Washington

Chris Addison (comedian-actor-director): "What a huge loss. She lit up many a film set and many a life. Urbane, funny, unflappable, deeply knowledgeable and wildly talented. The secret sauce in a million performances."

Tindyebwa Agaba Wise (humanitarian): "I can't stop thinking about the profound impact she left on me and the laughs we had together. I am so pleased I had the chance to let her know what she had done for me, and she changed my life immeasurably because of the skills she gave me. I am comforted that she will always be with me. She was a truly wonderful, beautiful person."

Cate Blanchett (actor): "Having worked with Joan for twenty years, I can personally attest to her unparalleled skills as a vocal and dialect coach. But her work goes far beyond merely teaching an accent. Through her rare ability to unlock the historic and cultural context of a script, and practically translate this into action, Joan has become one of the most sought-after professionals in her field. Joan has been an integral secret weapon; an unsung and elevating part of any and every production that she has worked on."

Jessica Chastain (actor): "I have been so lucky in my life and career to work alongside her and be graced with the brilliance and humility that she brings to her art form. Beyond her distinctive skill set in dialogue coaching, she also offers incredibly honest perspectives on embodying a character."

William Conacher (dialect coach): "One of the most often asked questions after telling someone I am a dialect coach is: Do you know Joan Washington? Rest in peace to the doyenne of coaches."

James D'Arcy (actor-director): "The world is a lesser place without her. She was a truly remarkable woman and had a greatly positive impact on my life, and that of many others."

Neil Dudgeon (actor): "We had such a laugh crammed in the tiny room she taught in at RADA. Joan had the most beautiful way of laughing and smiling, like she was trying not to, to keep us under control. She was THE BEST at what she did."

Sir Richard Eyre (director): "Joan is universally respected and has been outstanding in her field for forty years. She is one of the great unsung heroines of the British entertainment business."

Ralph Fiennes (actor-director): "I benefited from her skills countless times, especially in *Schindler's List* and *Great Expectations*. As a director, I relied not only on her phonetic skills but also on her extraordinary insight into the interpretation of a role—Coriolanus and Charles Dickens in *Invisible Woman*. I loved her for all her wisdom, humour and compassionate perception."

Martin Freeman (actor): "You knew you'd done all right when she gave you the thumbs-up. She actually helped, you know? Someone who truly deserved their reputation. Also, she was a right fucking laugh."

Dawn French (actor-writer): "Joan Washington will ALWAYS be remembered by those of us that knew her and were taught by her as a PHENOMENAL WOMAN."

Brendan Gleeson (actor): "She has enriched many of my performances with her intuitive questioning, technical expertise and patient unearthing of the humanity of a character and its appropriate expression. In particular, she was largely responsible for my having won an Emmy in

2009 playing Winston Churchill. She is a consummate artist and a collaborative wonder."

Domhnall Gleeson (actor-writer-director): "Your beautiful Joan. I loved that woman. She is a shining star. Here's to the incomparable, brilliant, devilish, hilarious, gentle Joan."

Anne Hathaway (actor): "I am so grateful for the happy and profound hours I spent with your brilliant wife. They shaped me in ways that I will rely upon for the rest of my life. My God, what a generous and spectacular woman."

Douglas Hodge (actor): "She taught me at RADA and introduced me to so much blissful poetry. I then had the exquisite surprise of bumping into her on so many jobs over the years, with her astonishing ear and gifts as a teacher."

Nicholas Hoult (actor): "What an incredible woman. I will cherish my time with her and what she taught me. So many wonderful memories."

Becky Johnston (screenwriter): "She was one of the greats. A woman so disarmingly open and engaged and full of spirit and life, I'd think to myself, what a force of nature. My most powerful memories of Joan are being in your kitchen in Richmond and feeling so utterly at home while she made those amazing meals and we would talk and talk. She had the gift of being able to receive you and make you feel heard and understood."

Simon Kinberg (director-producer): "It's impossible to fathom. Her spirit was so indomitable and entirely infectious. The little time I got to spend with her was one of the very great gifts of my life. Sending you all of the love in my aching heart."

Chris Land (writer-producer): "The foremost dialect coach in the UK and a legend in our industry. She taught me at RADA and was so funny, gorgeous and smart, that every student slightly fell in love with her."

Jill McCullough (British accent coach): "Joan singlehandedly created the role of dialect and voice coach in the British film industry. She is effectively the doyenne of our profession and paved a way for all who came after. Her wise and creatively intelligent determination inspired thousands of actors, directors and other teachers. She is whom we all wanted to become."

Kelly Macdonald (actor): "She was wonderful and funny, and absolutely the best company on set. She was always so wise and supportive. I know you know how adored she was by those of us who got to spend any time with her."

John Madden (theatre and film director): "She has an immaculate ear and a magical ability to convey the essence of a dialect to the actors she works with."

Miriam Margolyes (actor): "I'm remembering all the things I love about Joan—her skill, of course, rescuing me gently and wisely, her humour, her beauty, her laugh, her domestic glory. She was unique, brave, fierce. How proud she was of her family and her glorious marriage."

Eddie Marsan (actor): "I always found her to be not only a fantastic voice coach, but such a kind and supportive soul. Whenever you felt like a role was beyond you, a few moments with her, and anything seemed possible."

Rob Marshall (director): "Joan was *the* grande dame and a force of amazing spirit. We are so fortunate that she was able to touch our lives."

Tim Monich (American accent coach): "Actually, it might be more accurate to say that she established a field of coaching dialects in theatre and film. She has not only raised the bar and set the standard for this work in the UK, but is as valued and influential in Hollywood as she is in London."

David Morrissey (actor): "Joan was so kind and wonderful to me. Always encouraged me and we had some great laughs together."

Emily Mortimer (actor-director): "Joan was incredible, one of the world's great teachers. It was a privilege to know her and to have been in her orbit. Her and Richard's love story was an inspiration."

Stephen Rea (actor): "She was, as you know, a dream to be with, if only in a rehearsal room. So sensitive to a guy with a Belfast accent you could cut with a knife. So encouraging. So shrewd in her advice. And hilarious. It wasn't work. It was utter pleasure. Joan is in our hearts forever."

Eddie Redmayne (actor): "She was my first dialect coach and set the bar absurdly high. On the play she was of course so much more—an inspirer, an invigorator, and truly unique. She emboldened me to take a stab at this bonkers existence."

Christina Ricci (actor): "Joan was such an incredible, warm, beautiful human being. She touched so many lives and left an indelible mark. She was, and is, so adored. Always."

Ian Rickson (former director of the Royal Court Theatre): "In the Kingdom of Theatre, we often give awards to the more visible, or shiniest players in the game. Joan is a largely unsung heroine, a best-kept secret, and in her quiet, egoless way she has transformed so many actors on stage and on screen."

Fiona Shaw (actor): "The colluding smile, the rich warm voice, and that ease of intelligence merging with wit and gentle understanding. Joan has always been an indelible presence in my mind. She was a glorious person, powerful, knowledgeable and kind."

Meryl Streep (actor): "What a light she was, and so funny, so smart."

Dame Emma Thompson (actor): "Her consummate skill in pushing for authenticity and accuracy in the use of dialect has enriched and defined the performances of many actors in many productions (theatre and film) for many, many years. She also worked with my son, an ex-refugee and child soldier from Rwanda, whom she helped to hone pronunciation and diction. Her personal contribution to the development of a once traumatised young man is outside her professional remit but witness to her profound humanity—the quality that, for me at least, defines her and her artistic contribution."

Claire Tomalin and Michael Frayn (biographer and playwright): "She was a wonderful friend, teacher, homemaker, and will live on in our memories."

Liv Tyler (actor): "She was just the best. Hands down. No other. What an incredible teacher. Kind woman. Completely honest and direct and absolutely hilarious, and God she loved her family so much. I'm so grateful to have known her as a professional and also as a woman. My favourite part was going to her house to work—to feel its warmth and love and see all your magical treasures. It has left an everlasting imprint on my heart."

Dame Julie Walters (actor): "For over forty years she has played a vital role in my career and the career of countless other actors. Her extraordinary ear for the delicate nuances of speech and accent has afforded me greater insight into several important characters that I've played."

Jason Watkins (actor): "Joan taught me dialects and accents when I trained at RADA and beyond. I owe her everything. Such a terrible loss for us all."

Acknowledgments

Saffron Aldridge, Lady Carole and Lord Anthony Bamford, Pete Banks, Isabel and Julian Bannerman, Dr. Mitch Besser, Daisy Bevan, Lucy Bevan, Sanjeev Bhaskar, Corinne Biagini, Tanya Bird, Cate Blanchett, Christopher Bollas, Helena Bonham Carter, Diane Borger, Nige and Jules Bowsher, Rob Brydon, Gabriel Byrne, Ryan Caine, Camilla, Duchess of Cornwall, Phoebe Cates, Charles, Prince of Wales, Alex Ciobanu, Kelly Clare, Richard Clarke, Jasper Conran, Sophie Conran, Carmela Corbett, Allan Corduner, Wanda Cui, Simon Curtis, Felix and Magali de Loose, Pat and Lesley, Abi, Patrick, Nula, and Elliot Doyle, Sir James and Lady Deirdre Dyson, Rupert Everett, Ben Falcone, Theo and Louise Fennell, Sally Field, Michael Frayn, Dawn French, Georgia Garrett, David and Suzanne, John, Sophie, and Cathy Geddie, Bob and Jeanne Geldof, Toti Gifford, Brendan Gleeson, Domhnall Gleeson, Zoe Graham, Sue Gutjahr, Skye Gyngell, Holly Harris, Marielle Heller, Harry Herbert, Florian Herbst, Tom Hiddleston,

Olivia Hills, Anya Hindmarch, Harry Hook, Eric and Tania Idle, Karen "Gin" Jones, Donna Karan, Lady Ruth and Lord Bruce Kennedy-Dundas, Kevin Kline, Lynda La Plante, Nigella Lawson, Julie Legrand, Annie Lennox, Andrew Lincoln, Olivia Lloyd, Longfield Hospice, Lulu, Nikki Lunt, Susan and Hardy Lynch, Melissa McCarthy, Elizabeth McGovern, Becky McKee, Clodagh McKenna, David Maguire, Imogen Major, Kathryn Mannix, Ashley Margolis, Amanda Marmot, Steve Martin, Stephen Merchant, Christine and Stephen Mitchell, Phoebe Nicholls, Catherine O'Hara, Vanessa Redgrave, Joely Richardson, Eugenia Rillman, Bruce and Sophie Robinson, John Robinson, Vicki Russell, Carlos Schuster, James Seymour, Fiona Shaw, Brooke Shields, Jenny Shircore, Martin Short, Sting, Barbra Streisand, Trudie Styler, Ben Sullivan, Tim Sullivan, Meera Syal, Mark Tandy, Dame Emma Thompson, Claire Tomalin, Binti Velani, Ian Wace, Julian Wadham, Dame Harriet Walter, Dame Julie Walters, Tom and Amelie Washington, Emily Watson, Bo Welch, Jeff Whitty, Nicole Wilcox, Owen Wilson, Francesca and Boodle Zampi.